PENGUIN BOOKS
MY DEAR BAPU

Gopalkrishna Gandhi was born in 1945. Over the next three decades, his maternal grandfather, C. Rajagopalachari, oversaw his education, reading and commencement of a career in the Indian Administrative Service. Gandhi has held positions in the government of Tamil Nadu, was high commissioner for India in South Africa (1996–97) and Sri Lanka (2000–02), Secretary to the President of India (1997–2000) and Governor of West Bengal (2004–09).

He has written a novel, *Refuge*, on the ethnic conflict in Sri Lanka that first appeared in 1987 and a play in verse, *Dara Shukoh*. His other books are *The Essential Gandhi* and *Of a Certain Age*, the latter a collection of his biographical sketches on twenty notable Indians. More recently, he has translated into English the Tamil classic *Tirukkural* and written the book *Abolishing the Death Penalty*.

PRAISE FOR THE BOOK

'A fine book . . . The letters [reveal the two leaders sharing] each other's hopes and anxieties about the country and the people, about the freedom to be won and the ways of winning it . . . [Gopalkrishna Gandhi] has a fine mind of a historian which enables him to stand, provisionally, outside to evaluate the many relationships that the letters conjure up'—*The Hindu*

'It is difficult to get a full sense of the past, the pushes and pulls and shoves that won us independence; the immense struggle against splintering; the fine muslin of emotional appeal and inclusion of dissident voices that was woven into khadi. This is one of the precious reveals of *My Dear Bapu* . . . CR's erudition and Bapu's keen, contesting mind are in fine display throughout'—*DNA*

'The academic and literary value of this volume is immense'—*Caravan*

My dear Bapu...

LETTERS FROM C. RAJAGOPALACHARI

TO MOHANDAS KARAMCHAND GANDHI,

DEVADAS GANDHI

AND

GOPALKRISHNA GANDHI

EDITED BY

GOPALKRISHNA GANDHI

PENGUIN BOOKS

An imprint of Penguin Random House

PENGUIN BOOKS

USA | Canada | UK | Ireland | Australia
New Zealand | India | South Africa | China | Singapore

Penguin Books is part of the Penguin Random House group of companies
whose addresses can be found at global.penguinrandomhouse.com

Published by Penguin Random House India Pvt. Ltd
4th Floor, Capital Tower 1, MG Road,
Gurugram 122 002, Haryana, India

Penguin
Random House
India

First published in Viking by Penguin Books India 2012
Published in Penguin Books by Penguin Random House India 2017

Copyright © Gopalkrishna Gandhi 2012

ISBN 9780143428886

Typeset in Bembo Std by Eleven Arts, New Delhi
Printed at Manipal Technologies Limited, India

www.penguin.co.in

MIX
Paper | Supporting
responsible forestry
FSC® C043100

To the memory of Lakshmi, dearly beloved daughter to CR and daughter-in-law to Gandhi—a son's grateful obeisance

Contents

Photograph by William Vandivert, *Life* magazine

Introduction

Chakravarti Rajagopalachari was a man of letters in more senses than one. He was a man of books, both as an attentive reader and a writer of masterpieces. But it was in the writing of letters that he spent the largest part of his affair with pen and ink. He seemed to enjoy both the substance and the form of correspondence, with brief letters drawing the best from the effervescence of his wit and the longer ones, from the ripeness of his wisdom. When those two talents—wit and wisdom—combined and drew from the dictionary of trenchant words, we got what may be called 'vintage CR'.

If Mohandas Karamchand Gandhi had an addiction, it was to the same universe of written communication. Few have written letters as prodigiously as Gandhi, fewer with his thrift, cogency and clarity, his letters remaining, mostly, strait-laced and serious, but sometimes bursting into a laugh. There were days when Gandhi did not eat, when he did not speak. There was scarce a day when he did not write a letter.

This volume of letters from CR to Gandhi is therefore one of letters between two men of similar age (CR was nine years younger to Gandhi) who were devoted to the art of letter-writing as much as they were close to one another. They also happen to be letters written by two men who shared four grandchildren between them. Above all, the volume presents letters sent by a political disciple, CR, who had (in his own words) surrendered his heart to his 'Master', but never fully his mind or his choice of method of struggle in their common cause—the freedom of India from British rule and her emancipation from the chains tied round her by the follies of her own children.

CR and Gandhi shared about thirty years of colleagueship, hardship and friendship. Letters or postcards written on handmade paper and posted from different locations and also from wayside railway stations sustained the association no less than time spent together.

Even when most other limbs of British India 'polluted' by the imperialist ego were boycotted by Congress, the postal system was not. It was not only not disassociated from but actively patronized by these eminent rebels. Legislatures were to be shunned, law courts abjured, colleges and schools run by the government declared noxious and out of bounds for the patriotic, but not so the post offices of the Raj and its systems of collection and delivery.

From 1919 until Gandhi's assassination in 1948, postal correspondence linked CR to his leader. It did the same with others as well, and the pace and volume of correspondence between Jawaharlal Nehru, Vallabhbhai Patel, Rajendra Prasad and Gandhi were no less substantial. But, as any reader of the letters in this volume will see, there was to the CR–Gandhi line of postal talk a quality and a spirit that was its very own.

During these three decades CR was based in India's south—either in Madras or in his ashram at Tiruchengodu, in the parched part of Madras Presidency's Salem district. And Gandhi was wherever his two feet and a million concerns carried him, restless and composed, agitated and at peace, ever giving and ever demanding of trust. Not for nothing did CR get to be known as Gandhi's southern warrior, his flag-bearer. And, by some, as a barrier between them and the Mahatma, a wall that Gandhi leaned on for support and as a protective guard for his own spiritual sustenance.

Whenever Gandhi came to the south, CR was the visit's pivot and its 'petrol'. Not surprisingly, CR's access to Gandhi, intellectual more than physical, did not fail to occasion resentment. On his part, CR joined him often enough but always fleetingly. He was frequently at Gandhi's two ashrams, Sabarmati and Sevagram; dropped in on him in his great march to Dandi; was by his side in Bombay and in Delhi; at Congress sessions all over the country; at the sites of his incarcerations in Poona; for the longest spell they ever spent together—in a tour of Ceylon in 1927; and, finally, in Calcutta where the two were both present when India became free and divided—CR as the state's first Governor, and Gandhi as the Father of a Nation at once triumphant and torn.

The gaps between their meetings had to be and were much longer than the meetings themselves. On these spaces of time and separation grew the correspondence that is offered in this book.

Well over a hundred letters each way, at least, must have gone from one to the other. I give this conservative figure of 'over a hundred', for no more than that number survive. They lie preserved, among other venues, in family archives nurtured by Devadas Gandhi; in the excellent record room in Gandhi Ashram, Sabarmati, Ahmedabad; the Gandhi Smarak Museum at Rajghat, New Delhi; the National Archives, New Delhi; and among CR's papers lodged at the Nehru Memorial Museum and Library, New Delhi, along with those of Devadas Gandhi and Pyarelal.

———

A substantial number of their letters are reproduced in this volume. Wherever required for completeness of dialogue, Gandhi's communication—either as a 'cause' for CR's letter, or, more often, by way of a reply or response to one from him—is also given with the CR letter. *The Collected Works of Mahatma Gandhi* set has altogether 160 letters written by Gandhi to CR.

This volume carries eighty-eight entries in the main section that contains CR's letters to Gandhi. There are twenty-five each in the sections containing CR's letters to his son-in-law Devadas Gandhi and to his grandson, being me.

As the volume's compiler and editor I have written the headnotes for the entries in the first and second sections, and provided footnotes. The footnotes are meant to offer at first glance some information supports to the reader who may or may not require them, but could find them useful as aids to contextualization. When they refer to individuals, I have tried to make them comprehensive because each of those persons was a player, often definitionally so. Ellipses in the letters reflect illegibility in the original or elisions dictated by my editorial judgement as to relevance or suitability.

The letters to Gandhi are of value as the intellectual and never unemotional outreach of Gandhi's 'conscience-keeper'—the Mahatma's oft-used term for CR. They are also a cardiograph of the national struggle for freedom and for social reform, as recorded on the sensitive disc of CR's observations. But, above all, they are the testimony of an age when idealism had never been stronger and, ironically, when it had never been under more formidable strain. India's sense of destiny wrangled with a callous state's indifference towards Indian self-esteem and also with several weaknesses within itself that ran the idealism to the ground and made the struggle both protracted and complex.

CR's letters to Gandhi are like a family diary in which truth must be told but without jeopardizing the family's pride in itself or its future in dignity. They are frank, they are brave. They are often bitter.

The letters from CR to Gandhi show the evolution of a relationship between leader and follower that leaves both free to differ but not to part, free to berate but never to let down, free to persuade but never to dominate. That was the basis on which their lasting comradeship was founded.

The section containing CR's letters to Devadas Gandhi, the Mahatma's youngest son and his own younger son-in-law, speak of another relationship in which Gandhi figures prominently and yet does not dominate proceedings. Devadas's esteem for CR amounted to an obedient respect next only to that which he had for his own father and mother. CR's affection for Devadas equalled if not surpassed that which he had for his own children. The last of his children, Lakshmi, was to marry Devadas after a celebrated courtship and an equally celebrated serving of injunctions upon the love-struck couple by their doting if cautious fathers.

The third section is there because the letters are there. CR happened to write a few more letters to me than to my siblings for a sombre reason. When my father died in 1957, I, the youngest of his children, was twelve. CR felt, quite typically, that he had to fill in for my father, and since he was in Madras and I, with my widowed mother, lived in Delhi, a kind of 'distance education' exercise commenced between 'Anna' (the Tamil word his grandchildren used for 'Nana') and 'Gopu'. With fewer disruptions of home life than those of my sister and two brothers, I managed to preserve the letters from Anna, whereas my siblings, who were to move house and sites of work far oftener than I, were unable to do so.

The twenty-five letters of CR to this grandson take his letter-writing engagement with the Gandhi household, which started in 1919, to 1971—a half-century and more. The engagement is about struggles undertaken, privation suffered, love lavished, hope entertained, prayers offered, love of 'high' literature and of 'good language' taught. It is also a sequence of wise counsel given, intelligent caution administered, dark fears expressed, huge setbacks endured, high office entered upon with humility and relinquished with dignity. And overarching all this, a faith kept, flickeringly firm, in a benign power that all but loses out against the visitations of personal tragedy, political reverses and self-doubt.

'Come back,' CR writes to the Mahatma on 16 June 1920, 'and give us life.'

Is that a prayer or an admonition? Counsel or a subtle warning? Is it an individual's appeal or a collective pleading? Perhaps the words are a blend of all that and more. I believe they are written by one whose faith in his leader did not indemnify the object of his faith from misjudgements, error or even folly. Can faith be judgemental? The writer addresses Gandhi as 'Master'. Can one admonish one's Master? Not usually. But then CR is not 'usual'.

CR was never 'usual'.

Acknowledged in later years as a master of Tamil prose, possessing a very distinct speaking and writing style in that tongue, he managed to actually fail in his Tamil BA paper set in January 1896 by the University of Madras. Recognized as a deft user of the English language and, in fact, an adept in it, he was placed in the second division in the English test the same year. Celebrated during all his years as a politician and statesman as something of a phenomenon in argument and reasoning, CR passed the Bachelor of Law examination in January 1900 not in the first, not in the second but in the third division.

And yet, this non-medallist, non-topping, unremarkable student's was the only hand raised when a visiting Swami Vivekananda asked his student audience at Ice House by the Marina Sands in Madras, in January 1897, if anyone could tell him why Krishna is painted blue. 'Why?' asked Vivekananda. Replied young Rajan: 'Because the sky and the ocean, symbols of infinity, are blue.'

Under three years of that question being put and answered, CR was married and established as a lawyer in Salem alongside the politically minded C. Vijiaraghavachariar. If his fees soared to a thousand rupees per case, his mind turned increasingly to the national question. CR went in 1906 to the Congress's session in Calcutta presided over by Dadabhai Naoroji. He became an ardent Tilakite in the Congress's division between moderates and extremists at the Surat Congress, which he attended in 1907.

He had the identity of a Congressman with extremist views if not programmes of personal involvement when, in 1907, an Indian deported from South Africa called Asari met CR in Salem and told him of an Indian fighting for Indians' rights in that far-off land. The man was described as 'small in size' but possessed of a heart 'bigger than the Shevaroys seen from Salem'. Three years later, his practice peaking, and his extremist views being reconsidered as a result of the growing cult of the bomb, CR got to read Gandhi's *Hind Swaraj*. The little tract's multiple messages coalesced with his own innate sense of social reform and self-reliance for India.

Gandhi's accounts of his three jail terms in South Africa published by *Modern Review* in Calcutta and a new biography of the man, *An Indian Patriot in South Africa*, by the Revd J.J. Doke gave CR just the example he was looking for, of someone seeking a goal larger than professional success, and working for that goal through self-denial and suffering.

Unbeknownst to his future leader, CR reprinted the text of Gandhi's South African jail experiences and, in an introduction, the thirty-four-year-old Salem vakil asked for public funds to be sent to Gandhi with the following words: 'Shall we sit happy in our homes, or shall we give only tears? It is not given to all to exhibit the strength of M.K. Gandhi. He must be ranked with the *Avatars* . . .' The appeal led to the modest collection of fifteen hundred rupees which CR sent to Gopalkrishna Gokhale in Poona, who in turn sent it to the Indian patriot who was to 'discover' the fundraiser some six years later, in Madras.

This volume begins with a handwritten letter written just after that first meeting of Gandhi's with the forty-year-old advocate, now a widower with an ailing father and five children, who has moved from Salem to Madras.

Politics dominate most of the letters, as they would—inter-se politics within the Congress; inter-party politics between the Congress and the Swaraj Party, the Nationalist Party, Madras's Justice Party; and, of course, the larger politics of Congress vis-à-vis the British Raj. Letters sent by CR from behind prison bars strongly reflect the political pulse with beats missed and beats found, fresh reading done, new interests, even new talents discovered.

Print-propaganda by CR for the Congress and, particularly, for Gandhi's positions on the struggle, is a major concern in the letters.

His writing for *Young India* that appears in the correspondence is absolutely seminal.

Khadi occupies a larger than expected share of the CR–Gandhi preoccupation in their letters, occasioned by CR's setting up of the ashram almost on the rebound after Gandhi softened his opposition to the Swaraj Party's programme, an opposition that CR had spearheaded.

CR shows himself to be quite a master spinner and khadi-organizer, to Gandhi's unconcealed admiration. But CR is not a 'Centre's appointee' in khadi's outlying districts. He does not accept diktats from the 'headquarters' and, as a result, earns Gandhi's ire. He returns ire with ire.

The letters abound with all that ties true friends together. There is banter, there is laughter. There is candour, there is remorse. What is not to be found is the mintiness of sanctimony, the lavender of flattery. Also missing, refreshingly so, is anything that can diminish the tone and tenor of the dialogue. CR and Gandhi show how disagreement can outdo convergence in the manner of expressing it and in the method of receiving it.

CR's last letter to Gandhi is what might be called 'official'. It is indeed on an official matter, pertaining to his ministry, sent by sixty-seven-year-old CR, as minister in the interim government of free India in charge of the department of industries and supplies, on official letter paper, to the Father of the Nation. Though addressed, like the others, to 'My dear Bapu', it is signed as CR would sign all official letters, in full—'C. Rajagopalachari'. And, as is only to be expected from the unusual in CR, it demurs. CR declines to place 1900 bales of yarn per month at the disposal of a non-government agency for distribution in Noakhali on the grounds that only the Bengal government can and should distribute yarn, then a commodity in short supply.

Noakhali, as we know, was the scene of a millennial intervention by the Mahatma on the eve of the Partition of India, following brutal communal riots. Life in Noakhali was ravaged beyond recognition.

As part of a process of healing and restoration, it would seem that Gandhi wanted to have (non-khadi, 'mill') yarn placed at Noakhali's disposal for providing weaving and wage-earning opportunities to the affected people there. The idea was that a non-governmental agency would distribute the yarn on a monthly basis. But, no, the minister did not agree with the Mahatma. Procedures were procedures. Officially procured yarn was to be officially, not unofficially, distributed. And then, in the quantities that were feasible, according to the government's calculations, not Gandhi's. There is nothing to show the Mahatma pressed the point.

The nearly ninety communications that pass between the first and the last reflect the same unusual nature of their relationship, where respect is given, affection exchanged, but nothing taken for granted except the genuineness of the equation, its truth, its faith. They show CR as the faithful dissenter or the dissenting faithful.

In these letters as elsewhere, dissent marks CR's spoken thought, his written word—dissent over detail when he agrees with the larger picture, dissent with the larger picture when he disagrees with the detail. Dissenting with eloquence, dissenting with passion, dissenting with respect, CR brings to his argument the conviction of a Socrates, the veracity of a Marcus Aurelius. But he does something else that bears notice: he dissents to persuade the 'other side' and at the same time is prepared to lose the argument. He dissents without ego.

That is where a certain grace informs CR's contrariness. It can sound weary, sad. It does not sound affronted or disoriented by defeat. The strength of CR's intellection lies in its being exempt from two drawbacks: an eagerness to win the argument and the fear of losing it. He seems to find a careful exposition, a subtle elaboration, a syntactically apposite formulation laced with unexpected turns of humour to be sufficient to the purpose.

CR emerges in these letters as one wedded to, instinctively, deeply and irrevocably, certain ideals and values, essentially those of a liberal political order and a conservative social order. He is unabashedly God-minded and pious, placing his talents and his time very consciously at the altar of reverential belief. He writes on scripture as a sacrament, on politics as a duty, on social issues as an obligation. He writes on Gandhi as Ananda would on the Tathagata or Mark, Mathew, Paul and Luke would on the Prince of Nazareth.

And yet, it must be acknowledged that if style was nearly as important as substance in any of Gandhi's principal exponents, it was so in CR. There was an artist in CR of the telling phrase, of the clinching, scoring, crowning point. And he knew there was that artist in him. He was aware of his intellectual vigour, as an athlete may be aware of his physical stamina, a cricketer of his finesse on the crease, a musician of a mastery of the higher octaves. Being so aware, CR placed that artistry of his, that talent of intellection, at the service of his causes and beliefs.

Revelling in the delineation, and not so much in the culmination, of his thinking, more often than not CR won the debate but lost the argument. But never, ever, did he lose faith in his many differentiated faiths—political, social, philosophical, religious, existential.

Was CR, then, principally a mental phenomenon, an intellectual, a theorist lost among practical men? That assessment would be erroneous. CR was too much of a devotee, or what, in the Indian idiom, is called a 'bhakta', to be regarded so. In his celebrated commentary on that intellectual colossus, Adi Sankara, CR finds the devotional facet to be the most mature of the Advaitin's many-faceted sensibility. Devotion, in CR's case, was an energy, not an attribute. And he directed it towards India, towards its greatest leader, Gandhi, towards ideals such as good governance, religious tolerance, good citizenship, philanthropy, among other 'large' issues. Equally, he was devoted to 'lesser' ideals and affiliations like frugal living, 'high' reading, 'chaste' writing, elegant diction, refinement in human behaviour, temperance (though he knew more about what went into which alcoholic spirit than any tippler), gallantry, chivalry and, curiously, personal labour as in washing one's clothes and showing respect, not just courtesy, towards those who labour physically to earn and feed their dependants.

The designer of statesmanship tries various moulds. Some work well as ideals, some do better as 'moving items' in the market of public life. CR did not belong to the latter kind.

CR was designed to leave a mark on the stage of endeavour, not on the stage of achievement. His achievement was in his endeavour, as a freedom fighter, as a public intellectual, as an opinion-maker, and as a statesman in high office and outside it.

The letters in this volume are about endeavours, large and small, ephemeral and abiding, made in the public arena and in the inner domain of friends, of home and hearth. As in Gandhi's case, the personal and the public coalesced in the lives of his associates almost indistinguishably. Families were often foils, oftener supports. Sometimes, they were serious obstacles. In any event, they were not to be ignored. And ignored they were not.

Devadas Gandhi's premature death at fifty-seven is to be bemoaned. One among the reasons is that CR's correspondence with his son-in-law could not extend further into the post-Independence history of India. Had Devadas Gandhi been around to receive letters from CR until he turned seventy-two, that is, until CR's death in 1972, we would have had some fascinating insights into CR's disenchantment with Nehru; the rise of his opposition to what he called Congress's 'Statism' and 'one-party rule'; the 'permit-licence-quota raj'; and his amazingly courageous action to establish a democratic alternative to the Congress from the right, in the shape of the Swatantra Party. It is debatable if Devadas Gandhi, a consistent supporter of Nehru's prime ministership, would have tried actively to dissuade his father-in-law from becoming so strong an opponent of Nehru. It is, however, not to be doubted that there would have been some lively correspondence between the two, as there was over CR's dissenting voice in the Quit India phase of the freedom struggle.

CR just about mentions the Swatantra Party's electoral experiences in his letters to me. My inexperience and self-excludingly young age at the time ruled out any detailed political discussions in letters to me. They could not of course be kept out of home-talk, nor were they meant to be. CR invariably stayed with us when he came to Delhi, in our flat atop the *Hindustan Times'* building in Connaught Circus. But on his first visit to the national capital after the formation of the Swatantra Party, CR wrote to my mother to say he would not like to embarrass her by the politics that will surround his presence in Delhi and will stay instead at the home of a Swatantra enthusiast, Sir Sobha Singh. And so he did. But after that initial experiment at a non-family billet in Delhi he returned to standard practice and, on later visits, stayed with us as before.

Soon after the 1962 elections, in which Swatantra did surprisingly well, CR came to Delhi. His newly elected MPs were to take their seats in the Lok Sabha. I asked him if he would not like to watch the proceedings from the visitors' gallery. 'It will be a sensation, Anna,' I ventured. CR thought awhile and said, 'It will be sensationalism.' He went that significant year on a brief political Sabbath as well. This volume contains a couple of letters written by him from what was his one and only visit to the West or anywhere abroad, barring Ceylon.

I went to see him board the international flight out of Bombay to Washington, to appeal to President Kennedy on behalf of the Gandhi Peace Foundation, to halt nuclear weapons testing. Friends had insisted he take his physician, Dr C. Satyanarayana, with him. He and his colleagues on the delegation, R.R. Diwakar, chairman of the Gandhi Peace Foundation, and B. Shiva Rao, veteran journalist and expert on India's Constitution, were to stop over in London en route. Maharashtra Governor Vijayalakshmi Pandit was at the airport, among others, to see CR off. Sitting beside him in the lounge before his emplaning, I asked, 'Will you be meeting Bertrand Russell in London?' 'Who?' he asked, cupping his good ear. I repeated the philosopher's name and referred to the remarkable pacifist's opposition to nuclear weapons. 'Oh no,' CR replied, 'he is too old.' Russell was ninety that year. And CR, eighty-four.

A little flutter occurred at the airport. Shiva Rao, holding a boarding pass, came up to CR looking crestfallen. 'What is the matter?' CR inquired. 'I have been put in the Economy Class, whereas all the others are in First Class . . . You have to be there, you are a former Governor General, your doctor has to be near you, but Diwakar is also in the First Class as he is a former Governor . . . I as a nobody . . .' CR smiled and then turning to Governor Vijayalakshmi Pandit said, 'Oh, that is so very short-sighted. They should know that Shiva Rao is the only future Governor, President among us . . .' Everyone broke into laughter and Shiva Rao's sullenness was replaced by a broad smile as he proceeded to travel Economy without a trace of resentment in his heart.

Who or what was the 'essential CR'?

CR has composed a piece of verse in Tamil of which the opening line is '*Kurai onrum illai . . .*', which can be rendered as 'No regrets have I . . .' Sung famously by M.S. Subbulakshmi in a plangent tune, the versification is now a celebrated song. In my view, it bears the essence of CR's mind and heart. How could one who had been called by Gandhi 'my only possible successor' and became nothing of the kind; who was the first Congress premier of Madras, hailed as the most successful of all Congress premiers in that experiment in provincial autonomy, and had to give up office following the outbreak of the Second World War; who could be asked to be the first Indian Governor General but obstructed from becoming India's first President; who could be implored to become chief minister of Madras by an electorally enfeebled Congress, only to be asked to stand down after the party had found its feet; and then see the party he had served all his life turn cold to him, adopt policies that were anathema to him—how could such a one have no regrets? How could one who lost his dearly loved wife at age twenty-six, his son and then both his sons-in-law have no regrets? How could such a one not have, in fact, a sense of deep hurt? I do not believe CR had no regrets. He did, and they were huge. In a man of lesser spiritual and intellectual fibre, the regrets would have led to dejection, depression or a simpering resignation to 'Fate'. Not so with CR. He did not oblige his regrets, he sublimated them into an intellectually arrived-at position of peace with the hand of destiny.

CR was pious, he was not pietist. He was traditional, not orthodox. He could rebel but not dally with heterodoxy. He prized intelligence but did not pickle his brains in the vinegar of cleverness. He was accepting of what Time served him, but did not become servile before its buffetings.

CR's last recorded words in hospital, as life ebbed away from his ninety-four-year-old frame, were 'I am happy'. This book is of letters written by a man who rescued happiness from the debris of disappointments, and faith from shattered dreams. Contradictory? Of course. But then, nothing less could have been expected from that most unusual man.

Portholes
to the
Letters

CR to Gandhi

'Words fail me altogether. I hope you have pardoned me'

12.6.1920

'I shudder to think how near to unutterable shame and ruin, not you, but all saintliness, all purity, all asceticism, all India's hopes [were] ... Come back and give us life'

16.6.1920

'The South will fully wake up to Swadeshi only after you bestow attention to it'

8.9.1921

'Seasonable things are uttered by everybody, and what is useful may be out of season in that sense'

31.5.1928

'Flattery from you is not like other people's. Their flattery can be absorbed with ease and satisfaction, but yours is a load of responsibility'

11.9.1931

'Unless we develop a new efficiency, honesty and public spirit, I don't expect to be happier under Swaraj than under the British Government'

24.9.1931

'Like the scientists that discovered truths and gave weapons to the warmongers you have given "Satyagraha" to the world, to the curers of social and political diseases, as well as the mischief-makers'

28.2.1938

'What I say would, if you only accepted it, produce immediate fruit and strength to the nation. But I cannot make you accept it!'

10.6.1942

Gandhi to CR

'You are my greatest hope'

22.3.1924

'Am fasting to live not die ... Don't worry'

18.9.1924

'You are ... perhaps the nearest to me. My innermost being wants your approbation of what I am doing and thinking'

16.7.1925

'I am most anxious that I should not become exclusive and should be humble enough to arrive at truth no matter from what source it comes'

28.3.1928

'[Your] views about Hindu–Muslim unity are entirely unseasonable'

27.5.1928

'Not a day has passed but I have thought of you and also felt the need of your presence ...There are two men whom I would like by my side in London, you and Jawaharlal'

28.9.1931

'You are dearer to me than life itself'

5.5.1933

'Let things take their course. It is enough, you and I have acted right'

5.3.1946

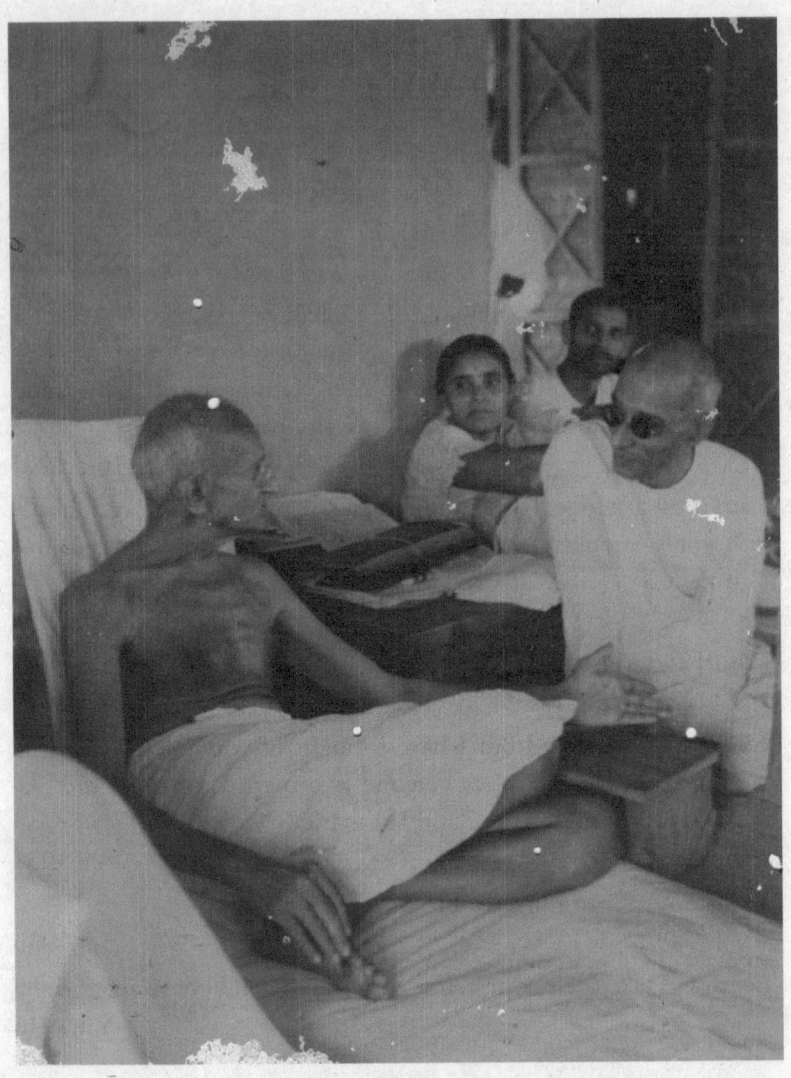

CR in discussion with Gandhi, Sevagram, June 1940.
Photograph: Kanu Gandhi

CR to Mohandas K. Gandhi

1

The stream of postcards, letters, telegrams, notes connecting Rajagopalachari to Gandhi begins with a four-page letter, handwritten, from CR. Dated 28 April 1919, this may not be the first letter he wrote to that destination, but it is the first to come to my notice. Like many in that stream, it is addressed not to Gandhi but to Gandhi's secretary, Mahadev Desai.[1]

Not surprisingly in a 'beginner', the letter starts in hesitant, self-conscious English. His misspelling of Devadas's[2] name also reflects lack of familiarity. But by the time the letter enters its postscript, it shows CR's mind as being quite 'his own', and one that is, on men and matters, already made up. It also shows how assessments of persons and politics have begun to find common ground between him and Desai and, by extension, between him and the Mahatma.

CR and Desai are to run an active system of communication between themselves that flows around Gandhi. Desai invariably shares CR's letters and his own replies with Gandhi; indeed, that is the assumption with which they are written.

---

[1] Mahadev Desai (1 January 1892–15 August 1942), lawyer, freedom fighter and writer, was Gandhi's personal secretary for over twenty-five years, from 1917 to 1942. Arrested with Gandhi during major campaigns, he wrote most of his important works on Gandhi during his imprisonment in Yeravada, Poona, between 1931 and 1934. Arrested, with Gandhi, on the morning of 9 August 1942 after Gandhi's call to the British to 'Quit India', he was sent to the Aga Khan Palace prison to serve his sentence. He died of a massive heart attack on 15 August, at the age of fifty, leaving Gandhi and his wife Kasturba, who had regarded Mahadev Desai as their son, desolate.

[2] Gandhi spelt his youngest son's name, when using English, 'Devdas', without the middle 'a'. CR consistently used the 'a', as is required in correct phonetics. And the name's owner quickly followed suit, though he did not attempt to change his father's practice.

*The original of this letter, written shortly after CR's return to
Madras from his first visit to Gandhi's ashram in Sabarmati, is preserved
in the ashram.*

Gandhi is fifty at the time, CR forty-one and Desai twenty-seven.

*As befits an 'inaugural', the letter is given here both in facsimile and
typed form.*

2 Cathedral Road[3]
Royapettah, Madras
28 April 1919

My dear Mahadevbhai,

Swami Satyadev[4] and I arrived here after an uneventful journey.
Leaving Satyadev in Sowcarpet, I met Devidas who is quite
well. Kindly convey this with my respects to Mahatmaji and
Mrs Gandhi.

A special message now from Mahatmaji is very necessary for
Madras. Otherwise it looks as if people will go to sleep. They feel
that everything has stopped. Of course I shall try and communicate
the life and activity that I saw in your place. But a specific message as
to the immediate work from Mahatmaji would greatly help. I should
desire his insistence that . . . preaching the duty of civil disobedience
should be continued as vigorously as ever.

---

[3] This house belonged to Kasturi Ranga Iyengar (also spelt 'Rangiengar'). CR, as
a tenant, hosted Gandhi and Mahadev Desai in it in March 1919. The building does
not exist any longer. The Hotel Chola is located on the site, with a plaque at its front
acknowledging the heritage.

[4] Swami Satyadev Parivrajak (1879–1961), a social reformer, was deeply influenced
by Swami Ram Tirth, Lala Lajpat Rai and Gokhale. Satyadev became a wandering
monk visiting America during 1905–11 and the European continent. He campaigned
against the maltreatment of women, idolatry, caste, child-marriage, purdah and
untouchability. He differed with Gandhi on many points but could never quite shake
off Gandhi's influence.

Mr Satyamurti[5] has fled to England. I understand he was sent off by Mr Kasturi Rangiengar[6] yesterday to Bombay to take ship there. I understand that Mr A Rangaswami Ayyangar[7] also is to leave for England in two weeks. I hope there will be work for Satyagraha in England.

---

[5] S. Satyamurti (1887–1943) was a lawyer, writer, dramatist, politician and patriot. An adherent of S. Srinivasa Iyengar, Satyamurti was the political mentor of K. Kamaraj. CR's equation with Satyamurti was marked by mutual unease from early on in their careers. Satyamurti's gravitation to the Swaraj Party, where he acquired a powerful presence next only to that of Motilal Nehru and Chittaranjan Das, sharpened the differences. CR nominated Satyamurti to succeed him as president of the Tamil Nadu Provincial Congress Committee in 1930. Satyamurti tirelessly orchestrated the Indian National Congress's successful election campaign in 1937. CR's emerging as the Congress's choice for the premiership of Madras after those successfully fought elections is seen as a moment of injustice to the younger leader. Satyamurti served as mayor of wartime Madras in 1939, striving vigorously to improve the quality of its citizens' daily lives.

Like many others in the Indian independence movement, Satyamurti was jailed repeatedly. Arrested in 1942 for performing 'individual satyagraha' at the height of the Quit India movement, he was tried and deported to Amaravati Jail in Nagpur and suffered injury in the spinal cord during the journey. He passed away at General Hospital, Madras, on 28 March 1943.

CR's reference is to Satyamurti's going to London to be at hand when nationalists were protesting the Montagu–Chelmsford reforms and the Rowlatt Act before the Joint Parliamentary Committee (of the UK). When Satyamurti was in Britain, he also functioned as the London correspondent of *The Hindu*, to fill in for a correspondent on leave.

[6] Kasturi Ranga Iyengar (1859–1923) was a lawyer, freedom fighter and politician. He was the managing director of *The Hindu* till his death at the age of sixty-four. In 1905, the year he purchased it, *The Hindu* demanded complete independence for India. The paper put its weight behind the Home Rule Movement and strongly condemned the Rowlatt Act and the Jallianwala massacre of 1919. Gandhi stayed at his house as CR's guest and, while there, on 22–23 March 1919, in the 'twilight condition between sleep and consciousness', had the idea for an all-India hartal to protest against the Rowlatt Act. After the enactment of this law and the Jallianwala Bagh massacre and Khilafat, Kasturi Ranga Iyengar and CR worked closely together, the former presiding over Nationalists' Association and CR functioning with T. Prakasam as secretary. CR moved to a smaller house, 'Venkata Vilas', on Luz Church Road, Mylapore, towards the end of 1919.

[7] A. Rangaswami Iyengar (1877–1934)—nephew of Kasturi Rangiengar, journalist and editor of *Swadesamitran*—was an active proponent of Council-entry, along with S. Satyamurti.

Hind Swaraj[8] Tamil Translation is getting ready—only 30 pages yet to be done—I shall get the same printed here.

You did not give me copies of Mahatmaji's recent leaflets. I happen to have the No.1 and No.2 from the Bombay Chronicle. I want No.3 and No.4 in English either newspaper cutting or manuscript or printed copy.

Can you arrange for 2000 copies of English Hind Swaraj for us when you get . . . ready there. Let me know when ready so that I can send a man to bring them.

Let me know who can supply in Bombay honest—mill spun—Swadeshi yarn. I shall arrange Salem handlooms for weaving the same.

I am very glad I went to Bombay and the Asramam. I feel much encouraged to work. I wish more people from Madras went likewise.

My kindest regards to all brethren and sisters there.

Yours sincerely,
C. Rajagopalachari

P.S

1. I hope the letter from Simla re. Whipping is reassuring really and not a successful piece of diplomacy.
2. I do hope Mahatmaji is not travelling and has got over the cold.
3. I wish you sent me important news from time to time, whenever you find time to breathe.

C.R.

---

[8] *Hind Swaraj*, or *Indian Home Rule*, a slim work in Gujarati and English by Gandhi, written while returning from London to South Africa on board SS *Kildonan Castle* between 13 and 22 November 1909.

/
S. N. 11696

2 Cathedral Road
Royapettah - Madras
28. 4. '19

5,3

My dear Mahadevbhai,

Swami Satyadev & I arrived here yesterday
after an uneventful journey. Leaving Satyadev
in Sowcarpet, I saw Devidas who is quite well
Kindly convey this along with my respects
to Mahatmaji & Mrs. Gandhi.

                Special   now
        A message from Mahatmaji is very
necessary for Madras. Otherwise it looks as
if people will go to sleep. They feel that
everything has stopped. Of course I shall
try to communicate the life & activity
that I saw in your place. But a specific
message as to the immediate work from
Mahatmaji would greatly help I should
desire his insistence that the preaching
of the duty of civil disobedience should
be continued as vigorously as ever.

        Mr. Satyamurti has fled to
England. I understand he obtained

54   (2)

J.n. 11656

was sent off by Mr Kasturi Ranga iyer
yesterday to Bombay to take ship there. I learn also that Mr.
A Rangaswami Ayyangar also is to
leave for England in two weeks. I hope
there will be work for Satyagraha in England.

Hind Swaraj Tamil Translation is
getting ready — only 30 pages yet to be done —
I shall get the same printed here.

You did not give me
copies of Mahatmaji's recent
leaflets. I happen to have No. 1
& No. 2 from the Bombay Chronicle.
I want No. 3 & No. 4. in English
either newspaper cutting or manuscript
or printed copy.

Can you arrange for 2000 copies
of English Hind Swaraj for us when you
get them ready there. Let me know
when ready so that I may send a
man to bring them.

Let me know who can supply
in Bombay honest mill spun —

S.n. 11696

Swadeshi yarn. I shall arrange Salem handlooms for weaving the same.

I am very glad I went to Bombay & to the Asramam. I feel much encouraged to work. I wish more people from Madras went likewise.

My kindest regards to all brethren & sisters there.

Yours Sincerely

C. Rajagopalachari

P.S.

1) I hope the letter from Simla re whishring is reassuring really & not a successful piece of diplomacy.

2) I do hope Mahatma is not travelling, & has got on the cold.

3) I wish you sent me important news from time to time, whenever

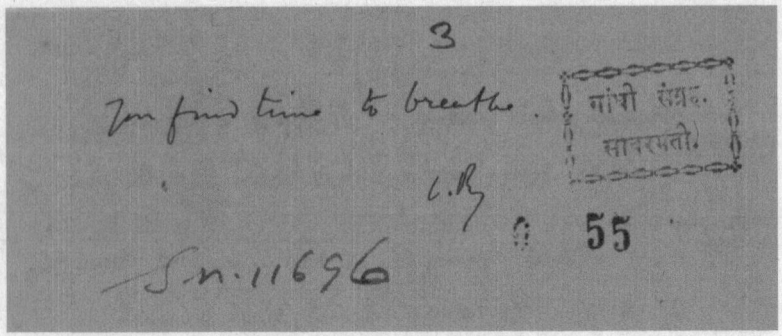

*The context of 'Whipping' mentioned in CR's letter is given in the
telegram reproduced below, which Gandhi had sent to the private secretary
to the viceroy.*

BOMBAY

21 APRIL 1919

JUST READ ASSOCIATED PRESS WIRE DATED 19TH SAYING PERSONS ARRESTED
FOR DISOBEYING ORDERS ISSUED UNDER MARTIAL LAW ARE BEING WHIPPED
IN PUBLIC STREETS. UNDERSTAND ORDERS HAVE REFERENCE TO OPENING
SHOPS. IF PRESS WIRE CORRECT, RESPECTFULLY SUBMIT THAT SUCH
WHIPPING WOULD ROUSE GRAVEST INDIGNATION. HOPE THERE IS SOME
EXPLANATION THAT WOULD REMOVE ALL CAUSE FOR ANXIETY AND IN ANY
CASE I WOULD LIKE TO BE ASSURED THAT NO AUTHORITY HAS BEEN GIVEN
TO GENERAL OFFICER COMMANDING, MARTIAL LAW OPERATIONS, TO WHIP
PEOPLE PUBLICLY OR PRIVATELY FOR OFFENCE DESCRIBED ABOVE.

N.A.I.: HOME: POLITICAL (DEPOSIT): MAY—1919: NO. 4.

2

*This five-page letter is the earliest communication from CR to Gandhi in
the holdings of the Gandhi Ashram, Sabarmati. It shows a relationship
of mutual trust and frankness between the two, marked by a clear*

recognition by him of the leadership of Gandhi, best reflected at this stage by his addressing Gandhi as 'Mahatmaji'. If CR acknowledges Gandhi's complete control over the civil disobedience being planned, he also reserves and exercises the right to advise him on specifics and strategy. The legal expertise of both is evident in the letter. Gandhi, on his part, is already reposing in CR the role of his 'Southern eyes and ears'. And, at a personal level, he has entrusted his eighteen-year-old son, Devadas, the first Hindi 'pracharak' (propagandist) in Madras, to the care and tutelage of CR.

Cathedral Road, Cathedral
Madras
29 June 1919

My dear Mahatmaji,

Your letter written Wednesday morning and the proof copy of instructions reached duly. The resolution you have arrived at, that you should first, and alone, offer civil disobedience, I must confess, produced what I must call a kind of grief—at any rate my feelings were mixed.

I showed the letter and enclosure to Devadas. Your instructions are being reprinted for private circulation among Satyagrahis, so that they may be in full possession of information as to their duties and your expectations of them. I have arranged for a general meeting of all Satyagrahis on 15 July in Madras.

It is a coincidence that Messrs Ganesh & Co.[9] have just got Hind Swaraj (English Edition) ready for issue. The Tamil edition was to be taken up as soon as the English was printed off. But Sri Harisarvottama Rao's[10] press which was to do both, is now unable

---

[9] S. Ganesan, Triplicane, Madras.

[10] Gadicherla Harisarvottama Rao, a nationalist from the Andhra segment of Madras Presidency.

to do it as the security is forfeited, and he is not likely to furnish fresh security.

It is difficult to contain oneself when one reads that the Viceroy has refused to stay the death sentence pending appeal to the Privy Council. This single telegram of the API is worse than a hundred articles in the 'Nationalist' or the 'cult of the bullet'!

I have sent yesterday a copy of the issue of the Nationalist containing the article on which the security was forfeited. New India has, unfortunately, declared that the article was rightly objected to. Apart from the merits of the question, the matter is still *sub judice* as an appeal lies yet to the High Court on the forfeiture, and the High Court has held it could go into the merits of the articles on which forfeiture is ordered.

I return the cutting about the British India Press. The fact of the matter is this. 'Desabaktan' is printed in a press called the British India Press. The press is financed and in so far as the real beneficial interest goes, owned by Mr Kamath[11] and another. But the declaration under the Press Act was originally made for some reason or another by the editor, Mr Kalyanasundara Mudaliar[12] and the same declaration continued up to date. When the security given by the press was forfeited some time before your last visit to Madras, Mr Kamath found it difficult to furnish the increased security demanded of the press. I understand that they were advised that they could under the law transfer the press to a third person, who could, then, in spite

---

[11] M.S. Kamath, friend of Subramania Bharati, started *Desabhaktan*, a Tamil equivalent of Annie Besant's *New India*. Later, he became founder-editor, printer and publisher of the Madras-based *Sunday Times* and founder-editor of the Tamil weekly, *Hindusthan*.

[12] Thiruvarur Viruttacala Kalyanasundara Mudaliar (1883–1953), better known as Thiru Vi. Ka, started out as a bookkeeper at the Madras store, Spencers, and taught at Wesley College, Royapettah, before joining *Desabhaktan*. Renowned as a Tamil scholar, essayist and activist, whose works helped define modern Tamil prose, Thiru Vi. Ka was active in the freedom struggle, becoming the president of the Tamil Nadu Congress Committee in 1926.

of the increased demand of the former declarant, apply for a fresh declaration and continue the paper, on an original security instead of the former proprietors giving the additional security. Under this advice, they agreed to transfer the press to a friend of theirs, Mr Dandapani. He applied on the strength of the agreement which was entirely oral. Though the arrangements were to be completed and possession transferred only after the Magistrate accepted the declaration, he appears to have stated that he 'purchased the press for cash'. Of course, if the arrangement was completed, the cash was to be paid. Subsequently, however, the public subscribed, and the old proprietors decided to pay the increased security and go on, and Mr Dandapani withdrew his application, and the transfer arrangements came to an end. The Police who were always desirous of giving trouble to Mr Kalyanasundara and Mr Dandapani, decided to take the opportunity and have ordered the prosecution on the ground that the statement that the press was sold was a false statement. I have advised them to state the bare truth.

If in breaking the internment order, you leave the Bombay Presidency, I suppose your objective will be, the Punjab. Before you start, I believe you will make a public statement directly connecting your civil disobedience with the laws that take away from the Indian citizen, the fundamental rights of liberty so that your resistance may not be associated too narrowly with the Punjab infamy by itself. Then I shall take the liberty of placing a suggestion before you. In leaving Bombay and committing civil disobedience, may you not add to it going to the Viceroy to offer yourself up for trial as the 'conspirator' that you were shamelessly termed in the martial law cases. Why should you not demand that you should be tried as so many others were charged with acts in pursuance of the same conspiracy of which they had the audacity to charge you with behind your back? It is not for the insult which, of course, you do not mind at all, but the substance of it that when they have hanged and imprisoned men stating that you 'conspired' and so on, it becomes their duty to try you and punish you. Of course, the whole thing may very probably end with only your own offer, for the Government will be only too glad to arrest you as soon as you leave Bombay and confine you indefinitely under some one of the beautiful regulations of the early 19th century,—or the Governor General may issue a Special Ordinance to confine you! It seems to me that in committing civil disobedience, and proceeding to leave Bombay, you may put this forward as your objective of the journey.

Regarding 'Young India' I have spoken to several friends, who have promised to contribute. I shall remind them.

With abiding love,
I remain,
Yours sincerely,
C. Rajagopalachari

The following letters from Gandhi to the private secretary to the Governor of Bombay are of relevance:

As at Laburnum Road
Bombay
22 June 1919

Dear Mr. Cowie,

I have just seen the petition submitted to His Excellency for mercy in the case of one Chand, a lad of 15 or 16 years, who has been sentenced to be hanged for the murder of the late Sergeant Fraser. There is in my opinion no doubt that the young boy was one of the murderers of an innocent police officer. I do not share the view taken by Chand's pleader in his petition. But I do respectfully share the view taken by the prosecuting counsel who is reported by The

Times of India (12th instant Dak Edition) to have said in his address before the Court: 'The only extenuating circumstance in favour of the 1st accused (Chand) was his age.' There is no doubt too that this was not a murder deliberately planned by Chand or anybody else but that Chand evidently did the act in a fit of mad excitement. Regard being had to all the circumstances of the case I venture to submit that the ends of justice will be better met by tempering it with His Excellency's prerogative of mercy and by commutation of the sentence in any manner that may appear to His Excellency to be most proper. I may observe that Chand has a widowed mother. I trust that His Excellency will be pleased to give favourable consideration to the petition for mercy.

Yours sincerely,

As at Laburnum Road
Bombay
29 June 1919

Dear Mr. Cowie,

I received your letter about Chand as I was leaving for Ahmedabad. I have just received news that the sentence against Chand has been commuted into transportation. May I say that this great act of mercy will be much appreciated not only amongst the poor family of the lad, but widely amongst all those thousands of men and women who have been following the proceedings of the Tribunal with more or less interest, amongst whom I count myself as one. Will you please place this letter before His Excellency?

Yours sincerely,

3

This handwritten two-page manuscript on the letterhead of the Cosmopolitan Club, Madras, is preserved at the Sabarmati ashram. On receiving the letter, Gandhi has written down at the end of the second page the name of the 'young man' in pencil as 'Chaturvedula Venkata Krishna ayya', with the 'ayya' scored out. Gandhi's follow-up letter to his nephew, who was managing the administration of the ashram, describes CR as 'the well-known satyagrahi'.

Cosmopolitan Club
Mount Road Madras
4 July 1919

Dear Mahatmaji,

The bearer is a young man who persists in his enthusiasm to be with you or in the Ashram in spite of my explaining to him everything about his venture. I do not know him, but from what Mr. Nageshwara Rao[13] writes about him, he seems to be a young man of character.

Can you possibly find him a place near you or in the ashram?

Yours Sincerely,
C. Rajagopalachar

---

[13] Kasinadhuni Nageswara Rao (1867–1938), better known as Nageswara Rao Pantulu, was a journalist and politician from the Andhra region of Madras Presidency. A front-ranking Congressman, he was a contemporary of 'Andhra Kesari' T. Prakasam and served as president of the Andhra Pradesh Congress Committee for four terms from 1924 to 1934. Active in the programmes unveiled by Gandhi, especially khaddar, Nageswara Rao participated in the Salt Satyagraha and was jailed in 1931 for six months as a result.

Following up, Gandhi wrote to his nephew Maganlal Gandhi
(in Gujarati):

Wednesday
[16 July 1919]

Chi. Maganlal,

This note will be brought by one Mr. Venkat Krishnama. He has been sent by Rajagopalachari, the well-known satyagrahi. He wants to do manual work. He says he will be able to get us Rs. 10 every month.

He will be satisfied, he says, if he gets a verandah to himself, and is ready for any kind of work. His own wish is to learn weaving. You may put him on to any labour you like, starting him, at the same time, on spinning. He may stay if he works well and leave if he is not happy. I may, thus, send on any person I think fit; if you find the thing embarrassing any time, let me know immediately. I am to see the Governor on Friday. I shall know better on that day what the future holds for me . . .

Blessings from
Bapu

4

The following six entries, namely three telegrams and three letters, are
in the nature of replies, sent by CR from Madras during the month of
June 1920. The correspondence occurs against the backdrop of a national
development of huge public salience—the first non-cooperation movement
about to be launched—with Gandhi then stationed at Mani Bhuvan,
Laburnum Road, Gamdevi, in Bombay, preparing for that struggle. The
first letter from CR is occasioned by one from Gandhi to CR, which does

not figure in The Collected Works of Mahatma Gandhi *(hereafter, the* Collected Works*), and which, we can infer from CR's letter, has been sent to CR with a covering letter from Mahadev Desai. In his letter Gandhi apparently informs his friend of a mental 'battle' within him over Saraladevi Chaudhurani.*[14]

The telegraphist's spelling mistakes have been retained in the address entries of the telegrams[15] *for integrity of vintage. The original of the first letter is among the Rajagopalachari Papers at the National Archives, New Delhi. The originals of the three telegrams and the second and third letters have been among Devadas Gandhi's personal collection since the mid-1920s, when Mahadev Desai handed them over to Devadas Gandhi. At the time of publishing, these five were in the family's possession.*

The ellipses in the transcription of these letters indicate the loss of legibility due in part to paper damage and in part, on account of the adhesive of a cellophane tape that had been amateurishly pasted across, eating into the ink.

First telegram from CR to Mahadev Desai received at destination at 2146 hours on 12 June 1920:

MAHADEV DESAI C/O GANDHI SABURNUM ROAD GAMDEVI BOMBAY
ARE WE NOT INDEED HAPPY CARRYING OUT DECISION DIFFICULT

---

[14] Married to the distinguished writer, nationalist, member of the Arya Samaj and the Indian National Congress Pandit Rambhuj Dutt Chaudhuri (1866–1923), Saraladevi (1872–1945) was Rabindranath Tagore's niece (sister's daughter), a graduate and gold-medallist of Calcutta University, and a noted poet and singer. For further details on the episode, refer to the *Collected Works*, Volume 21 (page 196), Volume 22 (page 119) and Volume 59 (page 196); Martin Green, *Gandhi, Voice of a New Age Revolution* (New York: Continuum, 1993); and Rajmohan Gandhi, *Mohandas* (New Delhi: Penguin Books India, 2006).

[15] The telegrams are on standard P&T stationery with the text pasted on them in the running strips that characterized telegrams at the time. Age has taken its toll on the letters, which are handwritten in black ink on now very browned letter paper, 18 cm in length and 11 cm in width.

SENDER HELP HASTEN RELENTLESSLY RESERVE PITY FOR NATION =
RAJAGOPALACHARI

*Second telegram from CR to Gandhi received at destination at 2235
hours on 12 June 1920:*

MAHATMA GANDHI LABURNUM RD GAMDEIR BOMBAY
YOUR TELEGRAM GAVE ME NEW LIFE PRAY ACT WITHOUT ANY DELAY
WHATEVER = RAJAGOPALACHARI

*Third telegram from CR to Gandhi's nephew, Mathuradas Trikamji,
received at destination at 2241 hours on 12 June 1920:*

MATHURADAS TRIKAMJI 93 BAZARGATE FORT BOMBAY
THANK GOD WATCH AND PREVENT WAVERING HASTEN ACTION =
RAJAGOPALACHARI

First letter from CR to Gandhi:

Madras

12 June 1920

My dearest Master,

Had your telegram. Words fail me altogether.
I hope you have pardoned me.

Yours most sincerely,

C. Rajagopalachari

Second letter from CR to Gandhi:

Venkata Vilas

Luz, Mylapore

16 June 1920

My dearest Master,

I enclose your letter. I am unworthy to hold such a confession. I thank you for your affection which I treasure in my heart.

Your confession surpasses my apprehensions. Mahadev is too much . . . His short account . . . He appears on the whole exhilarated with the richness of beauty, of the fresco of greatness . . . sin . . . confession . . . He speaks of 'not standing between me and the invaluable gift enclosed herewith'. He speaks with intoxicated admiration how you wove the 'wonderful gift'. I cannot take such an altogether artist's view of it. The thing is to me too awful. Mahadev is lost in admiring the beauty of the cobra's head. But I shudder to think how near to unutterable shame and ruin, not you, but all saintliness, all purity, all asceticism, all India's hope . . . were. There would have been no place in the world for India to hide its head.

What right had you to . . . your impregnability and dally with such ruin?

How could you venture out when in your boat was the faith and fate of millions of simple souls who if the boat had capsized would have seen neither beauty nor love nor grandeur, but unspeakable shame and death.

I do not like abstractions and figures of speech in this matter. Satan is an expression that will deceive us. It is a mere apologetic expression for the evil for which we are responsible . . . throne of a whole people's implicit trust—my dearest Master—allow me to be harsh, I speak with tears in my eyes—you have no right to act thus. The attack that you describe is a figure of speech. In itself is a great lapse. The struggle towards which we might cast a satisfied look behind after seeming victories, are all lapses from the very beginning. The battle is but a trick of language for expressing partial indulgence . . . All this proves how indestructible flesh is. The encasement of the divinest soul is yet flesh and nerves which have subtle tricks of their own simulating the spirit and the higher functions. You had found strength to conquer love of wife, child and all the passions that normally devour men . . . Your affectionate nature was trapped by long suppressed flesh into a most dreadful delusion; and your weak health and nerves made it all easier.

I utterly fail to see any 'greatness' in the lady. She is like a hundred other women, whom a little education makes very attractive. I have seen scores of bigger-minded—better souled women. There are no more . . . women,—certainly no more than in me, and you are not in love with me—not to speak of Mahadev or Devadas or Surendra[16]

---

[16] Surendra of Gorakhpur was an ascetic who joined the Sabarmati ashram at a very young age in 1916 and worked there as a tanner and cobbler. A gifted writer in Hindi and a linguist, he was one of the Dandi Salt Satyagraha marchers and later travelled extensively in the Himalaya. He was among the very small number of people who took

who simply dote on you as no woman ever loved man. She is not worthy to unloose the latchet of Miss Faring's[17] shoes and as to Mrs Gandhi,[18] it would be comparing a kerosene oil Ditmar[19] lamp to the morning sun . . . creature who lost her bearing in the familiarity of your glory and who neither truly returned your feelings nor suffered any struggle . . . . She . . . sailing in the . . . having enslaved an effulgent saint such as all the world adored. I do not take as answer her vocabulary of English poetry which come like ready-made wings to anyone sailing with Satan.

Anyway it was not a stormy passion—it was a weakling Satan in her case. It is difficult to forgive her reckless indifference to consequences . . . pray disengage yourself at once completely: No delay is allowable when you hold such great trusts. No . . . true Hindu culture and conduct can be . . . by you.

I have chosen to err on the side of harshness, rather than fail to strengthen. It is not the Christ, but the shell that I presume to warn and criticize. Come back and give us life.

Yours sincerely,
C. Rajagopalachari

a portion of Gandhi's ashes to be immersed at Lake Manasarovar in 1948. 'Surendraji' or 'Sadhu' Surendra, as he came to be called, lived in later years at Samanvaya ashram, near Bodh Gaya. He passed away on 16 June 1990.

[17] Esther Faering (1889–1962), a Danish missionary who first came to Gandhi's ashram in 1917. By 'not worthy to unloose the latchet' CR means 'not coming anywhere near, in comparison'.

[18] Kasturba Gandhi née Kapadia (1869–1944), satyagrahi and freedom fighter; colleague and wife of Mohandas Karamchand Gandhi; mother of his four sons, Harilal, Manilal, Ramdas and Devadas; imprisoned during Gandhi's campaigns in South Africa and in India; and vigorous campaigner in Bihar and elsewhere against the custom of purdah and for the propagation of khadi. She died during the course of his last sentence which she shared with him, in Poona.

[19] A kind of table lamp then in vogue, manufactured by R. Ditmar, Bombay, and advertised in the Statesman, Calcutta, in September 1905, as 'especially constructed for use in India' and 'noted for their splendid illuminating power'.

Third letter from CR to Gandhi:

Madras
29 June 1920

My dearest Master

I was no doubt harsh . . . been amply and deservedly punished by your forgiveness which has . . .

But my anxiety and anger overpowered me and . . . wrote harshly.

She[20] must have . . . it so hard to have . . . write to one who ha . . . letter anything of the affection which I undoubtedly felt—for one who loved and sacrificed so much for my Master. This feeling did try . . . itself. I remember . . . well. She m . . . treated her so well. But she rose to the height and has written justly and nobly. I fondly hope she has forgiven me, or at last one day will do it.

Hari Har Sharma[21] has not yet come back to stay at Madras. He has gone to his Native village.

My father's condition is not satisfactory.

I had your advice regarding my Madras letter for Young India. I quite appreciate the criticism—but it is another thing to be able to do what you ask me to.

I begin to think Hakim Ajmal Khan's[22] point is right and that we had better secure pledges to each stage of the programme for the time being put in place, so that we may carry a large number

---

[20] Saraladevi Chaudhurani.

[21] Pandit Harihar Sharma first met Gandhi at Santiniketan in 1915 and soon after joined the Ahmedabad ashram. He had been a teacher at the Ganganath Bharatiya Vidyalaya, Baroda, and was later secretary, Dakshina Bharat Hindi Prachar Sabha, Madras. Gandhi wrote in *Navajivan* (18 May 1924) that Harihar Sharma had 'taken up the work of propagating Hindi in the Dravida region and, for that purpose, he and his wife studied Hindi in Prayag. Both of them passed the Hindi examination there and they started the work of spreading Hindi in Madras.'

[22] Hakim Ajmal Khan (1863–1927) was a Unani physician, politician and freedom fighter. He founded the Tibbia College in Delhi. Working closely with Gandhi, he participated in the non-cooperation movement, played a leading role in the Khilafat

of men as possible each time with us. The number of nominated
and elected . . . officers—Taluka, District and Municipal Boards'
memberships—held by persons is so large in number—is so
important a part in the administration that it is not so hopeless to
do something effective even in the first stage.

S. Srinivasa Iyengar[23]—late Advocate General—who has in a
friendly manner defeated Mr Kasturi Ranga Iyengar in leadership
is actively denouncing non-cooperation as impracticable asceticism.
In fact he denounces Satyagraha itself in the same way.

Yours sincerely,
C. Rajagopalachari

5

*This handwritten letter is about an individual not figuring in later
correspondence.*

Madras
5 July 1920

My dearest Master

I had made up my mind long ago that Shanti Prasad was an
unsteady, quarrelsome and unreliable young man. I am inclined to

---

movement and became the president of the Indian National Congress, chairing the
Ahmedabad session in 1921.

[23] S. Srinivasa Iyengar (1874–1941), an eminent lawyer, freedom fighter and Congress
politician who favoured entry in legislatures as opposed to non-cooperation. Iyengar
presided over the 1920 Madras Provincial Conference held at Tirunelveli and participated
in the Congress sessions held at Ahmedabad (1921), Gaya (1922), Kakinada (1923), Delhi
(1923), Belgaum (1924), Kanpur (1925), Gauhati (1926—presided over the session),
Madras (1927), Calcutta (1928) and Lahore (1929). His work gave an impetus to the
Congress in Madras for about ten years, and brought to the fore his junior in the legal
profession, S. Satyamurti, and the future leader K. Kamaraj.

think that the complaints about Harihar Sharma are the result of his refusing to have Shanti Prasad as one of the Hindi pracharaks. I shall investigate as soon as Sharma comes back to Madras and write to you.

I am certainly at your disposal in regard to this work, and you need not get sad over it.

Yours sincerely,
C. Rajagopalachari

6

This is a telegram sent by CR from Madras to Gandhi in Bombay. The original is at the Sabarmati ashram. Gandhi scribbled a reply on it in pencil: 'View All India Committee meeting other obligations two weeks impossible before August'.

6 JULY 1921

MAHATMA GANDHI LABURNUM ROAD GAMDEVI BOMBAY
MUST COME HERE SOON FOR TWO WEEKS TOUR AFTER STARTING WORK
BOMBAY

RAJAGOPALACHARI S. SRINIVASA IYENGAR

7

At the time of his writing this letter, CR is one of three general secretaries of the Indian National Congress, the other two being Motilal Nehru and M.A. Ansari. This is a time when a significant tranche of talent leaves the courts of the Raj for the chessboard of lawbreaking. Motilal and Jawaharlal in the north, C.R. Das in Calcutta, Rajendra Prasad in Bihar, Vallabhbhai Patel in Gujarat and CR in the south are legal minds on the

warpath, aided by non-legal leaders like the Ali brothers, Dr Ansari and
Maulana Azad. Thirty-six lawyers including T. Prakasam leave the courts
in the Tamil region. Hindu–Muslim unity has been dramatically fostered by
the resistance to the Rowlatt bills and by the Khilafat movement.

But the camaraderie is shaken by a wholly unexpected turn of
events—the outbreak of the Moplah riots in Malabar, then part of
Madras Presidency. Reported insults to the Moplahs' priests trigger a
rebellion by the Moplahs, originally descended from Arab immigrants.
Directed first against the government, Moplah ire soon takes on Hindu
landlords. The Raj deploys troops on a massive scale. Over two thousand
are killed and nearly 25,000 convicted of rebellion and other crimes.

As Congress secretary, CR asks the authorities for permission to organize
relief. The permission is denied. This letter (with an important postscript)
is a report from the 'Southern lieutenant' to the 'General'. The original is
preserved in the National Gandhi Museum, Rajghat, New Delhi.

It is to be noted that by now 'Master' has turned into 'Mahatmaji'
whether at Gandhi's request or, more naturally, in the course of the
increasing frequency of communication and association.

At the domestic level, CR arranges the wedding of his elder daughter,
fifteen-year-old Namagiri, with twenty-four-year-old Varadachari, a
journalist in Rangoon. CR takes an even smaller house on rent in Madras,
'The Gem', on Poonamallee High Road, but in the middle of 1921 gives
that up too, selling his Darracq and furniture and going back to Salem. It is
clear he is expecting an escalation of the struggle and possible arrest.

Calicut
8 September 1921

Dear Mahatmaji,

Ever since the Bombay All India Congress Committee meeting[24] I
am sorry I have not been well. I am suffering from asthma; occasional
low fever and troublesome boils in the skin.

---

[24] AICC meeting, 28–30 July 1921.

About the same time that the joint letter written as you were going into Assam[25] reached, news of the terrible happenings in Malabar came to us. It is no exaggeration to say that the events have inflicted a mortal wound on the movement here. The doings of the Moplah bands have made man, woman and child among the Hindus here lose faith in Hindu Muslim unity. It is true there was great provocation which makes the outburst understandable; and the rebel bands consisted of different varieties, one the violent Khilafat kind, another the angry and suffering tenantry, another the pure religious fanatics, all acting independently according to opportunities. It is true also there is many an incident which brings satisfaction to the Congress and Khilafat workers. But nothing can make up for the universal feeling of distrust and hatred that has taken the place of the Hindu Muslim amity that had been built up with so much trouble.

The killing has been most in fighting and not in cold blood. But the looting of Hindu houses was carried out wholesale over a large area and the stories of forcible conversions are though exaggerated as regards number, still true in substance in at least 50 cases. The 50 is made up of one family of 33 and other stray cases. Hindu temples were generally immune. But two temples were broken open. This was probably for loot, and some important temples even in the worst centres of the disturbance were absolutely safe.

Martial law still continues. Calicut is calm. The chief lines of communication are all kept in hand. But in the interior there are still roving bands; and the soldiery are engaged in trying to get at them.

No meetings are possible, not even small ones. Opinion is unanimous that your immediate coming to Malabar can serve no purpose, and that it would be better if you finish the Tamil districts before coming here.

As regards the internal politics of Madras, the Tanjore Conference has on the whole eased the situation. The President's ruling has had

---

[25] This was a twelve-day visit—Gandhi's first—to Assam.

no practical effect. The objectors (most of them) have joined[26] in confirming the proceedings to which objections had been taken, and the Working Committee's decision has been accepted and work is going on. Of course personal anger continues in some cases.

The South will fully wake up to Swadeshi only after you bestow attention to it in the shape of a prolonged visit. I think this is the psychological time for it; as there are signs of spontaneous waking up also. Our drink campaign has succeeded wonderfully.

I have not received here a reply to my telegram to you to Calcutta as to date of your arrival at Madras. Perhaps telegrams are censored here at Calicut and not delivered.

I am at Salem on account of my bad health. I shall be at Madras when you arrive there. Let me have a wire at Salem.

Yours Sincerely,
C. Rajagopalachar

The wholesale looting by the Moplahs of Hindu houses in the disturbed areas and the terrible slaughter among the Moplahs has created extreme distress and starvation over a large area. Famine relief is urgent. If this work is organized by the Congress Committees here, there is hope yet to recover the lost ground. To organise this at once and efficiently is the essential work before us now. Money cannot be had here. I am not very hopeful that Tamil Districts either will immediately rise to the occasion. Anyway there is no time. The

---

[26] S. Srinivasa Iyengar opposed the Congress's decision to boycott Councils. He contested and won a seat in the Madras legislature. Satyamurti and Rangaswami Iyengar did contest but did not join the boycott with enthusiasm, while Kasturi Rangiengar, as president of the Tamil Nadu Congress, at first opposed boycott and in *The Hindu* criticized CR editorially. So also did the *Madras Mail* and *Swadesamitran*, which accused CR of keeping 'well-known leaders' out of Congress committees and, generally, of being self-willed. But three prominent Congress workers threw their weight behind CR: E.V. Ramaswami Naicker, T.V. Kalyanasundara Mudaliar (Thiru Vi. Ka) and Dr Varadarajulu Naidu.

reports about starvation are terrible. It would be a beautiful thing
if the Mussalman communities of India came now to the rescue of
starving Hindu families. Can the central Khilafat Committee spare
any funds at once. 75% of the Hindu houses in one half of Ernad
Taluk, almost the whole of Walluvanad Taluk, and the northern
half of another Taluk have been looted. Standing crops have been
either also removed or left to destruction now. The situation is very
pitiable. 2 lakhs would not be too much for immediate investment
in the work of relief if only we had the money.

Yours
C.R.

8

*This is a three-page letter written by hand. Civil disobedience has acquired
an edge by the visit of the Prince of Wales, whose arrival on 17 November
sees a comprehensive boycott. The Raj retaliates by banning volunteer
organizations of the Congress and the Khilafat, and disallowing gatherings.
CR defies the ban through a meeting attended by 5000 at Vellore, asking
them to maintain communal amity and 'to keep to the oath of non-violence
under all provocation'. He is brought to trial. His three sons are in Salem
at the time of his trial and sentencing, while his two daughters are in
Rangoon where the elder one, Namagiri, and her husband, Varadachari,
are based. This letter is written just before the Vellore meeting.*

Salem
9 December 1921

My dear Mahatmaji,

I sent you a telegram yesterday but I am told by the telegraph office
that it is 'objectionable' and won't be transmitted.

Our P.C.C. has permitted individual disobedience. On 4th inst. the Provincial Congress Executive Committee met at Vellore. The local Congress Committee taking advantage of the presence of the leaders from various districts announced a public meeting. Immediately, notices were served under Sec. 144 Cr. P.C on me, Dr. Rajan,[27] Erode Ramaswami Naicker[28] (Joint Secretaries of the Province), & on Subramania Sastri (President of the Provincial Congress Committee) prohibiting us from addressing any meeting at Vellore for 2 months. Such orders have been served on workers everywhere now. The situation is such that the only alternative is standstill or imprisonment by disobedience. The Executive Committee met and after prolonged deliberation they agreed in pursuance of the Prov. C.C's resolution permitting individual disobedience that Ramaswami Naicker & I should disobey the order & it has so notified. Police Sports occupied the only ground available till today. The meeting is announced to be on the 14th inst. So unless I withdraw now, I must go to prison on that day. Probably earlier also, as I hear Government is just thinking of arresting me

---

[27] Dr Tiruvengimalai Sesha Sundara Rajan (1880–1953) was a doctor, politician and freedom fighter and was minister of public health and religious endowments in Madras Presidency between 1937 and 1940. He obtained an MRCS degree in 1911 and worked in Middlesex Hospital. He was an acclaimed surgeon besides being good in physical medicine. While in England, Rajan was closely associated with V.D. Savarkar and V.V.S. Aiyar. On his return to India in 1914, he met CR and joined the Congress.

[28] Erode Venkata Ramaswami Naicker (17 September 1879–24 December 1973), born a year after CR, passed away the year following CR's demise. He was known by the initials 'EVR' and later came to be known with affectionate respect as 'Periyar', the Elder or the Senior One. He brought to his political engagement in the Congress a passion for justice and the creation of a casteless, just society. Leaving the Congress, he joined the Justice Party and clashed famously with CR on intra-party issues and later, when CR was premier of Madras Presidency, on the teaching of Hindustani in schools. He did all this maintaining a warm personal cordiality with CR throughout his life.

Periyar started the Self-Respect Movement and the socio-cultural organization, Dravida Kazhagam (DK). Periyar's impact on Tamil society was decisive in relegating caste-based discrimination to the past. Periyar's prestige as a social reformer grew formidably in later years, and not just within Tamil Nadu.

under Sec. 124A. Meanwhile I got a telegram yesterday from Allahabad (it was delayed over 36 hours) about Panditji's arrest.[29] Godbole[30] and Raja Rao[31] wire for instruction. Under the circumstances set out by me I am not in a position to take up Panditji's place. If I withdraw now from disobedience it will demoralize people. So I made out a telegram to you suggesting that the All India Congress Office may go to Ahmadabad, Godbole and Raja Rao cooperating and getting on. Jairamdas[32] may be drafted from Sindh if you approve.

I wish this to catch at least today's post. It is nearly post time. I expect a wire from you as to your wishes in the matter, addressed to Salem.

Yours sincerely,
C. Rajagopalachari

9

Being under the shadow of arrest for the first time, CR sends the following telegram to Gandhi saying he would be asking for a full sentence. Gandhi wires back: 'Good. Hope you will get the maximum penalty'. CR also

---

[29] Pandit Motilal Nehru and Jawaharlal Nehru, along with George Joseph, then editor of the *Independent*, were arrested on 6 December 1921. Motilal Nehru had suggested that CR should guide the AICC office, then functioning from Anand Bhavan, Allahabad.

[30] M.S. Godbole was assisting with the production of the *Independent*.

[31] Raja Rao, appointed assistant secretary of the AICC in 1917.

[32] Jairamdas Daulatram (1891–1979), one of the Congress's foremost leaders from Sindh, was an activist in the Home Rule Movement and the non-cooperation movement. He took part in the Salt Satyagraha, being shot and wounded when the police opened fire on agitators in 1930. He also participated in the Quit India movement and was imprisoned. He was a member of the Constituent Assembly. After India's independence, Daulatram served as the Governor of Bihar and of Assam, Union minister and member of the Rajya Sabha.

sends to Devadas (the letter appears later in this volume) his daughters' names
and addresses by way of parental insurance. 'Namagiri and Lakshmi are my
daughters' names and they are at 36, Forty Fifth Street, Rangoon.'
Gandhi, on seeing the letter, reflexively takes the matter in hand and writes
on its top left corner in pencil the following Gujarati instruction to the ashram:
Chhokariyo naa naam thaam lakhi leyi Devdas ne mokalvo *(The girls'*
names and whereabouts should be taken down and sent to Devadas).

CR *and Subramania Sastri are sentenced to three months' simple*
imprisonment. The term is spent in Vellore Central Jail. CR is permitted
some change of clothes, a pillow, a jamakalam *(cotton floor covering),*
a shawl, a flask, a quire of paper and a copy of the Bible, the Kural*,*
a Shakespeare volume, Robinson Crusoe, *a work on Socrates, and*
the Mahabharata in both Tamil and English. And, a charkha. While
awaiting his transfer to prison, CR manages to write to Gandhi expressing
the hope, teasingly, that when he is released he hopes to find India free and
the Mahatma back at his favourite vocation, namely, research in dietetics.[33]
The term (21 December 1921 to 20 March 1922) sees him lose
weight dramatically and be harried by asthma, to Gandhi's great concern
which he expresses in Young India. *But vacant prison hours also enable*
CR to write, in English, a memorable Jail Diary *and a Tamil rendering*
of The Trial and Death of Socrates.

Vellore Fort
15 December 1921

Mahatma Gandhi Sabarmati

Summons served first case taken today made statement admitting
disobedience inviting maximum penalty still prosecutor unready
case adjourned Monday

Rajagopalachar

---

[33] Rajmohan Gandhi, *The Rajaji Story* (Madras: Bharathan Publications, 1978), vol. 1, p. 105.

10

*While CR is in prison, the Raj arrests Gandhi at Sabarmati ashram
(10 March 1922) and tries him for sedition. Pleading guilty Gandhi
says the overthrow of the British government in India is his duty.
Justice Broomfield sentences him for six years. This is Gandhi's first jail
sentence in India. CR has ten days more to go for his release. 'What
can I do outside,' he wonders in his diary, 'with . . . Mahatmaji in
prison?' When he hears the sentence awarded to Gandhi, the thought
that Gandhi has 'at the age of 53 to rot in jail for six long years' is
unbearable. On his release, CR, joined by Devadas, goes to Yeravada
jail, Poona, to see Gandhi. Both are shocked at the prison conditions.
Twenty-one-year-old Devadas cannot but break down seeing his father
made to stand while the jailors sit. Despite Gandhi's making light of it
all, CR writes to the press about what he has seen, saying the prison
officials do not seem to realize their 'privilege of being custodians of a
man greater than the Kaisar, greater than Napoleon . . . greater than the
biggest prisoners of war'. The criticism has its effect.*

*Into his second year in prison, Gandhi has to undergo an
appendectomy. The emergency operation is performed on 12 January
1924 by Bombay's Surgeon General Col. Maddock[34] at the Sassoon
Hospital, Poona. The procedure, in that era, is not known to be an
assured success. Scouting the Tamil countryside at the time for a khadi
centre, which is to be established shortly thereafter at Pudupalayam, near
Tiruchengodu south-west of Salem, CR goes to Poona again. Gandhi,
reduced 'to almost half his size' is unconditionally released on
5 February 1924.*

*CR wires his relief. The telegram is transcribed on the Raj's postal
stationery which carries advertisements for Lipton's Tea, Imperial Special
Cigarettes and Jute Soled Canvas Shoes, made by the Indian Jute Shoe*

---

[34] The operation was both successful and eventful. The electricity in the operation
theatre failed and the torch that was brought in got fused. Surgeon Col. Maddock then
proceeded to complete the operation in the light of a kerosene lamp.

Company Ltd, Calcutta. The original, which reposes in the Sabarmati ashram, is reproduced below with its typographical mistakes intact.

5 February 1924

Mahatma Gandhi
Sassoons Hospital Poona

Received devadass wire. Feel we are now in a changed world of gladness and hope going on with our arriving Poona tenth morning.

Shankarlal Deshpande Rajagopalachar

11

Out of prison, Gandhi goes to a seaside dwelling in Juhu, Bombay, to recuperate from surgery and incarceration and to attend to work in Bombay. CR's son Ramaswami, then studying at the non-governmental National Medical College in Bombay, meets Gandhi, leading to a letter (carried below) of trenchant criticism to the father for writing to his son in English rather than in Tamil, followed by another (also reproduced here), enclosing Ramaswami's first-ever letter in Tamil to CR.

CR's four-page reply is preserved at the Sabarmati ashram.

Andheri
Saturday, 22 March 1924

Dear Rajagopalachari,

This is hand–made paper. I understand it was specially got and printed for me. I am using it for the first time today. It is now after 3.30 a.m. I have hardly slept during the night after 12. You are one of the reasons. I had a chat with your son last night. Incidentally,

I asked him whether he wrote to you and you to him in English or Tamil.

When he told me it was English, the information cut me to pieces. We had then a discourse upon the possibilities of Tamil. Young Ramaswamy thought that it was not capable of being used for high and scientific thought. My brain then began to work and it is still working.

You are my greatest hope. Why this, as it seems to me, grave defect? If the salt loses its savour, etc. What are the Tamil masses to do, if her best sons neglect her? What is the future before poor Ramaswamy as a worker among the masses? Do enlighten me or promise henceforth to write to the young man in your best Tamil. It was good of the Hindu people to offer to lend services of the shorthand-writer.

With deepest love,
M. K. G.

⁓

Monday, 24 March 1924

My dear Rajagopalachari,

The son has begun before the father. That is as it should be.
You can see how the discovery has preyed on my mind.

⁓

Salem
28 March 1924

My dear Mahatmaji,

I did not know whether to weep or to rejoice when I read your letter written in the small hours of the morning. Your castigation was severe yet I feel so happy.

There must be a cause for everything though not a justification. I shall not trouble you therefore why I wrote my letters to Ramu in English. I promise henceforth to use the mother tongue.

Did Ramu really try to make out that high and scientific thoughts could not be reached with Tamil, you would say that my own conduct was responsible for this belief of his. Not quite. He has known me exert in the direction of claiming and applying the mother tongue for such uses.

You saw but one of my defects and were so much pained. What about the hundred other defects wherein I cannot hope to satisfy you. If I think about it, little do I really deserve your affection. A friend wrote to me the other day complaining that I denied Christ twice already, once when I allowed Mahomed Ali[35] to have his own way at Delhi and again at Coconada. I wrote to him that I was denying Christ—not twice or even thrice but a hundred times, in my inefficiency, in my laziness, and in so many other things.

I have not had friends often since coming here. I weighed myself yesterday. I am 93½ lbs. just the same as when I was at Poona. I feel no worse or better. It looks as if the milk diet has no effect on my asthma.

This is also handmade paper of which I received a little quantity at Erandal in Khandesh.

---

[35] Maulana Mahomed Ali Jouhar was a scholar and writer and, with his brother Maulana Shaukat Ali, a leading figure of the Khilafat movement. Mahomed Ali was present at the founding meeting of the All-India Muslim League in Dacca in 1906, and served as its president in 1918. In 1919 he tried to persuade the British government to prevent the deposition of the Caliph, or Khalifa. He was instrumental in the formation of the Khilafat Committee in India when the British rejected this appeal; Muslims all over India boycotted the government on the directions of the committee. While Gandhi got many thousands of Hindus to join hands with the Muslims in their struggle, Ali supported Gandhi's call for civil disobedience and served as president of the Congress in 1923. He parted from Gandhi soon thereafter and supported the Fourteen Points of M.A. Jinnah and the League.

CR to Mohandas K. Gandhi   55

Will you forgive me? And sleep well, as I have given you the promise and do repent?

With dearest love
Yours ever
C.R.

Ramu's Tamil letter with the magician's precious endorsement reached today.

Will you have the enclosed for Young India?

R

12

The Vaikom (Vykom) Satyagraha in Travancore (1924–25), which led to the 'untouchables', including the Ezhavas, gaining access to three sides of the temple, sees Gandhi's non-political social agenda coming to the fore in the south. ('Full temple-entry' was to be secured only in 1936.) George Joseph[36] gives the movement inspirational lead. Joseph wires Gandhi on 12 April: 'Am arrested. Satyagraha must continue. Overwhelming public support and numerous volunteers. Leadership only needed. Send Devadas or Mahadeo. Wife remains in Chengannur. Asking for blessings.' As the movement begins to gain momentum and draw national attention, Gandhi urges caution

---

[36] George Joseph (1887–1938) of Chengannur, Travancore, was a barrister, writer and freedom fighter. He was repeatedly imprisoned during the freedom movement, notably for leading the Vaikom (Vykom) Satyagraha. He was also the editor of the Allahabad-based *Independent* and Gandhi's *Young India* while Gandhi was in jail.

*and perspective.[37] The following telegram sent to Gandhi in Andheri,
Bombay, relates to that major event.*

Salem
13 April 1924

Joseph arrested telegram asks me take his place wire your advice.

Rajagopalachar

⎯⎯

Reply from Gandhi:

13 APRIL 1924

RECEIVED WIRE. IF HEALTH PERMITS YOU MAY GO NOT NECESSARILY
COURT ARREST BUT REGULATE MOVEMENT. YOU SHOULD NEGOTIATE WITH
DIWAN AND INVITE IF THEY WILL COME OTHER LEADERS PARTICIPATE
AFTER ALL YOU ARE BEST JUDGE SITUATION. DEVDAS AT YOUR SERVICE
IF REQUIRED.

GANDHI

---

[37] He writes:

Vaikom satyagrahis undoubtedly arrived at a delicate state, so many leaders having
been picked up by the Travancore authorities. Appeal has been made to all-India
leaders to lead the movement. It is a question how far a local movement, on reaching
a critical stage, can be turned into an all-India movement. All-India sympathy I can
understand and that Vaikom satyagrahis are having in abundance, but to concentrate
active energies of leaders from different provinces on a single local movement seems
to be a difficult, if not an impossible, task. I am hoping, however, that leaders in the
Madras Presidency will not allow the movement to die for want of proper lead. A
telegram was sent to Mr. George Joseph before his arrest advising dropping of fast. As
he is not likely to have received my letter which followed the telegram, I hand it for
publication, which sums up my position. It is not affected by recent developments.
(*The Hindu*, 14 April 1924)

13

CR monitors the Vaikom situation for Gandhi and seeks his advice on tactics and direction, as this telegram (lodged with the reply at the Sabarmati ashram) indicates. Style erraticisms have been retained as in the original.

Salem
15 April 1924

Kerala itself unable without outside help in leaders money myself physically unequal strain of campaign Tamilnadu can send workers dislocating Khaddar works if you consider campaign as conceived worth it. Regarding general question read letters already addressed devadas pyarelal. Volunteers not arrested now but road physically blocked. No alternative but hunger strike. Do you approve this. Wire advice.

Rajagopalachar

Gandhi's response was:

Andheri
[On or after 15 April 1924]

My reply regarding first published press. Hunger strike unlawful. Think Vykom struggle should be kept up under reservations suggested

Gandhi

14

The following two letters to Mahadev Desai are really as much letters to Gandhi as they are to the peerless secretary. Mahadev almost certainly 'put them up' to the Mahatma or at least shared their substance with him. CR pours his mind and heart into them, and there is a tender

exchange of confidences. Politics occurs in them, inevitably, but so do philosophy, etiquette, linguistics and, above all, the weight and charm of domesticity. Some allusions remain veiled by time and guessing at them would be both unreliable and intrusive. But some references, with names given and situations explained, are crystal clear. We learn from one of them, for instance, how precariously close CR came, in his unpredictable pattern of living, to giving away his twelve-year-old daughter Lakshmi in an absurdly early marriage. The Child Marriage Restraint Act, popularly known as the Sarda Act after its sponsor Rai Sahib Harbilas Sarda, was to be passed five years later, on 28 September 1929, fixing the age of consent for girls at fourteen years.

The ellipses in the second letter account for portions that are illegible or undecipherable.

Salem
17 April 1924

My dear Mahadev

Yours of 12th inst. reached yesterday. The Class Areas Bill[38] is withdrawn. But it is not dead by any means. This struggle is like the struggle of the elements, ever to go on.

The last use of Young India was altogether a 'Sarojini' issue.[39] I don't know about Bapu's spreading the net. Sometimes we think we are spreading the net, whereas the fact is we are all the time planting our feet in the snare spread for us. But this is not my concern. You don't know how I am struggling every day to purify and strengthen my heart, that other people's hatred should not be my concern. We should ever pray . . . I have . . . has been lost . . . that our own minds may be filled with love. This I have concluded is the true meaning of

---

[38] of South Africa.
[39] Sarojini Naidu (1879–1949). CR first met the poetess in Conjeevaram (Kanchipuram) in May 1918 when she presided over a conference of the south's politically minded intellectuals, addressed by Dr Annie Besant.

the Gayatri. I have so often found that while one is praying thus, one's mind wanders again into the old groove and sends up prayers that other peoples' hearts may be filled with love. This of course is an inversion of the true solution. Fill me with love should be a sufficient prayer.

But I am inflicting a fifth rate sermon on one who should be instructing me. Forgive.

Your news that Motilalji has accepted Bapu's position is strange. It must be wrong. Motilalji must be all disappointment and anger now. His love for Bapu is great but his pride is strong. You must have the 'rough unrevised draft' by now. I have had a copy too. It is splendid, isn't it? I have suggested a few very slight modifications more or less to remove doubts. Bapu can improve it I have no doubt, but too much time has been lost already and the thing should be out now.

The debates so far could not have fatigued Bapu. But the Hindu-Muslim Conference he has called will I am afraid be so painful that his nerves will be affected and his health may suffer.

The article on Md. Ali is in my opinion faultlessly beautiful. It is not only full of chivalry and charity as you say, it is also perfectly truthful. I see often faults enough in poor Mohammed Ali. But in the present controversy I see that he is not wrong at all. It is his absolute confidence that people could never underestimate or suspect flaws in his supreme attachment to Gandhiji that has led him into this trouble. He felt he should put his case beyond a shadow of doubt and chose the comparisons.

I think we are wrong in feeling it any way offensive to bring the adulterous person into proximity with Bapu. This is due to a kind of wrong sacerdotal feeling we have developed in regard to our ideal person. To the intensely religious man his faith in Mahomed or Christ is enough to wash every sin of its sin. There are I believe many passages in the Bible which can be brought to support the defence of Mohammed Ali. On the whole, slightly disagreeing from you I entirely approve of Bapu's article. If you read it again I am sure you will agree too. There is no cause whatever to feel uneasy.

Thank you for all the loving thoughts about Lakshmi.[40] Poor sweet girl, she *is* a charming little soul and so exceedingly loves her father, that the latter does not know what to do with her. Papa (Namagiri)[41] her elder sister is here now and does all the household work and cooking for us all. Papa wants that Lakshmi should be married away. If I were in the old style I would have insisted on marrying late. A practising lawyer can fight society and the rotten practice of early marriage. But a non-cooperating politician as poor as a copybook maxim is in a different plight. Looking at my poor health and all the complications of my existence, Papa is perhaps right in feeling anxious that Lakshmi should not be left unmarried or asked to fight society all her life. But I don't find a proper match either anywhere about.

You object to my calling Subbiah[42] my 'typist'. Do you want me to call him my 'secretary'. That would be calling myself a secretary keeper. You may say I should have used the proper name itself. But I wanted to bring in the idea that clerks, typists and others employed round about you should be brought into this occupation. It was not, I assure you, any sense of aristocracy.

With love,
CR

How is Maniben[43] now? I am really sorry she is ill so long.

Joseph[44] is a funny fellow. He has left his wife suspecting herself to be having tubercular fever and gone to jail. I was

---

[40] Lakshmi (1912–83), CR's younger daughter, who was to marry Devadas Gandhi in 1933. Later translator of her father's Tamil commentary on the Ramayana, his monographs on Marcus Aurelius, Sri Ramakrishna and many of his short stories into Hindi (published by Sasta Sahitya Mandal, New Delhi).

[41] 'Papa' means 'baby' in Tamil.

[42] A. Subbiah, devoted amanuensis, loyal associate and exemplary ashramite.

[43] Maniben Patel (1903–90), daughter of Sardar Patel, freedom fighter in her own right, imprisoned by the Raj in 1942, later member of Parliament.

[44] George Joseph (see n. 36).

asking him to send her to Dr Rajan who promised to build an open air shed for her in his own compound and look after her. He was taking time on account of the children who had come home for the school vacation and without doing anything has rushed to prison.

He wrote to me a letter saying he was in for Vykom satyagraha and was likely to be arrested and wanted all the Tamil Nad workers to be sent off to his camp at once. I was amazed at the unwisdom of the proposal and wanted him to slow his pace. Vykom is an inaccessible place without rail, post or telegram. I wired to him at once saying—I don't agree await letter—I posted a letter at once putting forth what a careful satyagrahi should offer but before getting . . . I should have used the proper . . . he dashed off a letter to another friend Dr Varadarajulu Naidu[45] saying Rajagopalachari has sent him a 'funny telegram' and quoting it and adding that he was in for it and couldn't retrace. This friend . . . was my staunch supporter once but all that is turned into poison ever since the advent of the Swarajya Party. He promptly published Joseph's letter to show that Rajagopalachari does not sympathise with untouchables! It not only has created misunderstanding. Joseph of course is not to blame for he used only a private letter but he knew the present state of feeling between Dr Varadarajulu and me and need not have communicated to him my telegram. However, this is Joseph, impetuous and good.

CR

---

[45] Dr Perumal Varadarajulu Naidu (1887–1957) was a physician, politician, journalist and freedom fighter, who converged and diverged from the politics of CR over a long and illustrious career within the Congress.

Salem
3 May 1924

My dear Mahadev

Your letter (from B . . . 29th April) reached this morning. Telegrams[46] from Bapu and Devadas, the ocean of love that surrounds me all around, and on the top of it all, your touching letter makes me cry.

I got Devadas' angry letter. Dear boy! He is so fond of me. He has every right to go into a rage at my seeming cold-bloodedness.

My son in law has developed pneumonia on the top of malaria soon after he arrived here. The lungs have not yet begun resolving. But the worst is he is in a temporary maniacal condition. This may be due to the brain poisoning of pneumonia or may be a . . . conjoint . . . of the concussion . . . in hospital for a fortnight and had to be relieved by spinal punctures! Anyway he has been for a week . . . and suffers much. I moved him to hospital day before yesterday. I don't fear any danger to life. But Papa is much distressed.

Bapu's wire came in the midst of this. How could I go to Nasik even though such love and concern are at the bottom of the peremptory order!

Yours most affectionate
CR

15

Gandhi's calling a sudden halt, while in prison, to the national struggle after the Chauri Chaura episode, in which twenty-two

---

[46] On 2 May 1924, CR sent a telegram from Salem to Devadas Gandhi, who was in Bombay with his father, saying, 'Son in law's pneumonia and mental derangement continuing distressing. Rajagopalachar', to which Gandhi replied, 'Wire received only comfort I can offer is send Devadas wire condition and reply. Gandhi'.

policemen were killed, leads to shock and dismay among his followers,
including CR. The nationalists begin to think of a major policy
change in favour of entering legislatures to leverage the
Raj's institutions for the nationalist cause. In December 1922—
after the Gaya session of the Congress where CR swings the party
resolutely towards the imprisoned leader's path of non-cooperation—the
'pro-changers' led by Deshbandhu Chittaranjan Das, N.C. Kelkar
and Motilal Nehru form the Congress-Khilafat Swarajya Party.
Das becomes its president and Nehru, one of the secretaries. Other
prominent leaders like Subhas Chandra Bose and Vithalbhai Patel,
who are dissatisfied with the Congress, also join the 'pro-changers'.
CR, now known countrywide as 'Rajaji', has steered the 'no-changers'
ideationally and inspirationally. But it is clear the party is no
longer cohesive.

Differing on tactics but anxious to avoid a 1907 Surat-type
split, the two groups remain within the Congress fold but work in
their separate ways. Gandhi emphasizes that there is no fundamental
difference between the two. Swarajist members are elected to the
Councils and Vithalbhai Patel becomes the president of the Central
Legislative Assembly. But with the legislatures having very limited
powers, Swarajists in the legislatures can only liven up some heated
parliamentary debates. Their mission of manipulating the Raj's
institutions does not really work.

As non-cooperation glides into low tide, all eyes turn
towards Gandhi, freshly released from prison. CR urges him
to accept the presidency of the Congress, which an increasingly
estranged Maulana Mahomed Ali is vacating. The letter
reproduced below is with the Sabarmati ashram. When after much
reflection Gandhi becomes Congress president—for the first and
last time in his life—later that year, CR's influence is doubtless
one of the factors that has persuaded him. This letter is part of
the Sabarmati collection.

Salem
24 July 1924

My dear Mahatmaji,

Your beautiful postcard[47] of Saturday 19 reached me duly. Sweet and beautiful though your protest is, I am of the same opinion still.

You and I believe that your programme is the only course for India. If anyone can induce her to follow it is only you. Success is not our concern. We cannot abstain from any step that offers even a small chance of inducing India to build as we want.

If you do not preside, do you still mean to move your propositions and appeal to the Congress or do you mean at once to give up the Congress and work from outside? I believe the former is your intention. If so, you must keep yourself free for contingencies. I use the same phrase as you did but intend just the opposite. If your leadership and proposals are sincerely accepted you can more directly and effectively guide the work as President yourself than through another President whose mind and methods may not always be as you want. If your advice is rejected or you feel that it amounts to it, you are free to resign. I believe that you are more free for either contingency if you accept the Presidency than if you at once reject it.

I feel that there is no halfway house between becoming President and at once deciding to leave the Congress. I think that your work as President of the Congress organisation may be more effective than efforts from outside. The latter is the last ditch which is of course always there. To give up the Congress now is to leave the national organization and the people to vacillate and drift. It soon means strengthening the forces that divert national attention and energy to futile things.

---

[47] Not included in the *Collected Works* and presumably missing.

You may say it is a necessary evil. But I say, not yet. Don't punish the nation for the sins of a few friends. Give them a fuller trial. The masses, it is so obvious, still feel that you alone must lead, whatever the intellectuals may think or do. Abdication now, it appears to me, will have the worst consequences.

Yours sincerely,

———

The churning in Gandhi's thoughts is clear from the following excerpt from a letter he wrote to CR the following month:

Sabarmati
24 August 1924

My dear Rajagopalachari,

. . . I am acting cautiously. All I am trying to do is to avoid an unseemly wrangle. I will take up the Presidentship, if I find that it will serve the country. There is plenty of time to decide.

The returns of spinning are proving most instructive. Is it much use my presiding if the returns remain as poor as they are? . . .

Yours,
M. K. G.

16

Meanwhile, floods unleash fury in the Malabar area of the Madras Presidency and CR, despite being racked by asthma and wanting to take a respite from hectic activity, has to engage with Nature's anger. The Moplah population bears the brunt of the floods. The first telegram here relates the scene from the spot, as it were, and the second gives a perspective from the Congress office, Allahabad, and Gandhi's dispassionate responses, as the next Congress president, to both. They are part of the Sabarmati collection.

Salem
31 July 1924

M K Gandhi Sabarmati

Flood ravages terrible magnitude advise whether we should attempt relief from Congress funds.

Rajagopalachar

———

Gandhi's reply to CR, superscribed on the incoming telegram, lodged at the Sabarmati ashram, says:

My opinion damage beyond our capacity. We must assist larger agencies with personal service. Gandhi.

———

It is interesting that he first writes 'beyond scope Congress' and then strikes out 'scope Congress', substituting those two words with 'our capacity'.

Allahabad
5 August 1924

Mahatma Gandhi Sabarmati

Srinivasa Iyengar proposes immediate grant fifty thousand stop Rajagopalachari requests conversion Tamil loan fifteen thousand to grant to enable give help floods stop all India funds now one lakh twenty five thousand fixed deposit twenty two thousand current account twelve thousand liabilities wire opinion on both requests = Congress

————

Gandhi's reply to the Congress office is:

Wired both last week floods too vast Congress capacity we should cooperate with neutral agency even government if they accept service. Personal service can and must always be given. If Congress can it may raise special subscriptions. Gandhi

17

Engrossed in flood relief in Malabar, committed like a soldier to the cause of the boycott of legislatures and government institutions, to khadi and to the 'spinning franchise' for membership of the Congress, CR is disturbed by the tensions caused to Gandhi by leaders of the Congress to whom boycott and khadi are anathema at worst or a time-consuming distraction at best. He despairs of Gandhi's courteous negotiations with the 'pro-changer' group. Gandhi tells CR there should be no decision on these matters by a divisive vote within the Congress, that the 'no-changers' must surrender to the 'pro-changers' if necessary. 'We must continue to surrender up to the very margin of principle,' Gandhi writes to CR on 6 September 1924.

If dissension has grown within the Congress ranks between the 'pro-changers' and 'no-changers', Hindu–Muslim unity is also suffering. Gandhi, in Delhi, and staying at Maulana Mahomed Ali's, goes on a twenty-one-day fast in penance for Hindu–Muslim discord. CR goes to Delhi to be by his leader as he fasts. CR feels Gandhi is giving too much of his time and his patience to the Swarajists whose aims are smaller than their size and, likewise, to the minority leadership of Mahomed Ali.

His letters to Devadas, carried later in this volume, reveal his thoughts during this period. A letter written by CR to Mahadev pertaining, we can infer, to Satyamurti and referred to by Gandhi is untraceable. Mahadev Desai perhaps had not accessioned it into the ashram archives. But Gandhi's response to CR—written on his way to Delhi for difficult parleys with the Swarajists and with Maulana Mahomed Ali—is important. It is supplemented by a whole article by Gandhi in Young India *(see Annexure I).*

The letter is as follows:

3 September 1924

My dear CR.,

I am on my way to Delhi for quarrel. I read your letter to S. I am sad because you are sad. I wish you were by my side. How can you continue when we [are] so hopelessly divided? Read my article in current Young India fifty times, if necessary and you will find out my meaning perhaps. It is written most for you. Your letter to S. suggested it. We are not giving up boycotts because they are removed from the national programme for a time. Surely, if we have courage of our convictions, we can revive them any moment. Why should suspension mean abandonment if we have trust in ourselves?

Yours,
M. K. G.

———

Gandhi's famous fast in Delhi for twenty-one days is part of history. CR implores him not to fast in a telegram dated 18 September for, CR argues, a fast 'would mean nothing short of death in view of his present health', getting the following reply:

[On or after 18 September 1924]

CANCELLATION FAST CANCELLATION SELF. AM FASTING TO LIVE NOT DIE
UNLESS GOD WILLS OTHERWISE. DON'T WORRY. GANDHI

The Hindu, 29 September 1924

*Despite clear dissimilarities of view, the following written on a postcard to
Mahadev shows CR's attitude to individual representatives and leaders
of the Raj. It also throws a beam of light on the similarity of approach
between the non-violent movement and the Raj's attitude to anarchism
and terrorism.*

Bangalore
10 January 1925

My dear Mahadev

Arrived here this morning and am taking train tonight and will
reach my place tomorrow. I wrote to you a letter (enclosing an
article) from the train and posted it at a wayside station. I addressed
it to Bhavnagar. I hope it reached you somewhere. The article may
be entitled 'Transfer Unperceived' i.e. to say some Gujarati phrase
briefly and sweetly explaining this idea.

I haven't forgotten to write you an introduction for your
'satyagraha ka maryada'. I am reading and admiring Morley.[48] What
a fine writer he is!

---

[48] John Morley, 1st Viscount Morley of Blackburn (1838–1923), was a British Liberal
leader, writer, biographer and newspaper editor. He became a member of Parliament in
1883 and was Secretary of State for India (1905–10 and 1911). CR is alluding to Morley's
classic *On Compromise*, which Mahadev Desai translated into Gujarati when he was working
in the Oriental Translator's Office. The Farbas Gujarati Sabha (established in memory of
Alexander Kinloch Forbes) had announced an award of Rs 1000 for the translation of *On
Compromise*. Mahadev Desai participated in that competition and sent three or four pages

Did you read Lytton's[49] speech in the Bengal Leg. Council? I hope Bapu did not miss it! If he did, you should make him read it. I like the speech very much. But for the fatal fallacy of asking for permission for tyranny as remedy for violence, the speech is a grand performance as an appeal against anarchy and terrorism. I am not prepared to put Lytton away as a diplomat or orator. I think he is a good soul. Whom if Bapu could come into touch with, great results could evolve.

I wish I knew Gujarati to read your Kathiawar impressions.

Yours affectionately,
C.R.

18

In 1925, CR has withdrawn from active politics and has set up on a four-acre plot in a challenging part of the rocky and rain-parched Salem district, Tiruchengodu. Pudupalayam village in Tiruchengodu has no more than 150 dwellings. The village has many from the weaving community, farming Gounders, 'untouchable' groups, one of them Telugu-speaking, and a small number of Muslims. Its new ashram, called Gandhi Ashram, is intended to promote khadi, counter 'untouchability' in the region, and wean men away from alcohol and drunkenness—tasks that are rather more difficult than making speeches and writing articles against the Raj. CR wins many admirers in the village but also creates sceptics who lose no time in attributing setbacks like drought to the ashram's conscious breaking of caste laws.

---

in translation as a sample and was chosen for the translation work out of many known literary personages. His translation was published in 1925, with a dedication to Mahatma Gandhi and CR's introduction (see Annexure II), rendered into Gujarati.

[49] 2nd Earl of Lytton (1876–1947) was Governor of Bengal, remaining there until 1927. For a short while, when there was a vacancy caused by change in incumbents in 1925, he also functioned as viceroy, his father's old post.

*CR is doing what is close to Gandhi and what has come naturally
to his own state of mind. This withdrawal also fits in with the Congress
leaving the stage for the while to the Swarajists. Led by Deshbandhu
Chittaranjan Das and Motilal Nehru and supported locally by men like
C. Vijiaraghavachari, Srinivasa Iyengar and Satyamurti, the Swarajists
support Council-entry, are opposed to Gandhian boycott of government
institutions and have but a dim view of khadi and spinning in the scheme
of nationalism.*

*CR is therefore irritated when he finds his leader being generous
and receptive to the Swarajists and to its chief representative, Das, to the
extent of being prepared to dilute his insistence on khadi and spinning
in order to accommodate Das. CR writes to Mahadev during Gandhi's
tour of Bengal in the course of which he and Mahadev spend a week with
Das and his wife, Smt. Basantidevi, at their home 'Step Aside'[50] in
Darjeeling. Tragically, the Deshbandhu passes away shortly thereafter.*

*The letter is preserved in the archives of the Gandhi Ashram,
Sabarmati.*

Gandhi Ashram
Tiruchengodu
18 July 1925

My dear Mahadev

The shocking news came to this village only today. I was prepared
for anything but not for a tragedy of this magnitude.

It looks as if the Gods drew Bapu to Bengal and to Darjeeling
on set purpose to sweeten the end of this friendship. The mystery
of it is almost like a dream or a page in romance.

The event must simply have taken away whatever self-restraint or
ballast there was in Bengal. His followers poor fellows must simply

---

[50] The house was restored by the government of West Bengal in 2007 and is now
a museum for C.R. Das and a dispensary for mothers and children.

be inconsolable. Maharashtra's loss in the death of Lokamanya was greater, far greater. But then Maharashtra has brains and sturdy power. Poor Bengal, brilliant and ever living in dreams, has been hit hard.

I suppose Bapu will be adopted as father over the funeral pyre. The nation in Bengal cannot do without some such epic succession. But all this means strain and yet more strain.

With love,
Yours sincerely,
C.R.

Unless Aurobindo chooses to shake himself free of yoga and goes to Calcutta to occupy the vacant throne.

———

Gandhi's reply written from Calcutta shortly after Deshbandhu's death, dated 16 July 1925, crossed CR's to Mahadev dated 18 July 1925. It is particularly important for what it conveys of Gandhi's psychological condition at the time and his reliance on CR for understanding, even sympathy:

16 July 1925

My dear C.R.,

Somehow or other I need your letter to feel that all is well with you. My position is this. My body and mind are living in a world by which I remain unaffected, but in which I am being tried. My soul is living in a world physically away from me and yet a world by which I am and want to be affected. You are a part of that world and perhaps the nearest to me. My innermost being wants your approbation of what I am doing and thinking. I may not always succeed in getting it, but it craves for your verdict.

Now you understand exactly why I want to hear from you apart from many other reasons. You must let me have if it is only a postcard every week. Mahadev, Devdas, Pyarelal should keep you posted with what is going on. And you must keep well.

Your sadhana is the development of the place where you are and a scientific test of our theory of the value of hand-spinning. Even if it proves untrue in the end, neither we nor the world will have lost anything, for I know that we are true in the sense that we have full faith in the programme and, if it is intrinsically not immoral, our theory can be claimed to be true, when a fairly large number of villages sustain hand-spinning and khadi without protection as the whole of India sustains home cookery without protection.

Surely this is a long introduction to what I want to say. Here is Pitt's letter and the letters from Kelappan. I am simply saying that we must keep nominally a satyagrahi at the Eastern gate unless the local men think otherwise. But you may come to other conclusion. You should write to Kelappan. He seems to be a nice, useful man.

With love, yours,
Bapu

Gandhi's letter to CR above affects CR profoundly, as is clear from a letter CR writes to Devadas (carried later in this volume). But there is no trace of the weekly postcard Gandhi has proposed, although they must have been sent, even if at a lesser frequency than the Mahatma wished. There is, though, a perfect nugget from CR to Mahadev Desai, clearly meant for Gandhi, written just as the year is drawing to a close.

Gandhi Ashram
Tiruchengodu
24 December 1925

My dear Mahadev

This letter won't reach you until after the Congress is over and perhaps after being re-directed from the deserted place. So it won't take your attention away from the all-absorbing national activities of the session. The enclosed cutting tells its own tale and will be a fuller statement of what you must have got in shorter form during the busy week. You and other friends including Bapu must have wondered what this news of my appearing in court meant.

A Panchama was convicted at Tirupati for having in a fit of devotion and exhaltation of senses, entered with other pilgrims at a famous shrine at the foot of the hill. I read a report of the case casually when at Madras and I was indignant that a man of that sort should be held guilty of having insulted religion and defiled a temple and punished under the provisions of the Penal Code. Later on I was requested to help in the appeal filed by him and I readily agreed. I went to Chittoor when the appeal was to be heard. The vakil appearing for the man asked me if I would argue. I said if I could appear as a private friend of the accused and not as a vakil I would. He asked the Court if it would permit me thus and the request was acceded to and I argued the case with a khadi chaddar on and neither coat nor turban.

I suppose every rule is observed best by the breach of the letter of it when an occasion demands it. The case of a simple devoted and earnest soul rushing in to the temple with cocoanut and camphor and clothed in bark and sacred marks and returning home and on the way a policeman catching him upon detection of his caste and taking him to Court where he is punished as having defiled a temple and insulted our religion was I felt one which should not be disposed of by reference to the letter of the Boycott of Courts rule. I felt I could serve the cause by explaining to the Court what I felt regarding the supposed crime of this Panchama.

He was not a satyagrahi, he was not a reformer, nor a hero of any kind. He was a panchama who believed in Hinduism and the God that he thought resided in the temple and invited his devotion and worship. I could not ask him to bear the conviction and sentence and repent his crime. He is not of that mould. Nor do I think that we have yet found a way to touch the truly pious Panchamas as a class and arm them sufficiently with the Sword of

Disobedience . . . who would revolt are those that would make a
shout for equality in religion because it means political ambition
and not because they want the temple.

He was a Panchama who year after year humbly and meekly
offered his cocoanut and camphor at the outer gate. This year, I
suppose, the rumblings of the Gandhi revolution had somehow
touched the inner chords of this meek soul. He asked somebody
whether malas (untouchables) could go. No, said the shopkeeper
who sold him the cocoanut. He was going as usual to the flagstaff
when a crowd of pilgrims came crying Govinda! Govinda!, the
Tirupati pilgrims' 'war cry'. They went in and he too went in. The
man was allowed to offer his cocoanut and camphor. Everything
was finished and he was on the road home to Madras when he was
caught and taken to the police station and charged. Who can read the
thoughts that took him into the temple in that sudden moment!

I argued the appeal and won it too! No wonder for I felt, as I
was talking, the old Advocate quite alive within me.

I suppose people have taken me too to have deserted non-
cooperation. What does Bapu think I wonder! I hope he will forgive
me anyway.

Yours affectionately,
C.R.

19

*Rajmohan Gandhi has written in his biography of CR: 'Congress's
national leader of 1922 and 1923 thus became, in 1925, an itinerant
preacher in an obscure corner in the south; instead of hurling defiance at
the Raj from the centre of the Congress dais, CR was now inveighing
against the toddy-mug from the back of a cart'. The next letter from
CR to Gandhi is of a year later, almost. It is written on the ashram's
letterhead which has become recognized 'CR stationery'. It has banter,*

*political gossip, hard evaluation. Gandhi has superscribed on the top of
the incoming letter a Gujarati instruction, 'Rakhvano', which means
'To be kept'.*

Gandhi Ashram
Tiruchengodu
7 January 1926

My dear Bapu,

Your letter from Sabarmati.[51] I am glad that you are after all going
to have some physical rest.

I have informed Shankarlal[52] that I shall join any tour he arranges,
in the latter parts of February.

Adventurous youths in Kerala seem bent on starting something
sensational. They are good at beginning things that they can't
manage afterwards.

The agricultural work has brought our spinning to a total stop.
It is the weavers' turn now to be wanting yarn and not getting it.
When we had overstock of yarn last year, we were foolish and gave
away 4000 lbs of yarn to Tirupur. If we hadn't done this, we would
have had just yarn enough to tide over the field season.

I am pushing my propaganda for the Council people taking up
the drink question. Srinivasa Iyengar[53] has a born incapacity for
concentration of effort or plan. He daren't commit himself any time
to any definite plan. However I hope to compel him to some kind
of action in this matter. He can't be saved from the non-Brahmana
attacks otherwise.

---

[51] Not available in the *Collected Works.*

[52] Shankerlal Banker (1889–1985) came in close contact with Gandhi during the
strike of the Ahmedabad textile millworkers in 1918. He was publisher of *Young India*,
secretary of the All India Spinners' Association (AISA) and was convicted with Gandhi
in 1922. There was a close bond between CR and Banker.

[53] S. Srinivasa Iyengar (see n. 23).

As you feared, the Swarajists refuse to understand me properly. They are afraid it is too tough and too definite a job to tackle successfully. They feel it is not fireworks enough, not knowing that a poor man's question like drink is the best fireworks even such as they want. Then they dread the incoming of the Moderates who tremble at and retreat at the last moment from any sort of strong action.

My difficulty is that as the Cawnpore resolution is framed (so far as a dull person like me can understand so long and intricate a resolution) the Swarajists must 'leave' their seats in the Councils and the Assembly in April after the Budget fireworks are over. Not only in the assembly but in the Provinces also. Can they go to the electorate with an election programme of Prohibition which means an effort inside the Councils? I believe they can and the A.I.C.C should sanction such a programme for the general elections. I suppose especially if any particular province should ask for such a plan being sanctioned it can and ought to be done. Any way let us see how people take the idea. It will at least keep the question before the public.

I see that Devadas is going away to look after Mathuradas[54] at Devlali. He must have left already. Girdhari[55] and Mathuradas have been writing to me that M is making progress.

I was at a meeting at Madras where Shraddanandji[56] spoke, on his way back from Malabar. His vanity is amusing but his stupid attacks on your principles are disgusting as they betray a kind of personal animus besides superficiality.

---

[54] Mathuradas Trikamji, nephew of Gandhi (see entry no. 4).

[55] Girdhari Kripalani, nephew of Acharya J.B. Kripalani and friend of Devadas Gandhi.

[56] Swami Shraddhananda (1856–1926) was an educationist and a leader of the Arya Samaj movement. He was a missionary who established educational institutions like the Gurukul at Kangri, played a key role in the consolidation of Hindu organizations and was associated with the Shuddhi (reconversion) movement in the 1920s. He was killed by a Muslim fanatic.

M.K. Acharya M.L.A[57] (who has given notice of a resolution asking permission for India to declare war against South Africa!) has written a long discourse in the press that untouchability cannot be removed as you want—that there is nothing wrong in refusing to go near 'untouchables' or excluding them from temples and houses— that the true way of reform is in asking them to purify himself and that it is absurd to talk of penance on the part of the 'higher' classes in this business for they have done no wrong whatever.

Andrews wires from Johannesburg on 30 Dec that a certain 'interview' I gave to the Swarajya about Mr Paddison (of the Deputation) is of great help and that the press may be reassured that all is going well. I told the Swarajya representative sometime early in December when every paper was attacking Mr Paddison and his deputation that from what I knew of Mr Paddison he was a European extraordinarily free from race prejudice and that he was a good and sympathetic man, and that I hoped that Indians in South Africa will render him every assistance in his work and not be prejudiced by the agitation in the press, and that there were some advantages in a 'Pukka' Indian ICS officer seeing things himself and placing the case before the Government of India in addition to what we may do unofficially. I gave this interview after some hesitation. I knew Mr Paddison when he was Labour Protector and I was a co-member with him in an advisory committee just

---

[57] M.K. Acharya, member of the Legislative Assembly from South Arcot, Madras, has been quoted by Katherine Mayo in her infamous book, *Mother India*, as having said during and about the constitutional parleys in Simla in 1925, which included the laws regarding the age of consent:

what is sought to be done is to make that an offence which is not an offence now, to make that a crime which is not at present a crime, and which we are unable to regard as a crime, whatever may be the feelings of some few people to the contrary ... There is very little opinion of any respectable body of men in India which wants this reform very urgently. It may come, and there is no harm in it, in its own course. Really this is . . . merely to give Honourable Members some legislative marbles and tops to play with during the time that we happen to be in Simla.

before Non-Cooperation and I felt justice demanded that I should tell what I knew of him, when everybody was against him and his venture.

But the S.A. situation is a hopelessly insoluble affair. How can England coerce that Dominion? Not until we have wrenched freedom from Britain and become an equal partner. I suppose Mrs Naidu will have a tour to England now to see the British ministers and meet people.

From one poet to another, even though I know my letter has become too long already—what an occupation for the latter days of Poetry to become a 'leader' of the Birth Control movement! Tagore has after firing off his pretty darts at the Charkha turned to this graceful business of organising family life in India with the help of French letters. The poor Rishis must be holding their sides for laughter.

Affectionately yours
C.R.

20

If Council-entry is the Swarajists' preferred mode of political struggle, temple-entry for 'untouchables' is a Gandhian priority. CR writes this letter, preserved at Sabarmati, with the satisfaction of one who knows his legal intervention in the Panchama's case has done well.

Gandhi Ashram
Tiruchengodu
19 January 1926

My dear Bapu,

The contagion has caught on. Another man charged for temple entry has been let off on the summary ground that a man giving to worship could not be said to have 'insulted religion'—And this time without any appearance or argument and in Malabar!

I hope your health is steadily improving. I see that so many people are parodying you out of the habit of going on a fast.

Mr Srinivasa Iyengar despite his unfocusable and labyrinthine brain is getting on famously with me. He has agreed to adopt prohibition. I gave one whole precious week to this work of proselytising Srinivasa Iyengar, Satyamurti and Rangaswami Aiyangar and making them shed their suspicions and alarms about me. The *quid pro quo* is that I should help the Swarajists in their work of capture of the Councils—a position you have entangled us all in yourself! But the more intimately I see them, the more clearly I see the logical end of their endeavours viz., accepting office after driving out other competitors in the field.

I believe my son Narasimhan has completed his training—as far as he can ever reach. If Maganlalbhai is of the same view, he may be sent home. The cashier's work here is wanting its permanent hand as those who took it up in Narasimhan's absence wish to be relieved.

With love,
Yours ever,
C.R

21

The follow-up on the well-being of Vaikom's hero, Kelappan,[58] is the subject of this letter at Sabarmati which gives us a glimpse of how satyagrahis were cared for (or not sufficiently).

[58] K. Kelappan (1889–1971), a teacher at St. Berchmans High School, Changanassery, fought for social reforms and founded the Nair Service Society. He was called 'Kerala Gandhi' for challenging the British Raj and following his notable roles in the Vaikom and Guruvayur temple-entry satyagrahas conducted for the rights of Harijans.

Gandhi Ashram
Tiruchengodu
30 April 1926

My dear Bapu,

I am very sorry for the delay in regard to Kelappan's affair. I returned here only on 23rd and there was a month and half of post to be waded through. I had intended to return from Patna but from there I went across to Ahmedabad and you know the rest of the delay.

Kelappan's case is hard. But how can we give him Rs 600 to complete the roofing of his house out of the Travancore fund?

He says his father gave him education and so he would give the house to his sister to equalize it between brother and sister.

But then he proposes to improve or complete the house at a cost of Rs 500.

This sum together with Rs 100 extra for debts = Rs 600/- will even if given, not solve the problem of his future, but only complete the sister's house. I think this payment of Rs 600/- cannot be made from the public funds. We may maintain Kelappan by a monthly allowance so long as he does untouchability work, but unless the money presented to you in Travancore is treated as a private fund it seems impossible to make the lumpsum contribution for the house.

I have written to Kelappan offering a monthly allowance of Rs 50/- (he is a bachelor) and remitted to him already in anticipation of your approval Rs 200/- for January to April 1926. This will enable him to pay off debts incurred recently for maintaining himself and for other urgent expenses. I have told him Deodhar Colony and school must be abandoned and he must take up some other work. I shall settle the work in consultation with him. Do you approve of the monthly allowance of Rs 50/-? The account of the Travancore Fund with me now is Rs 1755-10-4. I can therefore pay the sum monthly to him out of this fund for some time.

I enclose Kelappan's letter of 2nd March so that you may peruse it with reference to my remarks about the grant of Rs. 600/-.

Dr Dalal said that you ought to use the right hand in writing and not give it up all together! I suppose other doctors prescribed rest! That is their way, so that someone or other among them may prove wise in either event.

Your statement about Devadas is distressing. You say he is 'progressing' on 26.4.26. I thought on 13.4.26 he had almost recovered. Was there a set-back?

The lots for deciding Mussoorie[59] was good! I wish you did the same for Finland![60] What is it for? The students of Europe can help themselves quite well. At any rate they don't stand in need of an ocular demonstration of insufficient clothing! Pardon my levity.

Santanam[61] was here but had left again before my arrival. Narayanan[62] and his wife live away from the ashram in the village. The shock of the incident has not yet passed off. I am waiting for it to propose their return.

Ramanathan[63] who has been doing the Provincial Khadi work is showing signs of weariness. I shall write separately about it so that you may pass it to Shankarlal.

Yours sincerely,
Rajagopalachari

---

[59] Gandhi used, occasionally, to resort to lots to decide when there was no moral principle involved in the choice under consideration. He obviously drew lots to decide on a proposed visit to Mussoorie, which idea was, as a consequence, dropped.

[60] The reference is to a visit that had been proposed for the World Conference of the Young Men's Christian Association (YMCA) to be held that August in Helsingfors, Finland. Gandhi declined the invitation after having considered it seriously for a while.

[61] Kasturiranga Santhanam (1895–1980), follower of Gandhi and early associate of CR, joined the Congress at a young age. He was one of the first inmates of the Gandhi Ashram, Tiruchengodu, and in charge of khadi production. Santhanam was a member of the Imperial Legislative Assembly (1937–42) and the Constituent Assembly (1946). In 1948 he became Union minister for railways and transport in Nehru's cabinet. In February 1952, he was appointed as the lieutenant governor of Vindhya Pradesh.

[62] N. Narayanan, a lawyer from Madurai, who had given up practice, was manager of the ashram.

[63] S. Ramanathan was an AISA worker and later minister for local administration, CR's council of ministers, 1937–39.

All places are boiling hot now, and everybody is weary. I can imagine what Ahmedabad must be like. Even you must now cease praising the weather.

C.R.

Gandhi's reply:

The Ashram
Sabarmati
11 May 1926

I have your two letters. I enclose herewith Kelappan's letter. What you have done is quite right. He must render an account of his work to you from time to time.

I am writing to Santanam. Herewith a copy of my letter to him. About Ramanathan, I shall discuss with Shankerlal. I do not apprehend any difficulty.

Can't very well draw lots about Finland. And, even if I do, it is too late now. But I share your misgivings. I have prescribed my terms and if they have me in spite of them there may be something in the visit.

You will be ready in June, won't you, for touring even if you have to have somebody from here temporarily. How would Chhotalal suit you? He cannot be there for a long time. But it would be possible to induce him to come there willingly for two or three months if he can be of any assistance and give you some relief.

I have now seen Shankerlal. He thinks that if Ramanathan's salary is raised to Rs. 150 there is bound to be pressure from others for raising their salary. It is a risky thing for a public and universal body like the Charkha Sangh to depart from fixed rules. At the same time, I see your or rather Ramanathan's difficulty. My suggestion, therefore, is that so long as it is absolutely necessary, you should pay Ramanathan from the Seva Sangh. For this, perhaps, Jamnalalji will have to be consulted which you should do or if you want me to I will. If the thing can be postponed you should come here at the time of commencing your tour and discuss with Shankerlal. I take it that Ramanathan will not insist upon the increase coming from the A.I.S.A.

Yours,

22

Money and health, travel plans and politics interweave in the following.

Gandhi Ashram
Tiruchengodu
20 May 1926

My dear Bapu,

Herewith the requisition you suggested regarding the balance of the South Indian Flood Relief Fund. It is not possible, I fear, to get Srinivasa Iyengar to think of this. I wrote to him and sent a form long ago and have had no answer. I am reminding him today again. Sadasivaiyer has not replied too. Perhaps being President of the Religious Endowments Board he thinks he is in active Government service. The Who's Who of the signatories I have noted in pencil on the paper.

I fear I have gone in for a mild kind of pleurisy. I caught, I believe, a chill somehow, but I am getting over it and will be quite all right in a few days. What is the upshot of the Mahabaleshwar talk? Nothing but an attempt at reconnoitring for the new Viceroy's sake, I suppose and an abundance of mutual courtesies.

How is Devadas?

Yours affectionately,
C. Rajagopalachar

P.S. I am sure to be ready for the tour. I shall be at Bombay on June 15. I have written so to Jamnalalji and Shankarlal and have asked the latter to make the programme.

C.R.

―――

A little earlier before reporting his pleurisy, CR has reported to Gandhi (letter unavailable) that he is in 'excellent health'. Gandhi replies:

The Ashram
Sabarmati
29 May 1926

I am so delighted that you are in 'excellent health'. Shankerlal must have written to you. But, in any case, I expect you to report yourself at the Ashram on the 15th June. Whilst you are touring certainly leave Lakshmi here.

Chhotalal is just now travelling here, there and everywhere. He has got the blues. He went to Khadi Pratishthan and passed a few days with Satis Babu. He is now in Wardha. I suggested that he should stay with you for some months and help you in your work. He was not inclined to do so because he said he would gladly render personal service if you need it but otherwise he did not know that he will feel comfortable. Now, however, he writes asking me if you will have him.

He still harps on personal services. But whatever he does, whether he helps you in the khadi work or whether he becomes your cook, waiter and sanitary attendant or whether he weaves your khadi, I suggest your having him on his terms. And if you find him moody you may ask me to withdraw him. If he wishes to tour with you let him do that. But you know him best. Are you prepared to have him? Or will you rather discuss the thing when you are here?

Your curse on the Finland visit is likely to bear fruit; for, a letter I have written to K. T. Paul seems to have put him in a fix.

The Ashram,

Sabarmati, 29-5-26.

My dear CR

     I am so delighted that you are in "excellent
health". Shankerlal must have written to you. But,
in any case, I expect you to report yourself at the
Ashram on the 15th June. Whilst you are touring
certainly leave Lakshmi here.

     Chhotelal is just now travelling here, there
and everywhere. He has got the blues.   He went to
Khadi Pratisthan and passed a few days with Satis
Babu. He is now in Wardha. I suggested that he should
stay with you for some months and help you in your
work. He was not inclined to do so because he said
he would gladly render personal service if you needed
it but otherwise he did not know that he would feel
comfortable. Now, however, he writes asking me if
you will have him. He still harps on personal service.
But whatever he does , whether he helps you in the
Khadi work or whether he becomes your cook, waiter
and sanitary attendant, or whether he weaves your
Khadi, I suggest your having him on his terms. And if

-2-

you find him moody you may ask me to withdraw him.
If he wishes to tour with you, let him do that. But
you know him best. Are you prepared to have him ?
Or xxxxxxxx will you rather discuss the thing when
you are here?

        Your curse on the Finland visit is likely
to bear fruit; for, a letter I have written to
K.T.Paul seems to have put him in a fix. I have
told him that he must look upon this proposed
visit with complete detachment. But it appears to me
that that he has prompted the invitation and that
the World Committee of Y.M.C.A. is a passive
instrument in his hands. However, I shall know my
fate inside of a week now.

        We are boiling here at the present moment,
but I hope you will send us rain before you come.

            Yours,

            Bapu

Sjt. C.Rajagopalachar,
    Gandhiashram
        Tiruchengodu.

I have told him that he must look upon this proposed visit with complete detachment. But it appears to me that he has prompted the invitation and that the World Committee of the Y. M. C. A. is a passive instrument in his hands. However, I shall know my fate inside of a week now.

We are boiling here at the present moment but I hope you will send us rain before you come.

Yours,

23

This letter, soaked in the atmosphere and travails of the Tiruchengodu ashram, gives Gandhi an update.

Gandhi Ashram
Tiruchengodu
_ 7 June 1926

My dear Bapu,

I won't halloo until we are quite out of the wood as regards Finland.[64] Is it finally given up?

---

[64] Letter to K.T. Paul:

The Ashram
Sabarmati
6 June 1926

Dear Friend,

I have your letter and the original letters from the Committee of arrangements. The letters make it clear to me that the idea of invitation was prompted by you out of your

I was pained to hear that Devadas has another trouble besides the one he had been recently cut up for. This was Pyarelal's letter. Let me hope that as so often happens with Pyarelal the information is incorrect. If it is true then I am so sad that the poor boy has to be under the knife again.

Somehow the tour has not yet been definitely arranged by Shankarlal who expects me to run up to Ahmedabad and *then* arrange the tour. This is very inconvenient. I wish to stay here as long as possible. So I would like things to be definitely arranged and me to leave just in time to join the others at Ahmedabad.

Santanam was to come here about now to enable me to go. But his children have been having whooping cough by turns and himself an ear ache and fever. So he hopes to come here about 20th inst. I shall be here therefore till the end of the month and if so directed by Shankarlal at [Ahmedabad] in the first week of July.

The rains have mercilessly failed here. The water famine and the general distress among the poor folk in this area are terrible. People are flying to the plantations in Ceylon and Malaya. Is there any

---

great goodwill towards me and your exaggerated notion of my influence over people especially the young mind. But I feel more than ever convinced that the time is not yet for me to leave India on such pretext as is furnished by the correspondence before me. The call to go out of India for service has got to be pressing and overwhelming. The correspondence is really a response to your desire for my presence at the deliberations at Helsingfors. But I know my own limitations and recognize the difficulties in the way of my message going straight home. If there is any power in my message it would be felt without the physical contact.

I know that my decision will disappoint you but it has been my lot in life to disappoint loving friends. But I know that these disappointments have done good rather than harm. You will please forgive me for all the trouble that you have been put to on my account and ask for forgiveness from friends at Helsingfors who might have expected my presence there. Needless to say my prayers will attend your deliberations and my best wishes accompany you on your voyage.

I return the original letters.

Yours sincerely,
M. K. Gandhi

truth in what the miserable people here now and then say, that my
'ashram' here is the cause of the rains holding off! I am so luckless
a fellow that it may well be so!

To add poignancy to the situation, I have to read out and write
replies to letters received by relations from the poor fellows who have
gone abroad. The matter is the same terrible news over and over,—
'there is no rain, life is hard, shall I come over too?' The spinning
wheel seems to be a caste affair—It does not seem possible to some
of the castes to take to it at all. About Chhotey Lal I would not leave
him here for the first time in my absence. He may well accompany
me in our tour if he agrees. I shall find him very useful personally.

With love, yours,
C.R.

24

*This letter, from the Sabarmati archives, deals with not a single political
issue. It is wholly absorbed in khadi and the impact of the weather on
the hand-spun fibre and fabric. An altogether extraordinary achievement
for two lawyers and politicians. And yet, unsurprising for the times when
Gandhi had succeeded in profiling khadi and spinning to a national
enterprise of no less criticality than the winning of independence.*

Gandhi Ashram
Tiruchengodu
23 June 1926

My dear Bapu,

I have your letter as well as Maganlalji's.[65]

---

[65] Grandson of an uncle of the Mahatma, Maganlal followed Gandhi to South
Africa in 1903 'in the hope of making a bit of fortune', but instead followed Gandhi's

The deterioration noticed is seasonal and due to the heat and dry winds. The weavers are unable to put close texture on account of the weather. As a matter of fact it is only some of the weavers that dare to weave at all, hand-spun yarn during these months. The number of looms working is much less than during cooler months.

As Jerajani[66] has written to you the warp standard is at ten strands to quarter of an inch. During cool months eight or nine strands for quarter of an inch would be put into the woof yielding a good texture. But during the hot months so much cannot be put in. It is not as if the weavers put in as few threads in the wool as they like, this being examined each time the weavers bring in cloth. It is attempted to check the texture with regard to woof also. The proper thing during the hot months would be to reduce the standard for the warp and enable it to take more threads in the woof. But we are averse to doing this because when once the number of threads in the reed is reduced it is a job to increase it again during the normal season; hence the present deterioration.

I know that trouble is being taken to check the deterioration and to bring back the old standard quality.

I notice the same deterioration in the quality of cloth produced here at the Ashram. It will not do to compare the qualities of the cloth produced now with that of the cloth produced during better months in previous years.

---

self-imposed poverty and helped organize and run the Phoenix settlement. Maganlal Gandhi it is who, while in South Africa, suggested the word satyagraha (from 'sadagraha' or 'insistence on the good and virtuous'; see Tridip Suhrud, 'Reading Gandhi in two tongues', in *Decentering Translation Studies: India and Beyond*, eds Judy Wakabayashi and Rita Kothari [Philadelphia: John Benjamins Publishing Company, 2009], pp. 107–18) to give a defining name to Gandhi's non-violent method of resistance. He followed Gandhi back to India in 1915 where Gandhi came to regard and describe Maganlal as the soul of the Sabarmati ashram. To Gandhi's shock and dismay, Maganlal died in 1928. His daughter, Radha, was later to marry Dipak, a son of Saraladevi and Rambhuj Dutt Chaudhuri.

[66] Vithaldas V. Jerajani (died 4 October 1971), manager of the Khadi Bhandar, Bombay, leading light of the AISA and Swadeshi Co-operative Stores, was regarded as a khadi pioneer and role model for khadi workers.

I write this in reply to your letter at once so that you might understand the situation. But I shall advise Ramanathan to try his best to improve the quality.

I do not think a public statement will be very useful except it be a very general one referring to the effect of the hot season and the dry winds upon the weavers' work. It may serve but to raise a scare.

Yours sincerely,
C.R.

———

The letter to which CR refers in the beginning:

The Ashram, Sabarmati
12 June 1926

I have your letter. You will have misfortune. But there is as much connection between your being in Tiruchengodu and the water scarcity as there is between Z—a newcomer—being in the same district and the scarcity. Those who charge you with rivalry unconsciously give your presence an importance you did not deserve. But as there is not much danger of your becoming inflated, let those good people who so charge you have all the pleasure they can derive from their belief.

The Finland idea is dead and decently buried. Dr. Dalal has . . . Devdas. Even if it requires an operation it would be a minor thing. I certainly don't worry about it, perhaps, because I don't dread the knife so much as I dread drug-taking. Poor Santanam! It almost appears as if we in India have more than our share of domestic troubles. And in India the Southern Presidency seems to take the first place.

I shall speak to Shankerlal about the arrangements of the tour.

Yours sincerely,

25

This one continues the charkha's steady hum.

Gandhi Ashram
Tiruchengodu
13 October 1926

My dear Bapu,

I am very sceptical about the Khadi Service Rules.

I think we are still in the stage of personal selection of men. Men with good local connections and good service behind them are generally to be preferred. To induce young men who have such connections, and who can give cash or other security upon employment, to go through two years course at Sabarmati and a further eight months practical course, we must offer very attractive and guaranteed careers. Otherwise the rules will be a dead letter. The greatest difficulty is in inducing really capable and efficient hands to stick to our service. The wrong sort, who cannot get employment elsewhere, stick. The right sort get tired of the conditions. It is not an economical arrangement to train a number of recruits of whom many have to be rejected. It seems to me that we may rather choose and send for training to Sabarmati or elsewhere according to the nature of the work to which they have to be deputed, some of the men who have proved steady and efficient. The training in book-keeping and the like may be had, not necessarily at Sabarmati, but before they are sent there. The term of special training may thus be very much cut down. I am not sure that it is necessary even as regards weaving that the training should be given only at Sabarmati. There are plenty of opportunities, and even better and more suitable, in the provinces where the selected men have to be employed.

I think to form an All India Khadi Service and an All India Khadi Service Board, is too much centralization and will lead to inefficiency. If the idea is that no one may be employed in Khadi work in future unless he is trained at the Satyagrah Ashram institute, I strongly object to it. To confine Khadi service all over India, irrespective of province and nature of the work involved, to those who go for training to Sabarmati is I believe not the best method of recruitment. We will keep out many efficient men and take many inefficient but trained men for seventy five percent of the posts. We will not be able to judge a man's efficiency or character unless we actually see how he gets on at work among his own people in his own province.

I am as good a lover of Hindustani as anybody else, barring those whose mother tongue is Hindustani. Except that during the two years course proposed there will be plenty of time for learning Hindustani. I do not think that we should insist on knowledge of Hindustani as a necessary qualification for khadi service in provinces like Tamil Nadu. Amplification of subsidiary qualifications leads to the entertainment of men who possess such qualifications but who may not be efficient in khadi work. If a centralized service like the Indian Civil Service is finally adopted I hope that there will be room provided for entertaining others also, where the provincial authorities feel that for any work a non-central-cadre man would be more suitable, and no restraint imposed against such freedom.

Yours sincerely,
C.R.

26

During 1927, the correspondence between CR and Gandhi flows thin since they spend a great deal of time together over the year, travelling in south India and Ceylon. Gandhi's illness—apoplexy—sees CR rush to his bedside in Nipani, in the Bombay Province. He urges a holiday in Mysore State, which suggestion is accepted. The sojourn is to turn into a significant tour, both in terms of family ties, and in terms of the work that was engrossing the Mahatma at the time: khadi. The following letter written to Mahadev Desai after the Nipani visit describes the scene and gives something of a model in the matter of tour arrangements. Nothing is left out, no detail, no dimension, of advance planning.

Bangalore
10 April 1927

My dear Mahadev

I hope Bapu is steadily improving. His Highness the Maharaja of Mysore[67] has placed his bungalow on the Nandi Hills at Bapu's disposal for his stay and offers all facilities. We have accepted the offer and fixed it up with the Diwan[68] last night. They are all keen about having Bapu. Gangadhar Rao[69] and I saw the Diwan at his residence last night. He was very nice. Nandi Hill is an elevation 4850 feet above sea level. Maximum temperature in summer is ten degrees below Bangalore. It ranges from 60 degrees to 70 degrees F. Gangadhar Rao and I inspected the place and have found it quite satisfactory. It is right in the middle of Mysore State. It will suit our requirements all right. It is 35 miles from Bangalore good motor road as well as a metre gauge line to the foot of the hill. The hill itself is an ascent of 1800 feet from the ground level. There are steps over a 1½ mile walking road. There is also a bridle path

---

[67] (Nalvadi) Krishnaraja Wodeyar IV (1884–1940), Maharaja of Mysore (1902–40), was the twenty-fourth ruler of the Wodeyar dynasty. Gandhi once described him as Rajarshi or 'saintly king'.

[68] Sir Mirza Muhammad Ismail (1883–1959) was diwan of the princely states of Mysore (1926–41), Jaipur (1942–46) and Hyderabad (1946–47).

[69] Veteran freedom fighter from Belgaum, known as 'Lion of Karnataka'.

5 miles long. There are only 4 bungalows all managed by the State. One of the bungalows is reserved for the State and that is now given to Bapu. There is first class bureaucratic management for all requirements.

We met the President and other members of the Reception Committee here at Bangalore as well as the local committee at Chikka Ballapur (the town at the foot of the Nandi Hill).

All arrangements will be satisfactory. Bapu must leave on 19th morning as arranged by Poona Mail and reach Bangalore on 20th morning. Gangadhar Rao will explain everything in person. I have suggested that the party may divide into 2 batches. One batch arriving here on 18th morning taking train at Belgaum on 17th; Bapu himself taking train on 19th and reaching here on 20th morning.

This will enable things to settle down before Bapu's arrival and will make it nicer for him.

I want Devadas to come with you positively. Shankarlal should be asked to come over with assistants and carry on the AISA office work from Nandi. There is plenty of accommodation for this being done without any inconvenience to anybody. I have an idea that we should organise a big conference and exhibition at Bangalore to be opened as soon as the period of rest is over i.e. the first week of June. I should like Shankarlal to organise it on behalf of AISA for all South India. It will help the collection of funds and reduce touring. I hope you will in any case bring Shankarlal down with you so that we might talk over the idea and see what can be done. He also needs rest badly having done so much touring and Nandi Hills will be good. For Devadas it will be the best thing in his present state of health. I am in perfect health. No giddiness.

CR

The Diwan specially desired it to be conveyed on behalf of the Maharaja of Mysore that H.H. was deeply concerned to learn about his illness and wished to have the privilege of doing all he can on this occasion to make his rest comfortable and help speedy recovery.

27

Given below are two interloper-letters. They are not from CR, but from Gandhi. The first one is to Hermann Kallenbach, Gandhi's associate from his South Africa days whom Gandhi routinely addressed as 'Lower House', harking to the bicameral nature of legislative arrangements in the South African legislature. I give the letter here for three reasons:

1. *The description it gives of the illness that brought Gandhi to Nandi, Karnataka, and for the picture it portrays of the ambience of the Nandi sojourn.*
2. *The amazing invisibility of CR, the organizer of the Nandi rest-stay, in the description.*
3. *Its portrayal of the Gandhi–Kallenbach equation that has featured in a 2011 biography of the Mahatma,* Great Soul, *by Joseph Lelyveld.*

The second one is to the veteran C. Vijiaraghavachariar[70] who has asked Gandhi to be his guest at Salem. I give it for the glimpse it gives of the state of CR's preoccupations at the time and of Gandhi's perception of his southern warrior.

Nandi Hills (near Bangalore)
13 May 1927

Lower House,

As I lie in bed and look up old undisposed of correspondence and revive old and sacred memories, I chance upon your letter of 27th

---

[70] Chakravarti Vijiaraghavachariar (1852–1944), lawyer and political activist, came to prominence following charges that he had instigated a Hindu–Muslim riot in Salem. Although in jail for some time, he successfully proved himself innocent. A member of the Salem Municipal Council in 1882, he was closely associated with Allan Octavian Hume and became president of the Congress in 1920. He was also president of the Hindu Mahasabha in 1931. Though bearing an identical family name and a similar-sounding name, 'CV' was not related to CR.

February sent with Andrews's letter from your home at Inanda, and I revive so many pleasant and sacred memories. Every letter that you have written during the last two years—and you have not written many—has been a despondent letter, distrustful of yourself; but as long as I live I am not going to lose faith in you. I am hoping that some day as before you will have a fatigue of the exciting things that give you momentary pleasure and that you will at least come to India to meet an old friend and renew many old acquaintances. You have made a provisional promise to do so next September or October. Do come if you can and then stay as long as you like or as little as you like.

I am glad you are having short spells of Andrews's company. I have not come across a humbler or more godfearing man throughout my varied experience. You don't want me to say anything about my illness; because I see you do get Young India and read it. I am at the present moment taking my cure in a little hill in the State of Mysore where an army of devoted volunteers and many of my closest co-workers are looking after me. Mrs. Gandhi and Devdas are with me. The names of others would mean nothing to you. So I do not give them. But when you do come, you will see them all and recognize them as having been with had put such terrific strain upon the brain that I was afraid of a crisis and it came just when I was arranging to have a lighter programme. But God seemed to say, 'I shall demolish your pride before you recognize your mad method and show you that you were utterly wrong in rushing as you have been doing, thinking that it was all well because it was for a good cause. You fool, you thought that you would work wonders. Have your lesson now and learn whilst there is yet time that God alone is to wonder-work and He uses whom He pleases as His instrument.' I am taking the chastisement I hope in due humility and if He raises me from this sick-bed, I am making Him promises that I shall reform my ways and shall seek still more strenuously to know His will and do it.

I hope you are keeping in touch with Manilal. He has got a girl with a strong character as his wife. She is the best girl I could possibly have found for him. Chance put her my way. She belongs to a godly family. Remember you are one of the trustees for Phoenix and I look to you to discharge your trust.

Sastri will be in South Africa probably within a month of your receipt of this. I have had long chats with him about you and your associations with Gokhale. Do try to be close to him and bring all our old companions in touch with him.

Yours sincerely,

——

Nandi Hills
31 May 1927

Dear Friend,

I have your letter. Either Jamnalalji committed a blunder or the interviewer. There is absolutely no chance even if I become obdurate of my being able to resume my tour in the middle of June. Let alone the doctors, I have myself no such confidence. Nandi has done me good. But there is much leeway yet to be made up. I get easily tired and I cannot move about with ease. A month more is the very least I shall require. What I feel is that I shall not be able to venture out much before the third week of July.

Rajagopalachari is not just now here. He has gone to Bangalore to find and prepare quarters for me there as the weather here is now becoming too bracing for me. He is the jailor in charge and it is he who has to dispose of me finally, so far as this Presidency is concerned. But in so far as I have any control over my movements, I would certainly love to be your guest if Salem is on the list at all. And, if it is not on the list, you can easily have it on the list by collecting a fat purse for the dumb millions from among your innumerable friends in Salem.

I never knew that the European Association at Calcutta had passed such an original resolution as you have described. Yes, I do feel, without being able to assign any justification for the feeling, that behind all the seeming anarchy, order is being evolved and that we shall not for ever remain a damned country.

Yours sincerely,

Sjt. C. Vijiaraghavachariar
Fairyfalls View
Kodaikanal Observatory P.O.
Kodaikanal Hills

28

After the salubrious break in Nandi Hills, Gandhi undertakes a tour of the Tamil country, spread over the next three months, with CR travelling with him and interpreting his speeches. His work on khadi hailed now as an effective model for strengthening rural livelihoods, and his propaganda against untouchability and drinking gaining ground, CR is becoming Gandhi's most prominent 'voice', indeed as that of his 'successor'. But leadership is ever followed by the shadow of resentment. Peers within and outside the Congress, seeing politics through Brahmin/non-Brahmin tints, bring their misgivings about CR to the Mahatma. The radical Aiyangar does not suffer fools; the 'problem' is he does not suffer very intelligent people either, if their intelligence is not tethered by self-restraint. His sharp wit and undisguised impatience with human failings are not designed to make him popular.

That schisms and intrigues, allegations and slurs were no less a part of public life then as they are now is evident from the following entry, dating to when Gandhi was in Karaikudi, in the Collected Works.

Talk To Young Men
[On or before 25 September 1927]

You are telling me utter falsehoods. You do not know the man. If Rajagopalachari is capable of telling lies, you must say that I am also capable of telling lies. I do say he is the only possible successor, and I repeat it today. You young men in trying to kill him will kill yourselves. The pamphlet shows how you are fed on lies—you are bringing up your movement on lies which means violence.

You may offer stubborn battle if you like, but build your foundation on truth. I am giving you this time only because I feel for the youth of the country.

29

During the stay in Karnataka, Gandhi and Kasturba have had Devadas with them and CR has had the company of his daughter, Lakshmi. Something that is 'meant to happen' does happen, quietly and without any immediate finality. Twenty-seven-year-old Devadas gives CR a letter in Bangalore, sometime in June or July 1927, asking for Lakshmi's hand. That this is not a sudden 'Nandi Hills' development becomes apparent to the parents as they talk the matter over with the young man. Also clear is that Devadas is not speaking for himself alone. Lakshmi indicates that she too is in love with her suitor. The letter he has given to his future father-in-law is not in the family archives and is not at Sabarmati either.

Rajmohan Gandhi writes in The Rajaji Story: *'CR told Gandhi, and the surprised fathers discussed the idea. They were not sure of its rightness. Was this true love or infatuation? It was this question, not caste, that troubled them.'[71]*

---

[71] Rajmohan Gandhi, *The Rajaji Story, 1937–1972* (Delhi: Bharatiya Vidya Bhavan, 1984).

CR's initial reaction is unknown from any direct record. The fact that Devadas 'breaks' his intention to CR when Gandhi is also at hand, means that Gandhi's response too is oral, not written down, a gain to intimacy of communication but a loss to documentation. Rajmohan Gandhi adds: 'Separately, CR and Gandhi talked with her. Lakshmi said she was clear. Then test your truth, she was told. Wait, and have no contacts. No meetings, no letters. Devadas was similarly adjured.'

After three more months in south India, where Gandhi and CR spend a great deal of time together, comes a memorable and historic visit to Ceylon to promote khadi and raise Rs 1 lakh for the Khadi Fund. Devadas, ill at the time with more than one medical episode, does not accompany his father and the father of the girl he is in love with. But Lakshmi goes with them and with Kasturba and Mahadev Desai. One may assume that although Gandhi and Kasturba are not prejudging anything and have trust that the 'right thing' is happening (or the 'wrong', not), they begin giving Lakshmi a certain place in their hearts that might not have come quite that way in 'ordinary' circumstances.

CR interprets Gandhi's talks in the Tamil country and also in Ceylon, when the audience is largely Tamil-speaking, as in the island's central highlands and in its north. This, incidentally, is the largest span of uninterrupted time Gandhi and CR have ever spent together—a total of seven months.

The first—and only—written inkling of the 'family development' comes in a letter Gandhi writes to the faithful Surendra, whose friendship with Devadas is something both Gandhi and CR know of and value. Gandhi's letter, written in Gujarati from Jaffna, is harsh to the son and also conveys CR's initial reaction which seems to have been, for all his affection for Devadas, very negative to the proposal. Surendra's reply has not been preserved.

28 November 1927[72]

Devdas's state is extremely pitiable. Rajaji is not likely at all to give him Lakshmi [in marriage], and rightly so. Lakshmi will not take one

---

[72] From the Gujarati original published in *Gandhijino Akshardeh*, Khand 35, item 224, pp. 305–06, as extracted from the manuscript of Mahadev Desai's *Diary*. Courtesy: Narayan Desai. Translation mine.

step without his consent. She is living cheerfully. Whereas Devdas has gone almost mad repeating Lakshmi's name, pining and suffering. If he had such love for God, he would have been revered as a saintly man and become a great dedicated worker.

But how can even Devdas act against his nature? He wishes to obey me, but his soul rebels against him. He seems to believe that I stand in the way of his marriage with Lakshmi and so keeps getting angry with me. I do not know at present how he can be rescued from this condition. Try and see if you can help him get calm down, and explain to him his dharma. It is possible that I have not understood him and am, therefore, doing him injustice. See if you can give him peace of mind through a letter. I of course keep writing to him.

I myself clearly see that impure desires in his mind are the cause of his many diseases. Impure desires eat away a person without being aware, I have no doubt about that. Devdas is right in believing that he loves a life of pleasures. But pleasure-loving is rather a mild word. His mind is filled with sexual desires. Since he cannot see this clearly, sexual desires are consuming him.

29

On returning to India on 30 November 1927, Gandhi goes on to tour Andhra and Orissa, Kasturba goes to Wardha to stay with Devadas who is convalescing from illness and surgery, while CR and Lakshmi return to the ashram. That the 'moratorium' on Devadas and Lakshmi has become established and the two fathers are back to national duties, albeit at the moment non-political, is clear from the following 'business letter-cum-health bulletin' from Gandhi.

Bolgarh
10 December 1927

My dear C.R.,

You will be surprised to know that at last I have three days of quiet in a beautiful little village. Before that the Ganjam programme was worse if possible even than the Ceylon programme, though it yielded twenty thousand. Then a doctor came to take my bloodpressure.

Niranjan Babu has made the same arrangements for examination of blood-pressure that you had. And when the doctor read 190, he got frightened and the whole of the programme has been rearranged. Hence the rest. Personally I am inclined to disbelieve the doctor's reading. However, even if it was wrong reading, it has done good. A new doctor who has come today from Cuttack has read anything between 155 and 165. His own reading is between 155 and 160. Mahadev and Pyarelal read 165. The diastolic is 90-100. If these readings are correct, the blood-pressure is the same as before, and there is nothing to worry. However I am not writing this to tell you about the blood-pressure. Enough for you to know that I am all right. I am dictating this in order to send you the enclosed. If you can send someone to inspect the village and find out whether we can take up the proposition, please do so. In any case correspond with the writer Mr. G. Subramaniam yourself. I am sending him a postcard telling him that he may expect to hear from you.

I send you also Dr. Joseph's letter. His suggestion commends itself to me. I think we must do some work in Nagercoil, and unless you have anything to the contrary, please enter into correspondence with him telling him that his suggestion is acceptable and that it will be put before the Council of the Association and you will let him know at an early date. Meanwhile you may send the sample of yarn he wants. We ought to be able to take up the yarn, and if there are local weavers, we may be able to get it woven there. Please write to Dr. Joseph early. I have told him that his suggestion commends itself to me and that I have forwarded his letter to you for consideration.

I hope you have fixed up the quarters in Madras. Satis Babu was with me for a day. He will be in Madras and stay with us. You should have ready a moderate amount, no more than one pound at the outside, of goat's milk butter.

Here is a letter from . . . Please ack. to him. I am not writing

to him. His proposal seems to be quite good. Of course we will be
with you.[73]

Bapu

30

*Back in the ashram, leaving his field—the political field—to others, and
returning to the charkha's hum, CR probably reflects on the compensating
truth of Milton's line, 'They also serve, who only stand and wait',
modified to '. . . who just sit and spin'. But is CR 'just spinning'?
At one level, the external, visible level, yes. Non-political constructive
work was his preoccupation. But can politics and national debates on the
country's political future be far from the thoughts of one who was seen as
Gandhi's multidimensional voice?*

Gandhi Ashram
9 January 1928

My dear Bapu,

This letter has come over the Straits with a remittance of Rs 1190 to
the Khadi Fund. Mr. Kalyanasundara Mudaliar,[74] Editor 'Navasakti'
Madras, wants me to send the letter on to you for a reply.

The money has been duly credited.

Yours sincerely,
C. Rajagopalachar

---

[73] The reference is to their meeting up later that month in Madras at the Congress's
annual session, which CR attended but did not participate in by way of political speeches.
The identity of the letter writer (in the previous sentence) has been excluded from the
Collected Works.

[74] See n. 12.

31

Two spaces—Tiruchengodu and Sabarmati—occupy CR's mind, both as Gandhi's exemplar and his adviser. This letter from the Sabarmati archive describes the double engagement.

23 January 1928

My dear Bapu,

I did get very angry when I read your last letter about almond paste and cocoanut milk.[75] Knick-nacks like these are totally inadequate substitutes for food and milk. Do take the home-made bread and vegetable which agreed with you very well. It is cheap, common, easily prepared and substantial food. Stale almond paste or cocoanut juice is not food and may sometimes be positively harmful. Cocoanut juice daily taken may not be very good for an old man's liver. To make these things fresh, it must be very costly and which by itself must be enough to exclude these inventions from your dietary.

---

[75] Regrettably, Gandhi's letter to CR is not in the *Collected Works*. But the following letter to Suresh Chandra Bannerji is relevant.

Satyagraha Ashram
Sabarmati
19 January 1928

My Dear Suresh Babu,

I have your letter. I am glad at the happy termination of the Comilla afair. Is it a reform from within or a reform super-imposed? With reference to my health, I have not seen my way to taking the medicine sent by Dr. Roy. It is something extracted from the human body and I have the greatest repugnance to taking any such medicine. But I have made radical change in my diet. I am now living on simply fruits and a little almond-nut paste and coconut milk. So far I have not come to grief.

Yours sincerely,

Overwork of any kind must be avoided. I hope advantage is not taken of absence of touring, and correspondence work and worries of management increased. It is not alone the shouting crowds that are to be avoided to give you the rest. Between 12 and 2 p.m. and at night, eight full hours, of sleep must be secured at all costs. I am glad you are taking 'silence' between 12 and 3 every day. But silence should be deemed observed only if you lie in bed, and have not written or heard any one for more than 1 minute's duration!

I should like you to place at my disposal for untouchability work Rs 5000/- if possible. I am dealing with Kelappan as you have expressed. I wish to have a few wells dug for the Panchamas near about here.

Yours affectionately,
C.R.

———

Gandhi's reply:

Satyagraha Ashram
Sabarmati
28 January 1928

My dear C.R.

I have your letter. I wish you will cease to worry about me. I can only give you my assurance that I shall do nothing wilfully to impair my health. But you know my nature. I cannot exist without dietetic experiment if I am fixed up at any place for any length of time. You know too that it has always been my intense longing to revert to fruit and nut diet or at least a milkless diet if I at all could. I find now that I can easily do so and so I have done it. Now that I can pull on with it, it would be difficult for me to go back to milk until I am satisfied that it is not possible to do without milk. I can only tell you that I shall not do anything obstinately. In accordance with Dr. Muthu's instructions I am not having the blood-pressure taken at all, but I am flourishing.

I discovered in Kathiawar that I could bring my voice to almost the original pitch without fatigue and without any discomfort. It was a well-thought-out, very rapidly delivered speech lasting for full one hour, and there was no trace of exhaustion after it. Surely, that was some test of my progress. And I was able to talk, not merely attend committee meetings for two nights, successively lasting up to 11 o'clock. About work too, I cannot say that I am not doing very strenuous work, but it is not beyond my capacity.

What has given Lakshmi her fever? I hope that she is all right now. I hope to send you Rs. 5,000/- for untouchability work soon.

Bapu

32

Gandhi's health worries CR, even as CR's and that of Lakshmi—who had been briefly unwell—worries Gandhi.

Pudupalayam
8 February 1928

My dear Bapu,

Your loving letter.[76] Lakshmi is now up and moving about. There is still some cough. Otherwise she is well. I do not need any relief from there.

---

[76] The letter is unavailable. But another one given below reverts to Lakshmi's health at the end.

Now, will you not isolate yourself completely from work for a month at least and sleep as much as you possibly can, and avoid all hard thinking?

Yours affectionately,
C.R.

I am of the opinion that the nut diet should be given up and milk resumed.

The Ashram
Sabarmati
18 February 1928

My dear C. R.,

Herewith Kelappan's letter. I have asked him to discuss his scheme with you. Whatever you think is feasible should be done. You will not hesitate to sanction anything for fear of funds being exhausted. All I am anxious about is that whatever work is done is substantial and honest.

I hope you are now not worrying about my health. I have not yet taken any vow about the milk and I am not going to do anything unless I find the experiment to be absolutely successful. And not only I am carefully watching myself, but so also are the Ahmedabad doctors. It is open to them to veto the experiment at any time they like and I have promised to stop it. But I want you, instead of thinking of somehow dodging and making me to take milk, find out doctors or physicians who will help me to arrive at a proper, purely vegetarian diet which will be more than a substitute for milk. I am sure it is perfectly possible. Do please therefore think over my suggestion.

Have you heard from Singapore friends at all? If we are to go, I should like to start during the first week of April, because the hot weather commences in right earnest in April in Ahmedabad and it would be better to avoid it. And then there is the talk of a visit to Burma from Singapore. I should like to negotiate it and, if that also is to be done, there is very little time left. And then there are two invitations from Europe to go there during July and August. I am inclined to accept them. The idea is cooking in my brain. One is from the World's Youth Peace Movement. It seems to be an important movement managed by a good organization. You may also consider the propriety or otherwise of accepting these invitations.

Lakshmi must not have a relapse.

33

*By now, CR's ashram, named after and blessed by Gandhi, has completed
three years of successful if arduous experimentation in carrying out Gandhian
programmes. The place is also, in a sense, fifty-year-old CR's tapovana,
a site for self-mortifying meditations. Pudupalayam's heat and aridity give
it the look and feel of a place in perpetual drought and ceaseless want. CR
has become, from that crucible of challenges, an acknowledged khadi expert;
'the unquestioned leader of the prohibition movement in India' (Jawaharlal
Nehru's 1929 phrase); and a skilful organizer of drought relief.*

*And of course, all the while, CR's pen has not stopped. Young India
keeps getting from CR a string of contributions, both by way of polemical
pieces and 'creative' ones. Self-appointed nutritionist and health adviser to
the Mahatma, CR's passion for quasi-medical prescriptiveness remains a
major activity, as this letter from the Sabarmati archive tells us.*

Gandhi Ashram
Tiruchengodu
21 March 1928

My dear Bapu,

Your letter of 10th[77] reached me only now. It was put in the wrong
cover and so it had to go to Satish Babu and come to me after making

---

[77] The *Collected Works* has eight letters against this date, but the letter to CR is not
among them. CR's footnote refers to the proposal that Gandhi visit Europe. He reverts to
the subject in another letter that is not available. Gandhi's reply to that one is given below.

The Ashram
Sabarmati
28 March 1928

My dear C. R.,

I have your letter about the proposed European visit. I have myself no heart in it, nor have
I any confidence in myself about making it successful; but an interview with Rolland still

the grand continental tour. The sign of a healthy blood pressure is that you should not get upset over this.

Regarding the food experiment I accept your assurance that all my points are wrong. I myself was feeling that I had grown cantankerous. I am glad, however that you have suspended the experiment.

Andrews really loves you more than I do. So let his opinion prevail.

Love
C.R.

Send me a wire when things are settled finally as to time, who goes, etc

---

remains an attraction. All the reputation I enjoy in the West is borrowed from him and I feel that if I meet him face to face, there may be disillusionment on many points. It may be that we should come closer than we ever were. I do attach considerable importance to our knowing each other much better than we do.

I quite agree with you that there is nothing to gain from the health point of view. I might possibly suffer, and health is no consideration, whatsoever in the proposed trip. From that point of view, any hill station in India would be infinitely superior for me. I feel also with you that the withdrawal of my presence is likely to unsettle things a bit especially in Bardoli. Foreign cloth boycott can certainly make no headway during my absence. But now that you are all gathering together at Calcutta, I would like you to discuss the proposed visit at the Council meeting. I am most anxious that I should not become exclusive and should be humble enough to arrive at truth no matter from what source it comes.

I am sorry about the defalcations, but I shall accept your warning not to disturb myself or discuss them. I understand what you say about Ramachandran. I want you to write him a warm letter and go out of your way to draw him towards you. He is kind of 'Chetty' also, for he did wonderfully well in the way of khadi at Jamia.

I must not forget one thing, though, about your reference to the defalcations. If the defaulter gives you Rs. 500 and tenders an apology for publication, you should be entirely satisfied. But this is an unconsidered opinion of a layman.

What do you say to my exploit in conducting an exclusively milk experiment? I do not want to be told you swooned at my saying it is a literally milk-and-water experiment.

Yours sincerely,

34

*Gandhi is contemplating another invitation from Europe, and
considering taking CR with him in the early summer of 1928 when he
learns that his beloved and trusted nephew, and the pillar of Sabarmati,
Maganlal Gandhi, has suddenly died of typhoid in Patna on 23 April.
CR is in Bengal at the time, with Jamnalal Bajaj, to further khadi and
to collect funds for a C.R. Das Memorial. He wires Mahadev Desai:*

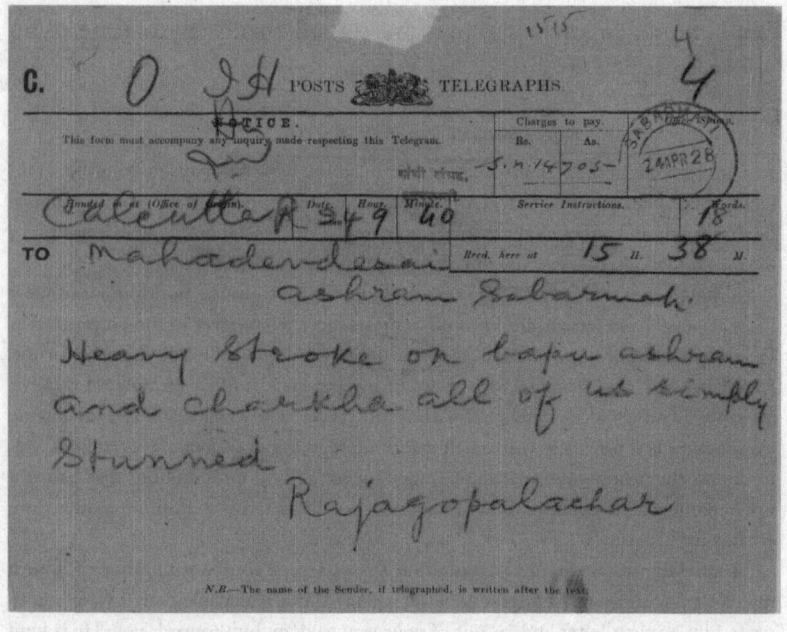

*And then, the following day, Gandhi. Upturning his earlier position
against Gandhi's going abroad and thereby leaving the scene of action,
he now urges him to go. A change of scene, he obviously feels, would do
Gandhi good. But Gandhi has already dropped the plan.*

Calcutta 7
25 April 1928

Jamnalalji gone Patna returning tomorrow you may resent suggestion but prayerfully press your going Europe now leaving scene of desolation in Jamnalalji's hands who must postpone pilgrimage remain ashram wire reply martaluminium

Rajagopalachari

———

Gandhi's reply:

Abandoned European visit before Maganlal's departure. Jamnalalji must go pilgrimage. Let me deserve inheritance left by Maganlal. Bapu

35

Back from Bengal, CR re-immerses himself in bringing livelihood to poor families in that arid countryside through khadi, anti-drinking work and the amelioration of Harijan lives. But writing—his natural métier—on the slice of life around him, translating into English the verses of Avvaiyar and of Subramania Bharati, and occasionally venturing into subjects fringing politics give him some relief. Not everything he sends to the Mahatma for Young India *appears in print, though. As this letter from the Sabarmati collection shows.*

26 May 1928

My dear Bapu,

Your letter[78] has not helped me to attain the peace which you intended it should do. I see your love and your reasonableness. But

---

[78] The letter is, alas, unavailable. Another letter from Gandhi adverting to the 'Comilla young men' of Abhoy Ashram is given below.

peace must come from within. As yet it is like a parched throat only causing pain if you try to find moisture and swallow.

Your refusal to publish my appreciation of the Comilla young men is, I think, unjust. I think they deserve the advertisement your columns would give.

Your unhappy C.R

36

Another 'regret' from Young India *follows soon thereafter.*

31 May 1928

My dear Bapu,

Your note about my conversational article[79] on Hindu–Muslim unity. I am not surprised. Every one dealing in gunpowder and sharp weapons is anxious that no others should come near. I fully expected you would put an embargo on such stuff. That is why I called the article 'unsold stock'; and unsold it is and you advise that it should not even be exposed for sale.

Satyagraha Ashram
Sabarmati
30 May 1928

My dear C. R.,

I did not argue with you about the reason for not publishing your tribute to the Abhoy Ashram. About the labourers, I think I gave you my reason. About the Abhoy Ashram, your tribute is well deserved. But instead of benefiting them, the tribute was likely to rouse all kinds of jealousies and I felt that it was better not to rouse any jealousy.

[79] This is unavailable.

But I maintain that what is unseasonable is most seasonable. There is a paradox! Seasonable things are uttered by everybody, and what is useful may be out of season in that sense. But if you think my views are wrong, after reading them again, I should like a criticism, if time and affairs permit. I think it is the only solution for the impasse about the Constitution.

Love
C.R.

⌒

Below is Gandhi's 'note' on CR's article:

Satyagraha Ashram
Sabarmati
27 May 1928

Mr Dear C.R.,

I just read your pencil notes 'Unsold Stock'. The views about khadi are purely introductory. The views about Hindu–Muslim unity are entirely unseasonable and are likely to be misrepresented if not resented. You must therefore keep them under lock and key for the time being.

Yours sincerely,
Bapu

37

The Hindu–Muslim question comes to the fore again, with a scheme proposed by a committee headed by Motilal Nehru and discussed at

*Lucknow. The scheme, meant to narrow the differences between the two
communities as a response to the Simon Commission, is not acceptable to
Muslim leaders outside the Congress. Motilal Nehru, scheduled to preside
over the Congress's annual session in Calcutta in December 1928, is
turning to Gandhi for support and Gandhi is turning to CR for advice.
This letter indicates a consequential return to political discussions in the
CR–Gandhi correspondence.*

17 November 1928

My dear Bapu,

Yours of 14 instant. If I had read your letter to Sir Habibullah[80]
I should have certainly desisted from the proposal. I was wrong
altogether and I am very sorry.

At Bangalore the news about Lalaji[81] came. It is a calamity too
great for words. Selfless patriotism personified, Lalaji was, and we
have lost him. Even if India could reconcile herself to the loss, how
is Punjab to bear it.

Yours sincerely,
C.R.

---

[80] Nawab Khan Bahadur Sir Muhammad Habibullah (1869–1948) was a member
of the Arcot royal family and awarded a number of titles and honours throughout his
career. He was chairman of the Vellore municipality (1905–19); India's delegate to the
first session of the League of Nations in 1919; and leader of India's delegation to South
Africa in 1926–27. He became member for revenue in the Governor's Executive Council
for Madras Presidency (1920–24); member of the Executive Council of the Viceroy
(1925–30); and served as the diwan of Travancore (1934–36).

[81] Lala Lajpat Rai died on 17 November 1928 after receiving a lathi blow across his
chest while protesting against the Simon Commission.

The letter CR refers to:

Satyagraha Ashram
Sabarmati
14 November 1928

Here is a letter and copy of my reply. You will either write
to the complainant yourself or enable me to send him a further
reply.

I have your telegram which surprises me. I could not possibly go
to the length you suggest. Enclosed is a copy of the letter I sent to
Sir Mahomed Habibullah. Please discuss the subject no more with
anybody and destroy the enclosed.

Yours sincerely,

38

*At the Calcutta Congress, Motilal Nehru's countenancing of dominion
status is attacked by Jawaharlal and Subhas Chandra Bose who want
'complete independence'. Gandhi suggests a compromise: if London does
not commit to autonomy for an Indian dominion within a year, Congress
would ask for complete independence.*

*The last month of 1928 and the year 1929 prove turbulent.
J.P. Saunders, the assistant superintendent of police at Lahore,
held responsible for the fatal lathi charge on Lala Lajpat Rai, is
shot dead in December 1928. Gandhi intensifies his programme
of boycotting foreign cloth which, though part of 'swadeshi' agitations
rather than 'swaraj' activities, is a political challenge to the
authorities. In a brief letter to CR, Gandhi asks him to plunge
headlong into boycott.*

Satyagraha Ashram
Sabarmati
22 January 1929

I have your letter. You will see from current Young India what I have done about the boycott of foreign cloth. You would do some such thing like that. I want you to throw yourself into that work.

———

As drought strikes the Tiruchengodu region hard, Young India *publishes appeals from CR for help. Help comes, but more is needed.*
    CR then sends Gandhi the following telegram:

In response to appeals in *Young India* in October and December last the Pudupalayam Gandhi Ashram has so far received over Rs. 769. Of this Rs. 225 were received by us direct and Rs. 544 through the Sabarmati Ashram. . . . We have restricted our relief work to *Adi-Dravidas* of five villages within a mile of the Ashram. . . . A card is given to each family entitling them to buy at concession prices from the Ashram every Saturday not more than five measures of *jovari* per adult and half this quantity for children below twelve. . . . So far 108 families with 344 adults and 179 children have been registered and are receiving relief as above from 2nd February, 1929. . . . Even then the cost of relief will be Rs. 1,312 of which we have received only Rs. 769. But there are other villages near the Ashram whose *Adi-Dravida* population is in a pitiable condition and is clamouring for relief. . . . Large numbers are emigrating. But very poor and old persons, especially women and children, have not even this escape out of an intolerable situation. . . . We would very much like to give them food free. But our funds are limited. . . . We need at least Rs. 5,000 more to do work fairly satisfactorily. The call is very urgent.

———

Gandhi publishes this telegram in Young India *with tributes to CR. But, privately, he finds fault with CR's methodology. He writes sharply:*

Satyagraha Ashram
Sabarmati
26 February 1929

I have your telegram. I am publishing it with a note. But I repeat my complaint. Whatever the cause, you fail to back your appeal with facts and figures from week to week. You may not plead want of time or if you want to plead want of time, then don't expect any response. You may not have the cake and eat it. I myself after the publication of the appeal was utterly in the dark as to what was happening. Surely Santanam or whoever is in charge can say from week to week how much relief has been given, what kind of relief has been given and to whom it has been given. You are talking about volunteers going to the villages taking notes. Some telling experience might be given. The condition of the homes of these people might be given. A hundred things suggest themselves to me. How do you expect people to respond when very telling figures [are not] thrust upon their attention from week to week, indeed from day to day? You can say if you send such reports they won't be published.

You will see from my notes that I have justified your telegram somehow or other. My complaint against you is that the telegram was not absolutely inevitable. The facts related in the telegram do not suddenly come under your notice. You can send telegrams about landslips, overflowing flood to a terrible extent, but you cannot telegraph about the daily happenings in a famine area, unless you send news to a distant newspaper from day to day. Do please wake up. I will find the Rs. 5,000/- somehow or other. But what is the use? That won't be in answer to your appeal, that would be merely from friend to friend and that is not how you want this relief, if I understand it rightly. And if you wanted it that way, you could simply have telegraphed: you must send me Rs. 5,000/- for my starving people.

Verb. sap.

39

Meanwhile, the Raj is tensing up. In March, Congressmen and communists are arrested and tried in Meerut. Jatin Das, arrested following the Saunders murder, fasts unto death in jail. Two bombs and pamphlets are famously thrown during a session in the Central Assembly on 8 April 1929. The country wants Gandhi back in a frontally political role. And CR prepares to attend a provincial conference at Vedaranyam, Tanjore district, in September 1929. CR believes the 'dominion versus complete independence' issue is polemical and asks for Vallabhbhai Patel to be sent to the conference to help deliberate on the urgent situation. The following telegram, preserved at Sabarmati, carries the weight of the political tension of the times, although it cannot help touch on a favourite CR–Gandhi topic, healthy food.

Gandhi Ashram
Tiruchengodu
19 August 1929

Convinced no harm will result by reason difference over issue which nobody takes as real. Vallabhbhai's presiding is like your presence important for moral effect pray avoid disappointing. Now you have doomed uncooked food forever hope inflammation subsiding.

Rajagopalachar

After an attack of dysentery, Gandhi had given up his preferred diet of uncooked food. Gandhi's reply to this telegram of mixed political and dietary views and suggestions is:

[On or after 19 August 1929]

RAJA

AM ADVISING VALLABHBHAI PREPARE GO. UNFIRED CAN NEVER BE
DOOMED. GETTING ON.

BAPU

40

Khadi dominates the year 1929 for CR and, through remote control,
Gandhi as well. Late into the year, CR shares with Gandhi his delight
over an instance of khadi-based honesty.

I admit that till now I have been indifferent regarding khadi. But I
have now realized that khadi men are men who follow truth. The
day before yesterday I went to Coimbatore khadi depot . . . I had
with me notes of the value of Rs. 10,000 . . . which I placed . . . on
the table. I quite forgot about the money and left the depot. After
some time, your manager saw the money and in the hot sun came
to Podanur . . . handed over the money to me

———

Gandhi is unimpressed. Giving a gist of CR's communication in Young
India, *he writes:*

This letter shows how unreasoning and illogical we are. Surely there
is no necessary connection between honesty and khadi. Even rogues
must cover themselves and therefore may wear khadi. I am sorry

also to have to confess that not all the workers in the employ of the A.I.S.A. have always been found to be honest. Would that every one of them was incorruptible. But alas! khadi service like every other service has its black sheep. And supposing for the moment that all khadi servants were incorruptible, it is still possible for khadi to be a huge mistake or an economic waste. But I know that many have come to khadi not on the strength of its merits but on grounds irrelevant to khadi, and I knew too that some others have left off using khadi not because it is an error but because they have not liked something some khadi men have done or not done. Whilst therefore I do not mind the adventitious aid such as the possessor of the ten thousand rupees notes promises to give, khadi to be stable must stand on its own unassailable merits. These are fortunately being proved day after day.

The other reflection the foregoing letter gives rise to is somewhat humiliating. Why should anyone run into ecstasies because someone is found to possess the ordinary honesty of not stealing other people's property? Have we fallen so low that a man forgetfully leaving valuables in a shop may not feel as safe about them as if they were in his possession? At any rate this letter has a lesson for men and women in khadi service. Their honesty may bring rich votaries to the altar of *Daridranarayana*. And He needs them all.

Young India, 5 December 1929

41

If the year 1929 has been spent by Gandhi's 'southern warrior' as a khadi, drought-relief and anti-drinking organizer, the absence of camaraderie within the 'Congress family', the withdrawal of his friend and erstwhile colleague E. V. Ramaswami Naicker from partnership and the unceasing intrusion of the Brahmin/non-Brahmin dimension have remained causes for disquiet. Gandhi receives a communication from someone saying CR is using khadi funds collected during Gandhi's southern tour 'to maintain idle brahmins'. In what can only be described as an epiphanic moment in July 1929, when CR, sitting outside his hut at Pudupalayam, is drafting a reply to this slur, a woman in rags comes crying. Her husband had borrowed five rupees from a moneylender, paid ten as interest and had died. Now the moneylender was threatening her for the principal amount, saying he would break up her daughter's imminent marriage. Hearing the account, CR tears up the draft he was writing and sends, instead, an article for Young India *on an altogether different key. It is carried by Gandhi, albeit without comment, in* Young India *on 11 July 1929.*

Almost every one of these people is in debt. A couple of rupees borrowed carries so much interest per rupee per month and the people earn so little that the debt can never be discharged but grows and grows. It practically sells the man into slavery. There is no legal process but assault and intimidation and coercion do the work of the courts. The creditor is his own bailiff. If no one lent money to these people they would be in a worse position. A debtor and slave feel more respectable than a mere starving beggar.

I tore off the worthless article I was writing in self-defence. What if I was calumniated? It was nothing to the miseries of these defenceless people. Our mutual quarrels and hates are God's retribution for our wicked indifference to the miseries of these children of His.

'Is your daughter to be married?' I asked.

'Yes, lord, this Wednesday', she smiled.

What fuss we make over a wedding in our homes! Think of a brute who lent a couple of rupees to your dead father, and he comes and stops the proceedings and pulls the carpet and paraphernalia out and assaults the assembled folk, for his debt is still due.

'Go on with it', I said. 'Don't be afraid. If the kantukaran [moneylender] comes and interferes in any way come and tell me at once and don't be afraid'.

'My Swa-a-mi! My protector', she cried in joy as she walked away.

I sent a message of stern disapproval to the tyrant's friends. Either he feared police proceedings or he relented, or what is more probable, he resolved to bide his time. I heard nothing more of the trouble.

42

The caste allegations rankling him, CR writes another nugget in his favourite genre, the short story, called 'Simplified Marriage'. While supporting Hindu marriage reform and 'change', he has his own take on it. Marriage's religious form, he says, must be preserved for its 'strength and durability'. His daughter's hand having been sought by a dearly loved young man of another province, another caste, the subject is not altogether academic for him. In a postscript to the story, CR writes something that could well have been a paragraph in a letter to Gandhi, his leader in the anti-casteism movement, and his daughter's future father-in-law:

I claim to be a greater changer than many that now beat up a great deal of dust. I have been an out-caste among my relations for the last twenty years. I have done and am doing things which my clamorous friends have not, I believe, in their own persons attempted.

43

In the midst of all this, politics, of the highest kind, beckons. The viceroy's announcement on 31 October 1929 that there would soon be convened a Round Table Conference (RTC) in London includes a statement that the 'natural issue of India's constitutional progress . . . is the attainment of Dominion Status'. But he declines, in discussions with Gandhi, to promise dominion status. As the Congress plans its annual session in Lahore to discuss these momentous developments, Gandhi is keen that CR should be there. CR himself is not planning to attend. This letter

is in the Gandhi section of the Pyarelal Papers at the Nehru Memorial
Museum and Library (NMML), Teen Murti, New Delhi.

12 November 1929

My dear Bapu,

I enclose a literal translation of a letter[82] received by me today. You
may find it interesting.

Why should I go to Lahore? I had made up my mind not to go,
when I got your note[83] suggesting that I should join you at Wardha.

How are you keeping? All well at this end.

As ever,

44

CR does go. With the battle lines clear, he wants Gandhi to assume
presidentship. But despite CR's and many others' entreaties, Gandhi
declines and secures the withdrawal of Vallabhbhai Patel from the path
to that highest office in the party and the movement as well. And, in a
step of long-lasting impact on the history of India, places the mantle on
forty-one-year-old Jawaharlal Nehru.

Along with 3,00,000 people CR witnesses, on the midnight of
New Year's eve, on the banks of the Ravi, the future prime minister of
India unfurl India's tricolour. After six years of voluntary detachment
from active politics, CR is now back in the Congress Working Committee
(CWC) headed by Jawaharlal Nehru.

The 26th of January 1930 is chosen as the day when the people
of India would adopt a pledge that declares acquiescence to alien rule
'a crime against man and God'.

---

[82] Unavailable.
[83] Also unavailable.

CR returns to Tamil Nadu geared for a fight, for sacrifice, and for what he describes as 'The hour . . . to make a supreme effort again'. Gandhi has given CR a mandate to do his best in and with Tamil Nadu. But the path is thorny.

On returning to home ground CR pens a hurried line. The original is among the Gandhi section of Pyarelal's Papers at Teen Murti, New Delhi.

Gandhi Ashram
Tiruchengodu
21 January 1930

My dear Bapu,

The 'Hindu' has practically closed its columns against Congress propaganda. Enclosed speaks for itself.

Mr. Srinivasa Iyengar to whom I spoke on the phone when I passed Madras was in a great passion over a letter[84] which he said you had written to him and to which he had suitably and lengthily replied! He did not wish to show the letter or the reply to me. He said he would work for Congress but could not accept any dictatorship, etc.

---

[84] Letter to S. Srinivasa Iyengar (from a Xerox copy: S. Srinivasa Iyengar Papers, courtesy NMML):

Sabarmati
17 January 1930

My dear Friend,

The prayer bell is just ringing 4 o'clock early morn.

Preoccupations compel me to burn after-midnight oil. I can no longer delay acknowledging your angry letter. Though I have an answer to every one of the statements you have made I must restrain myself. I can only give you my assurance that my affection for you is no more diminished because of political differences than for Malaviyaji for the same cause. But this I cannot prove by words. Future conduct alone can prove the truth of my assurance. I did not write my letter to hurt your feelings. I wrote in order to be true to you, a friend and associate, and to myself.

The Peshwa's sannad[85] you have given me for Tamilnad is not a bed of roses.

Yours,
C. Rajagopalachari

45

In this eager and ready-to-sacrifice mood, Gandhi conjures his magic 'throw'—salt. Is the Tamil country and its leading light not to be at the heart of the new agitation? Of course he is.

CR tells a large gathering at Tuticorin what he could well have penned in a letter to Gandhi, by way of a 'draft'—something he was always expected to give—spelling out the new narrative:

Suppose a people rise in revolt. They cannot attack the abstract constitution or lead an army against proclamations and statutes but have to capture a stronghold here, a stronghold there, seize an arsenal here and destroy a fortification there. As in armed conflict, so also in civil resistance, you must give up the general and apply yourself to the particular . . . against the salt tax—not that that is our final end, but for the time being it is our aim, and we must shoot straight.

46

Here follows a letter from the Sabarmati archive in which CR's 'typist'— as he had described A. Subbiah—portrays to the 'headquarters' CR's

---

We shall know each other better when the mists have rolled away. Meanwhile I anticipate your forgiveness for offence given utterly unconsciously.

Yours sincerely,
M. K. Gandhi

[85] The reference is, needless to say, to no written document but to a general signal given to CR to take charge of the post-Lahore agitation in Tamil Nadu.

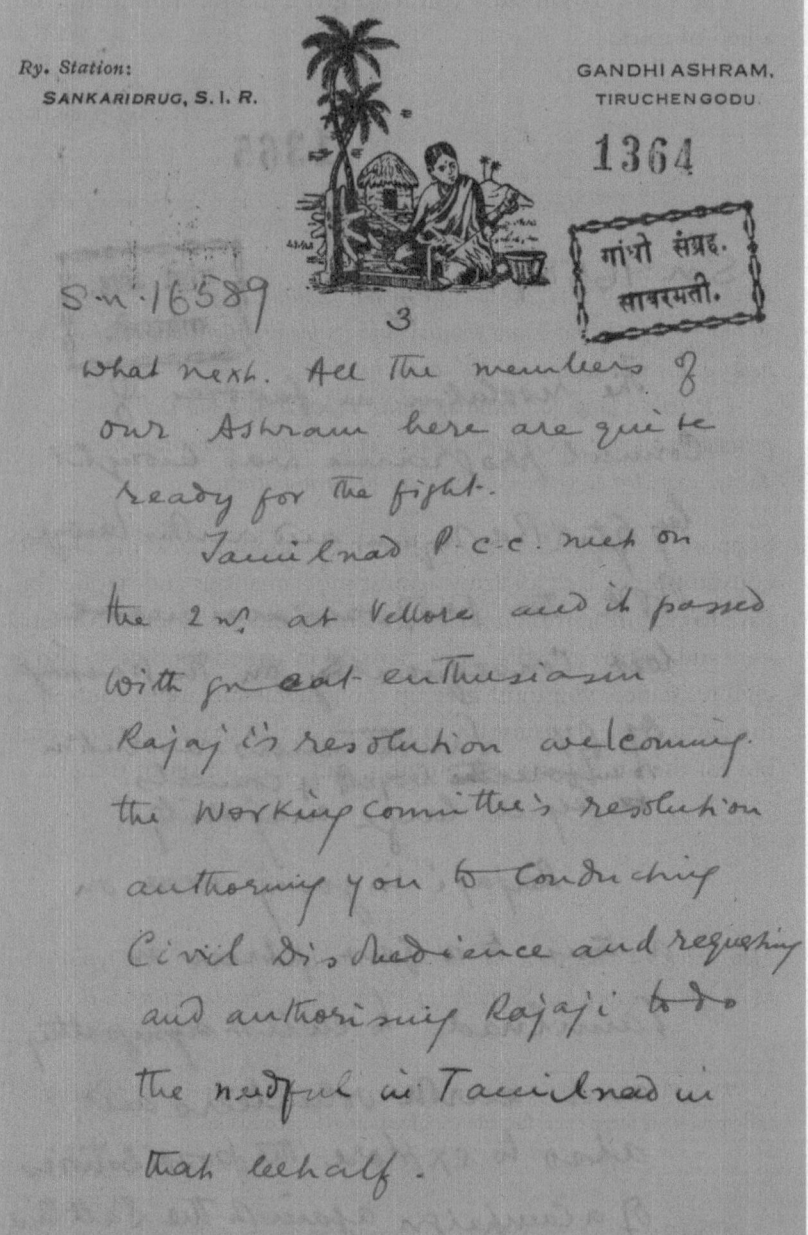

Ry. Station:
SANKARIDRUG, S. I. R.

GANDHI ASHRAM,
TIRUCHENGODU.

1364

S.n. 16589

3

what next. All the members of
our Ashram here are quite
ready for the fight.

Tamilnad P.C.C. met on
the 2nd at Vellore and it passed
with great enthusiasm
Rajaji's resolution welcoming
the Working committee's resolution
authorising you to conducting
Civil Disobedience and requesting
and authorising Rajaji to do
the needful in Tamilnad in
that behalf.

plans to do just that, 'shoot straight'. Subbiah has just returned from
Sabarmati where, one can infer from the letter, he helped prepare and
perhaps type the draft of the historic letter (see n. 88) Gandhi wrote to
the viceroy, intimating him of Gandhi's intention to break the Salt Law.
Subbiah, now back in Tiruchengodu working for CR, is agog with plans
for 'doing a Dandi' in the Tamil areas.

Excerpts from that letter, written on the Tiruchengodu ashram
letterhead with a lovely logo, are given below.

4 March 1930

My dear Bapuji

. . . I am now full of vigour and courage to do all the work that is
given to me by Rajaji and I feel happy in doing it.

By this time you must have sent the letter to the Viceroy. Papers
report that Mr Reynolds[86] is going to carry it. We are anxiously
awaiting to know what next. All the members of our Ashram here
are quite ready for the fight.

Tamilnad P.C.C. met on the 2nd at Vellore and it passed with great
enthusiasm Rajaji's resolution welcoming the Working Committee's
resolution authoring you to conducting Civil Disobedience and
requesting and authorising Rajaji to do the needful in Tamilnad
in that behalf.

The resolution in favour of Council programme was brought by
Sjt K. Bashyam and another lawyer. Both the propositions were lost
consequent on the passing of Sjt Santhanam's resolution to enforce
boycott of councils by a large majority.

Rajaji is going now on a tour to a few places in Tamilnad to

---

[86] Reginald Arthur Reynolds (1905–58) was a British Quaker, who spent some time
with Gandhi at Sabarmati in 1930 and carried Gandhi's letter to the Viceroy's House in
New Delhi. He was later general secretary of the No More War Movement (1933–37).
He published trenchant poetry every week in the *New Statesman* and his best-known
work is *The White Sahibs in India.*

enlist sympathy and enrol volunteers and to explore the possibilities of a campaign against the Salt Law.

I enclose a copy[87] of our programme for your use if necessary. We reach Ahmedabad on the 20th morning by Kathiawar Mail.

Yours obediently,
A. Subbiah

47

CR's letter sent four days after Subbiah's reflects the same excitement. 'It is not the salt but disobedience that you are manufacturing,' CR says in his typical way with words.

8 March 1930

Pyarelal sent me a copy of your letter[88] to the Viceroy.

I don't think the Government will let you remain free as some people imagine. They cannot let the conflagration grow on the ground that much salt cannot be made by you. It is not the salt but disobedience that you are manufacturing.

I don't know if this will reach you when you are still there. But I take the chance. It appears to me that picketing of liquor shops is

---

[87] Not included here.

[88] In that letter, dated 2 March 1930, Gandhi informed the viceroy, Lord Irwin:

I shall proceed with such co-workers of the Ashram as I can take, to disregard the provisions of the salt laws. I regard this tax to be the most iniquitous of all from the poor man's standpoint. As the independence movement is essentially for the poorest in the land the beginning will be made with this evil. The wonder is that we have submitted to the cruel monopoly for so long. It is, I know, open to you to frustrate my design by arresting me. I hope that there will be tens of thousands ready, in a disciplined manner, to take up the work after me, and, in the act of disobeying the Salt Act to lay themselves open to the penalties of a law that should never have disfigured the Statute-book.

best in this province. I am thinking of a march from Cape Comorin to a single picketing centre, gathering volunteers on the way.

I am fully alive to all the considerations for and against it, especially to the point that a unified attack all over India would be very desirable. What do you think about it? Do you advise me to desist and do what we can for salt only just now or do you bless the picketing programme?

Love,

Yours sincerely,

C.R.

48

CR goes to Gujarat and meets Gandhi on 23 March 1930 in the village of Buwa, near Broach. At that point, Gandhi is halfway to Dandi where he is to famously break the Salt Law on 5 April. Resolved to do the same in Tamil Nadu, CR rushes back and selects Vedaranyam on the Tanjore seaboard for the defiance. The coastal settlement has salt swamps and it also has an indomitable local leader in Vedaratnam Pillai who is daring enough to be the battle's ramrod.

With eight volunteers from the Tiruchengodu ashram as the starting team, CR puts together a hundred, drawn from all the Tamil districts, to march 240-odd kilometres from Trichy to Vedaranyam. The triumphant procession draws huge crowds as it goes forward. Tanjore's ICS collector, J.A. Thorne, proposes CR's arrest. The government of Madras turns it down, fearing it would confer martyrdom on 'probably the ablest and certainly one of the most intransigent' of the Congress's southern leaders. But Thorne issues orders against 'harbouring' CR and his band. Barring a couple of places, no one heeds the order. 'Thornes and thistles cannot stem this tide of freedom,' CR tells reporters. Almost immediately after CR bends to pick up some salt on 30 April 1930, Superintendent of Police Govindan Nair arrests him. He is tried in a salt shed by the sea.

Awarding him six months rigorous plus a fine of Rs 200—which CR refuses to pay, thereby 'winning' another three months—the judge who has known CR from Salem days, breaks down. From the train carrying him to Trichy jail, CR writes to Lakshmi:

My dear child, I am getting nine months leave . . .

———

Fellow marchers and others—375 of them—are similarly arrested, including Vedaratnam Pillai, Santhanam, Rukmini Lakshmipathy and Dr T.S.S. Rajan.

Gandhi's arrest at Karadi, near Dandi, in the dead of night, follows five days later.

CR is to spend a little over five months in prisons in Madras, Bellary and Vellore, being released before the expected time, on 10 October 1930.

Gandhi, undergoing his term in Yeravada, Poona, tells a colleague on learning of CR's release, 'Write to Rajaji and tell him that I generally do not write to eminent leaders and therefore I will not write to him either. But I remember him every day.'

On 25 January 1931, Gandhi is released as well.

Lord Irwin does not lose time in calling for talks. On 17 February 1931, Gandhi calls on Irwin in the new Government House in New Delhi's Raisina Hill, into which the viceroy and vicereine have just moved.

Meeting in Karachi in April that year, ahead of its annual session, the Congress elects Vallabhbhai Patel as its president. CR opts to stay out of the new Working Committee, preferring to continue with his khadi, anti-drinking and anti-untouchability programmes from Tiruchengodu, even as the Congress, following the Gandhi–Irwin Pact, prepares for Gandhi's visit to London for the second session of the RTC.

The 'truce' with Irwin goes through many vicissitudes, including the downward slide caused by the viceroy's refusal to heed Gandhi's urgings on behalf of Bhagat Singh, Sukhdev and Rajguru, sentenced to death for Saunders's murder. Despite all this, Gandhi goes ahead with his visit to London.

He asks CR to come to Ahmedabad and discuss matters but, on hearing that CR's daughter Namagiri is unwell, wires:

GURARAT VIDYAPITH
AHMEDABAD
15 AUGUST 1931

RAJAGOPALACHARI
CARE A.V. RAMAN, LLOYD CORNER
ROYAPETTAH (MADRAS)

DISTRESSED OVER PAPA'S HEALTH. UNDER ALTERED CIRCUMSTANCES YOU NEED NOT WORRY TO COME EARLY. AM HERE SOME TIME. WRITING.

BAPU

———

And writes (sourced from a Xerox copy—S.N. 17474):

15 August 1931

I had your letter.

You are going through a terrible trial. But I know that in the midst of it all you can remain cheerful and unruffled. I would not think of tearing you away from Papa. So long therefore as she needs your personal nursing, I have no doubt that your duty is to be by her.

What shall I write to you about the dramatic developments? I hope your reasoning fully endorses the decision. I have personally not a shadow of a doubt about it. I wish you would be able to attend the next meeting of the Working Committee, if I am free till then. I expect still greater dramatic developments now. But I feel that all will be well and as satyagrahis we have no business to want to peep

into the future. We must simply take care of the present and be sure
of the future.

Syt. C. Rajagopalachari
C/O Syt. A. V. Raman
Lloyd Corner
Royapettah (Madras)

49

*Gandhi is to attend the RTC as Congress's sole delegate. He takes with
him Mahadev Desai, Devadas, Pyarelal and Miraben.*
*A letter (from the Sabarmati archive) to Gandhi, after he has sailed
for London to attend the RTC:*

Gandhi Ashram
Tiruchengodu
11 September 1931

My dear Bapu,

It is not easy to write, feeling all the time that the letter you write
will take ever so much time to reach. And letter writing has always
been a difficult task with me. It is so hard to find words even remotely
expressing what one feels when writing to those near and dear.

I hope you are snugly ensconced in Kingsley Hall among good
and attentive cosmopolitans. I am sure you will have better attention
and better care of your personal needs than ever India was able to
give you with all its mad worship. People in the West are, I know,
much more considerate and skilled in the art of transferring affection
into active and unexaggerated attention. We, here, are so thoughtless
and clumsy. But this is an inferiority complex, or jealousy of your
English friends and I must avoid it.

I brought my daughter[89] down here in the first weeks of this month after a three weeks' stay in Madras. She is slowly, but distinctly, improving as the climate here is as dry as is good for her. The only difficulty is, it is so dry that we cannot get fresh fruits or vegetables for eating raw. This reminds me that a large part of your time must be now being spent on dietetics.

Your letter written on August 28th reached me duly, i.e, five days after you sailed. Kumarappa also sent me an extract from your letter[90] to him, the portion about 'Young India'. I am flattered by all your confidence. But flattery from you is not like other people's. Their flattery can be absorbed with ease and satisfaction, but yours is a load of responsibility and never a source of comfort. I shall do what I can for 'Young India'. I am so far down South, however, that dealing with 'Young India' from here feels like tilting the boat too much. And again you carry away the focus with you wherever you go. Everybody is

---

[89] CR's elder daughter, Namagiri ('Papa'), married to S. Varadachari.

[90] From a Xerox copy—G.N. 10098:

Unrevised
On the Frontier Down Mail
28 August 1931

My dear Kumarappa,

Will you please look after the columns of Young India? The idea is that there should be no change of name as editor. I do not think the law requires such change during the temporary absence of the editor-in-charge. But if such a change is required C. Rajagopalachari should appear as the editor, and in any case whenever you are in doubt or opinion among our own coterie differs, C. Rajagopalachari's should be the final voice when a reference is at all possible. When such is not possible Jairamdas's should be the final voice and when even that is not possible yours should be the final voice unless Kaka Saheb chooses to decide. I do not want him to bear this burden. But he has a right whenever he considers intervention necessary. I have already written to Rajagopalachari to send something regularly ...

Love,
Bapu

straining his eyes and ears, so to say, towards London. Things cooked in this Southern corner, whatever be the caloric value, will lack vitamin.

Till 29th August, I was feeling that you ought to go to London. But from that date, I am feeling like fractured in the arm, or orphaned or anything else you like, to denote helplessness. I feel like cabling to you 'come back as soon as possible'.

What a fine message[91] you gave to Reuters—the one that was wired from Aden, in which you hated the distinction between Foreign and Indigenous and set out your ideals about Free India. I know you don't care for my appreciation, but it set me quivering with joy to read that message. Newspapers in India have not made half enough use of that inspired outburst. But this is how India always wastes its treasures.

Yes, it is God within that is moving you, and may it all come about as we dream!

The work is going on here. As you are aware, I am mostly

---

[91] A statement to Reuters:

Aden, 3 September 1931

I shall strive for a constitution which will release India from all thraldom and patronage, and give her, if need be, the right to sin. I shall work for an India in which the poorest shall feel that it is their country in whose making they have an effective voice; an India in which there shall be no high class and low class of people; an India in which all communities shall live in perfect harmony.

There can be no room in such an India for the curse of untouchability or the curse of intoxicating drinks and drugs. Women will enjoy the same rights as men. Since we shall be at peace with all the rest of the world, neither exploiting nor being exploited, we should have the smallest army imaginable.

All interests not in conflict with the interests of the dumb millions will be scrupulously respected, whether foreign or indigenous. Personally, I hate distinction between foreign and indigenous.

This is the India of my dreams for which I shall struggle at the next Round Table Conference. I may fail, but if I am to deserve the confidence of the Congress, I shall be satisfied with nothing less.

concentrating on the Drink struggle. It keeps me tied down to my province. There has been great response and unparalleled success. But now I feel the clouds are gathering. Our operations have touched Finance to the quick. It is no longer merely interference with pickets and pin-pricks, but security sections to intimidate caste organisations.

I never liked the idea of sending you complaints and worrying you with the tiny troubles of your gift to us, the second-hand motor car, as I was frivolous enough to caricature the Truce when I was talking to you last. I felt always that we, your lieutenants should use it as best we can and leave you free. Much less should I now send you weekly budgets of troubles for you to worry over there. But I cannot refrain from sending you a tit-bit:

(Translation)

Copy of emergent order issued to all village officers in the Chittoor District by the Collector.

Chandragiri Taluk Office,
Dated 22-8-31.

Emergent Order to all Village Magistrates and Accountants.

It is published in the newspapers that the Pact between Gandhi and the Government has been broken. You must therefore consider that the Congressmen are the enemies of the Government. The District Collector has notified that every action of theirs, namely, meetings, processions, propaganda, etc., must be put down without being carried on in the least. Therefore whenever Congressmen or any one connected with them organize any meetings; processions, or propaganda in your village, you must forthwith send reports through the village servant in the report books to the Police and the Sub-Magistrate of Tirupati with full details and report to the Tahsildar on ordinary paper the fact. Severe action will be taken against village officers who are negligent in this matter. Very Emergent.

Sd/R. Krishnaswami,

For Tahsildar

I enclose a copy[92] of a letter I have addressed to the Governor on the subject.

---

11 September 1931

Dear Mr. Crombie,

I crave His Excellency's attention to the most objectionable and mischievous circular that has been issued and broadcasted in the District of Chittoor if I have to believe a communication that I have just received from the District Congress Secretary of Chittoor. It grieves me beyond expression that the authorities of the District should have on the 22nd August thought it fit to make up their minds that there should be war between Congress and Government . . .

We have no desire to do anything secretly and we do not object to reports being asked for. But what I respectfully consider to be objectionable in the highest degree is the creation of an atmosphere of war through such circulars. It is in the same District that, while the Flag displays were permitted all over India and in this province, it was thought necessary to issue a prohibitory order in respect of such displays on the strange ground that because the Congress claimed as party to the Delhi Settlement that it should be recognized as the intermediary between the peasants and the Government in connection with the disputes arising over the collection of land revenue arrears, the display of the Congress Flag would lead to misconceptions regarding the sovereignty of the British Government and endanger peace.

His Excellency is also aware that as mentioned in my letter to you of 8th September a magisterial offensive has been launched against the organization of castes hitherto indulging in the use of intoxicating drinks to give it up in the future on ground that such organization would amount to coercion, even though it is [a] long established right of castes and communities to regulate the personal habits of their members by excommunication and fines.

I feel it my duty to lay before His Excellency my apprehension that the affairs in Chittoor District present an ugly appearance and that the danger is great.

You ask me to send you my reflections on what I expect you to do in London. I expect you to go, see, and conquer, like Caesar of old. I believe the harvest of hearts is ready waiting for the reaper. I somewhat differ from you, and think that the people over there are now much chastened and changed and that we ought not judge them by what their proconsuls here do and think.

Polak[93] wrote to me totally misunderstanding a cable that I sent to him and Sastri, during the negotiations just before you went to London. I tried to express briefly the importance of attending to the question of land revenue collection in Gujarat before you went to the Conference: Gandhi would carry no power with him unless the peasants were behind him and the peasants cannot be behind him if he did not stand up for them in their present troubles. Don't therefore press him to go to London unless you there in London are able to get his demand for an enquiry or arbitration conceded. If you want him there at all you want him as a man with sanction behind his demands, not the mere shell of Gandhi. This is what I wanted to say. But Polak appears to have thought that I was sensitive about the prestige of the Congress, that I wanted the enquiry as a point of honour, and that though he agreed that the enquiry was a reasonable demand, my argument was irrelevant.

One wishes one had so much more strength, physical as well as mental, and so much more time, and so much more everything, to

---

I shall be very grateful if you will kindly place this letter before His Excellency as early as possible.

Yours Sincerely,
C. Rajagopalachari

A.D. Crombie, Esq. [M.C.S.],
Private Secretary to
H.E. The Governor of Madras

[93] Henry Solomon Leon Polak (1882–1959), born in England, moved to South Africa in 1903, met Gandhi at a vegetarian restaurant in Johannesburg and became an ardent supporter. He helped Gandhi edit *Indian Opinion* and, after becoming a lawyer, with legal work as well.

serve in these great days. It is tragic that things must wait on our limited capacities. But this is also an insidious kind of pride and want of faith.

Love
CR

Gandhi had written to CR before leaving for London:

On the Frontier Down Mail
28 August 1931

Dear C.R.,

What shall I write to you? Do you know that not a day has passed but I have thought of you and also felt the need of your presence? But I was not to have it and as ill luck will have it, I cannot have even a few words with you before sailing. There are two men whom I would like by my side in London, you and Jawaharlal. But I feel that even if both of you were available I must not have you by me. Somehow or other I do feel that you will both be helping me like the others by being here. Only your presence with me will have lightened my burden. But I must bear the Cross alone and to the fullest extent. When I think of myself with all my limitations and ignorance I sink in utter despair but I rise out of it immediately, as I think and feel that it is God within Who is moving me and using me as His instrument. He will give me the right word at the right moment. That does not mean that I shall make no mistakes. But I have come to believe that God as it were purposely makes us commit mistakes if only to humble us. I know that this is a dangerous belief which can be utilized to justify any error. But I have no doubt about its correctness in respect of all unconscious errors. But this is not a letter to air my philosophy. This is written to ask you to give me through weekly letters, sent even by air mail, what I cannot get through your presence. I would like you also to write for Young India every week. I do not think there is any legal necessity for advertising a new editor during my temporary absence. If there is a legal necessity I would like you to wear the editorial mantle.

I would like you to prepare a rejoinder to the Madras Government's reply to the Madras charge-sheet and bring the latter to date and send your rejoinder to the Sardar.

By way of preliminary send me by air mail your detailed reflections on what you expect me to do in London. Copies of whatever you send by air mail should be sent through the usual weekly service.

How is Papa? I do hope she is better.

50

The second RTC is overshadowed by a change in Britain's political climate. Three days before Gandhi sails out, the Labour Prime Minister Ramsay Macdonald affects a major change. Though he continues as prime minister, a new national coalition government dominated by Conservatives takes office, with 'Tory attitudes to India' dominating.

One hundred and twelve delegates are attending, twenty-three representing the princely states, sixty-nine representing British India and twenty the British government. The sessions are held in three parts: the Federal Structure Committee, the Minorities Committee and a concluding Plenary Session. Gandhi attends all.

On 15 September 1931, on his way to the session where he is to make his first speech, Gandhi is asked by G.D. Birla what he proposes to say. 'I am absolutely blank,' he replies. . . . 'I have no desire to appear extra intelligent. Like a simple villager all I have to say is: "We want independence".'

Direct versus indirect elections, and separate electorates for the minorities are important issues to be discussed. Gandhi stays firm on the

Congress concept of complete independence. And he makes no secret of his feeling that the ongoing exercise is 'unreal'. On the minorities question, he obdurately sticks to his claim to speak for the 'untouchables', firmly denying Dr B.R. Ambedkar's claim to do so.

The Times of London is to later say he 'made no real constructive contribution', while Sir Mirza Ismail, attending on the side of the princely states, says, 'He electrified us by the remarkable speeches he made.' The Secretary of State for India, Sir Samuel Hoare, is to say, 'With an eye and mind as pointed as a needle, he penetrated in a moment any sham.'

Outside the conference, Gandhi is reaching out to the British public and winning hearts. CR writes to him (from the Sabarmati archive) with news of all this trickling into his village retreat, and giving him news from home.

Gandhi Ashram
Tiruchengodu
24 September 1931

My dear Bapu,

I hope you have got my letter of 11th September in which I have acknowledged receipt of your letter written from the train on August 28th. I got yesterday your beautiful little letter[94] of 5th written from the steamer.

I notice you are using your left hand all through. Does it mean that you are having an attack again of finger trouble. I hope it is not very severe. There are beautiful pictures of your disembarking at Marseilles in the papers here. Judging from the face there I fancy you are keeping very well.

Papa is better. Though there are occasional set backs, she is on the whole slowly improving. She is still confined to her bed, and I am prevented from moving about in the country as much as I would like to.

---

[94] It is most distressing that this letter is unavailable. The *Collected Works* has seven entries against that date but not this one, a distinct loss to documentation.

Vallabhbhai writes to me generously excusing me for not being able to go and work by his side. He writes that he is suffering from nose and tooth trouble. But Jairamdas is working like a double-shift machine without any holiday both night and day.

The Madras Government is changed, the Chief Secretary[95] who began the Gandhi–Irwin Pact administration is dead—I believe of over-work. He was a fairly good sort, at least I liked him. The new man[96] seems determined to put me down and push all representations on behalf of the Congress to the District Magistrates. I suppose in their turn, the District Magistrates will ask us to settle with the Sub Divisional Magistrates and the Police Inspectors! Here is the latest. From the Madras Government: 'I am directed to say that the Government have investigated the allegations made in your letter of the 22nd July, 1931, and are satisfied that the District authorities are doing their best to observe the terms of the Settlement of the 5th March, 1931, in the face of considerable difficulties and provocative action. I am to suggest that in future cases of alleged irregularities by subordinate officials, the persons aggrieved should in the first instance approach the District Magistrate concerned for redress.'

This was in a case in which I was sure of winning, the facts were so clearly on our side.

I am enclosing a memorandum[97] showing tangible results so far achieved by the prohibition campaign in this province. There is an unprecedented awakening, unprecedented in extent as well as in depth.

There was a quarrel over the use of waste and unassigned land for making salt under your concession. We have secured exemption from encroachment proceedings in respect to such lands. But Government is claiming to restrict the use of the Delhi concession to a five-mile

---

[95] Charles Cotton, Chief Secretary, Madras, from 11 October 1930 to 29 July 1931.

[96] Geoffrey T.H. Bracken, Chief Secretary, Madras, from 31 August 1931 to 20 July 1933.

[97] See Annexure III.

radius round the salt tract. I am contending that the limitation to conveyance on foot was conceived as a practical restriction in regard to distance, and that no further arbitrary restriction by mileage should be added.

Will you accept my congratulations for the way in which you have been getting on there? You have plumped for indirect election. Have the orthodox nationalists swallowed this? There were two matters in which I felt differently from orthodox nationalists, indirect election and separate electorates. These two things were always opposed by nineteenth century nationalists and those in India who cut their democracy according to that mould. I always felt that in our country a wide franchise or anything like adult suffrage must be worked only by indirect election and group electorates.

Of course there is so much to be said against indirect election as well as against group electors. For one thing, there will be a lot of corruption in indirect election. But this is a common feature in aspects of the Swaraj problem. Unless we develop a new efficiency, honesty and public spirit, I don't expect to be happier under Swaraj than under the British Government.

How much I wish I had been with you at least to enjoy the fun if not to be helpful. I would have much enjoyed the white people's lionizing of you. Do not be too sure that you will not be able to achieve anything.

Love,
C.R.

My love to Pyarelal, Mahadev, Devadas and Miraben.

51

Gandhi is among the poor of London's East End and his visit to Lancashire—where cotton mills made the cloth Gandhi was boycotting in

India and wanting to replace with khaddar—is particularly momentous.
He is cheered by the millhands to whom he says if India, self-governing
and free, wanted to buy cloth without jeopardizing its own self-reliance,
he would advocate a partnership with the mills of Lancashire.

On Gandhi's sixty-second birthday, the Indian community in London
fetes him in Guild House. Sabarmati has preserved the letter in which
CR remembers him on that day thus:

Gandhi Ashram
Tiruchengodu
2 October 1931

My dear Bapu,

I waft my love and greetings to you today when all over the country
millions are celebrating your birthday and thinking about you and
your wonderful work. This will take many days to reach you, but
I suppose the thought will reach you much earlier than this letter.
When I think of all that has happened these twelve years, one thing
after another, it looks all like a glorious dream and I am filled with
thankfulness for the privilege of love and intimate association that
I have enjoyed at your hands.

I entirely and thoroughly endorse all your statements about
preference for Lancashire, whoever else may have doubts. There is
no other cause open to you and your way of thinking.

Papa is not improving. She persists in being just where she is. I
have put her in perfect sanatorium conditions.

We are all praying that Shaukat Ali will carve out his niche in
history and go down to posterity in the same glorious association
with you as in the early days of the movement it was the joy of the
people of India to witness. I for one am still full of hope.

Love from me and Lakshmi and all of us,

Raja

52

Another status report-cum-comfort letter from Tiruchengodu to
London follows. It is written even as the RTC is breaking down,
with influential sections of the British government and of the British
press characterizing Gandhi as 'a Hindu leader' and the Congress
as 'one of several Indian factions'. More hurtful to Gandhi and
the Congress—and to CR who agonizes over the happenings in
Tiruchengodu—is that the Muslims claim Gandhi does not speak
for them, and Dr Ambedkar maintains that he, not Gandhi, is the
more authentic voice of the Depressed Classes. Gandhi has turned
down Ambedkar's demand for separate electorates saying that it would
splinter India.

Gandhi Ashram
Tiruchengodu
21 October 1931

My dear Bapu,

It is nothing more than what I expected, but it is all the same
wonderful, the manner in which you are conquering hearts in that
country.

It is a joy by itself, though the sad news of the minority conflicts
coming daily over the wires makes one sick.

The second hand car is still running. You must keep my cruel joke
in mind—I called the Truce a second hand car—It takes immense
quantities of petrol, and one has to stop and look after the parts
every now and then. Still, it is going.

Papa is wasting and wasting. It is awful to look at her sad eyes. I
am tied up to her, for I have not the heart to leave her. She breaks
down at the suggestion that I go out somewhere. I conduct work
from where I am here. It has not been possible for me to leave the
province. So Vallabbhai has not got any help from me. The work in

the province has been very heavy, as the picketing of liquor shops has been taken up most vigorously, and it is like dancing on the wire to maintain peace with the Government.

A meeting of the untouchables presided over by Mr. M.C. Rajah[98] at Madras has just described you as the greatest enemy of the 'depressed classes'! What further proof can one ask that you are their only friend. . . .

Love,
C.R.

53

Gandhi returns from the RTC aboard the SS Pilsna, *on 28 December 1931, 'empty-handed'. It is clear he is not going to be left free to fight for complete independence. Jawaharlal Nehru and the Khan brothers, Abdul Ghaffar Khan and Dr Khan Saheb, have already been arrested by the time Gandhi returns. Kasturba is at the pier to welcome him home, as are Vallabhbhai Patel and CR.*

Terrorism has reared its head in Bengal, meanwhile, and the spirit of the Gandhi–Irwin Pact is nowhere to be seen. Lord Willingdon, a very different man and viceroy from Lord Irwin, is in full charge with 'Willingdonism' the clear official policy.

CR and Gandhi meet up in those tense days in Bombay and discuss, political time permitting, the Devadas–Lakshmi matter. The young couple have been waiting, they note, for some three years now and have kept all the pledges. It is time, the fathers agree, with Kasturba at hand, that their

---

[98] Mylai Chinna Thambi Pillai Rajah (1883–1943) was a politician and social and political activist, originally in the Justice Party. He later joined Dr B.R. Ambedkar from whose comradeship too he separated. Rajah, a member of the Imperial Legislative Assembly from 1926 to 1937, represented the Depressed Classes along with Ambedkar and Rettamalai Srinivasan at the second RTC.

desire be blessed. But marriage has to wait, for Devadas is among the many Congressmen arrested and sent to Gorakhpur jail.

Gandhi is arrested on 4 January 1932. Congress President Patel is taken too, along with the entire Working Committee.

CR courts arrest in Madras on 9 January, with Satyamurti. They are arrested under Ordinance V of 1932 and charged with picketing and 'molestation'. CR and Satyamurti have a thousand Tamils following them to jail. Sentenced to six months, CR is first sent to Madras jail, then to his familiar Vellore jail.

Eleven days before his release, CR learns that even as his daughter Namagiri is recuperating under Dr T.S.S. Rajan's care in Trichy, her husband Varadachari has suddenly died.

Gandhi, from Yeravada jail, wires to CR: 'You stand in no need consolation from us. God must be your rock.' And to Namagiri he wires: 'Remember you are daughter of brave father.'

Pyarelal's Gandhi Papers have the following:

23 July 1932

My dear Bapu,

I hope you had my telegram which I sent on 11th July on receipt of your telegram to me and Papa. Your letter to Papa enclosed with another to Lakshmi[99] written on the 7th came just now. The post

---

[99]   7 July 1932

Daughter Lakshmi,

If Devdas had not sent me a wire, from where could I have got intimation of Papa's condition? I hope you are at present working like a brave woman. Please let me have all information about Papa. I have written a letter for Papa and I am sending it along with this. Now Anna must have come to the Ashram. Tell him to write to me.

Do not spoil your health by worrying. Fear of death and sorrow should be abandoned

marks show that the delay was at your end. It was 9 days before the Poona date stamp was put on the cover.

Papa is much braver than one could expect under the circumstances. I have no doubt the messages from you have put a great deal of heart into her. She and Lakshmi are staying for some time in Coimbatore with a nephew of mine. Her health is poor still. It got to improve, but just then this tragedy came.

I vividly remember the occasion in Feb 1919 that Mahadev refers to. We were staying in one of the late Mr Kasturi Ranga Aiyangar's houses in Madras that I had just taken up to start practice in Madras. My saman was all upstairs not yet unpacked, and you were put up on the ground floor as you were too weak to negotiate the staircase. That was the first time we met. You put her under a fire of searching and difficult questions as to whether she preferred Tamil or English. You attacked the girl of 13 quite vigorously; and she was answering away without flinching, quite as bravely as an English girl might do—this was your own expression when you admiringly talked about it to Mahadev—I don't know whether it was really what you thought, or whether you intended it to flatter her fond father in order to net him. Her answers were so good that you said I had probably coached her! I remember distinctly that I felt quite hurt by this unjust suggestion. I suppose I did my best to hide my feelings.

It was a case of Typhoid and broncho-pneumonia. Dr. Rajan did all that could possibly be done, but the violent delirium was so severe and continuous that the patient worked himself to heart-failure. They

---

altogether. Why should there be pain and fear for a thing which is inevitable for every human being? It is ignorance to regard death as a punishment from God. Death is a gift to man from God.

I expect a long letter from you.

Blessings from
Bapu

had gone to Dr. Rajan's place on his repeated invitation that they should stay with him for some time to enable him to X-ray Papa and help a proper diagnosis of her case. The man went there in perfect health, and the morbidest imagination could not have forecasted the event. He had left Rangoon in the middle of last year to join Papa and take my place as nurse. He was wonderfully attached to her, and served most diligently until a few days before his death. Death is a dear friend, quite true, and not a frightful enemy as men suppose. But then, we all fight so vigorously against him on his approach, and employ all the knowledge of the ancients and the modern sciences to drive the friend away, the truth is quite forgotten just when we ought to remember it most.

You appear to have written to me, so Lakshmi says. But I did not get any letter from you so long as I was in Vellore. Your telegram of 9th was the only message passed.

It is not grief but darkness that is around me. I am still praying for light. I do not complain about my share of humanity's lot. Do pray for me. Love to Vallabbhai and Mahadev.

Ever yours,

Raja

Papa has mostly forgotten her English. She does not know Hindi. Lakshmi has done her Tamil letter into Hindi for you. I wonder what the Y.M.[100] authorities will do with the Tamil!

54

Released on 9 July, CR is back to a shaken family and an unshaken government. Devadas, on being released, establishes contact with his

---

[100] Yeravada Mandir, Gandhi's name for the Yeravada prison.

father-in-law-to-be. Gandhi's responses from jail to the Ambedkar scheme of separate electorates and London's openness to it acquires an edge when, in August, London publishes the Communal Award, providing separate electorates for the Depressed Classes, Muslims and Sikhs. But it is the separate electorates for the 'untouchables' that rankles Gandhi the most because the people so described and treated are scattered all over India and it will divide the land vertically and horizontally. He announces a plan to fast.

CR seeks an interview with Gandhi, which is denied. He wires Gandhi to desist. Gandhi declines and wires CR:

No cause for distress. On the contrary, I expect you to rejoice that a comrade of yours has had this God-given opportunity for a final act of Satyagraha in the cause of the downtrodden.

———

CR is with Gandhi as he fasts; he is with him as the ordeal and the challenge end. He has played a part, a crucial one at that, in Gandhi and Ambedkar arriving at the 'reservation within joint electorates' formulation. Dr Ambedkar is to be quoted by Pyarelal (Epic Fast) as saying CR 'came to our rescue when we were almost at a breaking point and had it not been for his ingenuity probably the agreement would not have come into being'.

There is much to be glad about on the political stage, with the Gandhi–Ambedkar agreement getting London's endorsement and joint electorates with reservation of seats for Muslims and Sikhs also being agreed to at a meeting in Allahabad in November.

Back in his province (and acting as president of the Congress) CR returns to his anti-untouchability campaign. He writes to Gandhi from Calicut where a major struggle is brewing for getting the gates of the temple at Guruvayur opened to Harijans:

Calicut
12 October 1932

My dear Bapu,

Your note[101] of 7th reached me yesterday. Devadas must be telling you what we all felt about your 'little' fast. We had intended sending you a terrible telegram signed by all of us, your slaves here. But then we saw in the press (and also Devadas wired us) your fast had been definitely stopped and we contented ourselves by sending our anger in the shape of a letter to Devadas.

You have again begun I see using your left hand. That tells its story about your health. Please take proper care. I know you always do. But we are foolish and anxious: can't help.

The situation regarding the referendum is very satisfactory. I do not think it will finish as early as 15th Dec. It may take a week longer. I have given up Allahabad and am sticking here.

I don't quite like the change of name you have agreed to for the League. 'Servants of Untouchables Society' is good in itself, but it means a continued recognition of untouchables as such. 'Servants of India', or 'Servants of Bhils' or 'Servant of God', are all right, because 'India' must be there. 'Bhils' is a race name and not a name implying inferiority and God is always there. But servants of 'untouchables' or servants of 'slaves' would not be right if we intend to abolish untouchability or slavery. Suppose the American Abolitionists had a league called Servants or helpers of Slaves it would not have expressed the object. Of course the society may close down when the institution of slavery or of untouchability is abolished. But the argument is not right, for it is the abolition in the psychology of men that is wanted at once. You should have to say Servants of Untouchables 'so-called' which is cumbrous and in reality open to the same objection. I would have liked 'Untouchability Abolition League' (or society). As a matter of fact I did not like 'Anti-Untouchability'

_____
[101] Not in the *Collected Works*.

as a phrase. It is so barbarous. 'Untouchability Abolition Society' would be further a literal rendering of the names already in use in Hindi, Gujarati, and other Indian languages without any objection. It is really abolition of slave status and the phrase Abolition would have been suggestive and emphatic (as Prohibition has come to stay in connection with Drink and drugs). *Service* to a group of men is not really the object and aim, if we think about it. It is really the doing away with the evil. There is a school of thought which would keep the segregation, and ask us to do all we can to make them live and eat more comfortably. This is not all that we want to do.

Forgive my writing so much about a mere name. Ba and Urmiladevi are both well, and standing it all excellently. Their programme has helped greatly. Kerala is doing well.

Love,
Raja

Thakkar[102] told me you have wired to Principal Dhruva.[103] I am glad. The Agama objection is greater in the East Coast than in the West.

55

The issue of 'untouchables' being allowed entry in temples acquires
a sharp edge, and CR is at the head of an agitation which does not
preclude negotiations over their admission to the temple in Guruvayur.

---

[102] Amritlal Vithaldas Thakkar, later known as Thakkar Bapa (1869–1951), worked for the upliftment of tribal people in Gujarat and beyond. At one time a member of the Servants of India Society, Thakkar Bapa founded the Bhil Seva Mandal and was later general secretary of the Harijan Sevak Sangh. His initiative also led to the creation of the Bharatiya Adimjati Sevak Sangh in 1948.

[103] Ananda Shankar Dhruva (1869–1942), Gujarati writer and Sanskritist, later vice chancellor, Banaras Hindu University.

*A referendum is contemplated in the orthodox citadel to measure public
opinion of nearly 28,000 adult 'caste Hindus' on the matter. From the
Sabarmati archives:*

Calicut
29 November 1932

My dear Bapu,

I came here on 25th morning and have been at the work since then.
I was hustling them in the interior of the Guruvayur Taluk (Ponnani)
when your message about Srimati Urmila Devi[104] came. It did not
reach me in time for me to run up to Madras. I hope she has not
been put to much inconvenience. We are expecting her here now
at 11 am. Ba is also coming. Harihar Sharma will have met her at
Madras today. I came back to Calicut from the Ponnani Taluk late
last night. The communications in the interior are difficult. Ba
and Urmiladevi will stay in Shyamji Sunderdas's house in Calicut.
I saw the Zamorin[105] on Saturday last. He holds his head tight in
both hands as if to keep it from splitting and refuses to discuss the
problem. It is as cruel as useless to inflict any talk on him. It is also
true that over and above advanced age and threatening paralysis, there
is a determination not to yield. However the Referendum work is
independently going on. The enclosed copy[106] of a statement I have
issued to the press will explain matters.

I am also getting the legislation pushed through. I have given a
draft bill to Dr Subbaroyan and have made him fix up an interview

---

[104] Urmila Devi (1883–1956), sister of Deshbandhu Chittaranjan Das and one of
the first women to join Gandhi's non-cooperation movement.

[105] Descendant of the Zamorin (Nair) rulers of the erstwhile feudal state of
Kozhikode, Kerala. The Zamorins or Samoothiris ruled between the twelfth and
eighteenth centuries AD and were the most powerful kings of Kerala during the
Middle Ages.

[106] See Annexure IV.

with the Governor over it so that the necessary sanctions (of the Viceroy) may be asked for. The Government is not of itself inclined to move or take any helpful steps. Hence the need for special effort in that direction. I am going to Madras for that purpose today and will rejoin the work here about December 4th.

Sjt Ganshyamdas[107] wanted full information when he reaches Poona. I hope you will kindly show him the statement enclosed which will give him the necessary information. I am not going to Poona now.

Love,
Raja

Sadashiva Rao[108] has been here since 25th evening and moving about with me. I saw also your letter to Kelappan. I am glad you have made things clear to Kelappan.[109] Hope you are keeping well. Urmila Devi and her son arrived just now. She was met at Madras and looked after all night. She is in high spirits. C.R.

56

Kasturba Gandhi joins the campaign at a crucial point. The arrangements for the referendum are being closely monitored by Gandhi from his cell in Yeravada jail. To K. Ramunni Menon, who says public opinion was not for reform and was not with Gandhi, the Mahatma writes on 25 November 1932:

There should be no difficulty in getting an accurate referendum as to the wishes of the temple-goers. The reformers assure me with

---

[107] G.D. Birla.
[108] Karnad Sadashiva Rao.
[109] See Annexure V.

as much firmness that popular opinion is in their favour, as you assure me that it is against temple-entry. I suggest referees being appointed by either party and an honest referendum taken without any undue pressure being exercised on either side. The question on which vote is to be taken should be properly framed and explained to the voters. There need be no heat imported into what is a purely religious matter.

———

The Sabarmati Papers have this letter:

Madras
30 November 1932

My dear Bapu,

I came here this morning from Malabar. Ba was detained here for just a day, and it was well. Tremendous crowds gathered, I am told, to receive her at the station yesterday and at the Triplicane temple where a meeting was arranged to welcome her. These spontaneous demonstrations have great value. At the house where she is staying in Mint Street, there is a constant stream of men and women gathering to get 'darshan', such as was your lot alone to cope with in old days. Ba is leaving tonight (after doing three meetings today) straight for Calicut. Urmila Devi is there already. Both will have a busy programme in Calicut for a couple of days, and 3rd Dec onwards in the interior of Ponnani Taluka, where the Referendum arrangements have been made and will be in execution from 3rd Dec. It is expected the votes will be recorded before 15th. The votes will not be at meetings, taken in books by house to house visits. This had to be so by reason of the peculiarities of Malabar villages so as to be complete and systematic. It will not be 10 mile radius area, but 500 sq. miles. Kelappan's fast having been on public exhibition at Guruvayur, there having been intense feeling both ways, a small area around would not have been satisfactory. 500 sq. miles is big but Guruvayur temple being a very important all-Kerala temple we could not help taking at least the whole Taluka. The workers are hopeful of completing it.

I must here assure you that our fears that perhaps I was not wanted in Kerala, were wrong. I learnt that one N.N. Menon wrote absurd letters to you, Birla and others and sent similar communications to Malabar workers, but they all repudiate his views. The best and most trusted workers there insisted on my going to Kerala, and I went there. I was there with them from 25th Nov and what I saw assured me that I was not unwanted. It would have been a crime if I stayed away. They had no definite plan, and did not realize what had to be done. As soon as I explained what a referendum meant, they were all enthusiastic and have taken it up vigorously. They were so glad when the Allahabad meeting was postponed enabling me to stay on, and have taken my promise that I shall be back there again on 3rd Dec for as many days as I could possibly give until called away to Allahabad.

I have given them all the detailed forms and instructions for the referendum and I have every hope of good results. Ba is leaving tonight for Calicut, but I shall be here tomorrow. I have to meet Dr Subbaroyan and coach him for an interview with the Governor over the Bill for which he will ask the Governor to obtain the Viceroy's Sanction. This will be done tomorrow and I shall reach Guruvayur on 3rd where it is programmed all the Malabar workers and friends will meet there.

I sent a draft Bill to a few friends in the Delhi Assembly, copy of which, as well as the Draft I propose for introduction in Madras Council, I enclose. I see that C.S. Ranga Iyer[110] has given notice

---

[110] C.S. Ranga Iyer (1895–1963) was a journalist, politician and social reformer. As editor of the *Independent*, he wrote *Father India*, a parody of Katherine Mayo's *Mother India*. A member of the Legislative Council since 1923, Ranga Iyer proposed the Untouchability Abolition Bill—the year he was expelled from the Congress—but later withdrew his proposal.

of the former promptly. You could go over these and see if they meet our case. The draft I have sent to the Assembly friends will if passed dispose of all secular matters and serve as a general charter. The Madras Bill deals with the ticklish temple question in a manner not to savour of legislative coercion in social and religious matters, which objection will be made much of.

I do not know if the Assembly friends will take the necessary steps to push a non-official bill through which is generally a hopeless task. I don't know if you can write to Sir H.S. Gour,[111] or C.S. Ranga Aiyar or Sir Harbilas Sarda,[112] on the subject. My draft is with them all.

The mentality of southern people is sometimes curious. Because you have stated that an adverse vote on the referendum means withdrawal of the fast, some people talk and write as if it may actually be better to bring about that result! A favourable vote and an obstinate Zamorin may mean risk to your life, while an unfavourable vote may straightaway save your life. Read the enclosed cutting. I wonder if you will be able to turn the emphasis back to *the* thing. But pray do not threaten another fast.

I must explain to you that the Kerala workers insisted on getting Ba down. I had to withdraw my objection and wire for her.

Love
Raja

———

[111] Hari Singh Gour (1870–1949) was a lawyer, jurist and educationist. He was the founder vice chancellor of Delhi University and deputy president of the Central Legislative Assembly. He had progressive views on women's rights and was active in raising girls' age of consent for marriage under the Age of Consent Act.

[112] Harbilas Sarda (1867–1952) worked with the Maharaja of Jaisalmer and as vernacular superintendent of the Commissioner's Office, Ajmer. He retired in 1924 as officiating district and sessions judge, Ajmer-Mewar. He was elected to the Central Legislative Assembly in 1922, 1927 and 1930. Sarda sponsored the Child Marriage Restraint Bill, which was passed in 1929 and came to be known as the Sarda Act.

Gandhi had written about the referendum:

21 December 1932

My dear C.R.,

. . . You have not told me, and I have not worried you about the state of the law on the subject. What is happening to the Bill? I am told that before a Bill of a religious character receives the Viceregal sanction for introduction, he is to have clear two months. If such be the case, and if the law as it stands is admittedly against us, the fast has to be automatically postponed; whereas if the sanction is withheld or is delayed purely through want of popular expression of public opinion on it, the fast has to go on till public opinion is sufficiently mobilized, if it can be, so as to secure Viceregal sanction. If public opinion is against such legislation the fast must stand adjourned. I would like you therefore to instruct me on the law. Ba tells me you are to be expected here about the 28th, if it is not possible for you to come earlier.

Yours sincerely,

57

Those wanting change win the referendum. Fifty-six per cent of the caste Hindus support Harijan entry, 9 per cent oppose it, 8 per cent are neutral and 27 per cent stay silent. Kelappan and CR score a victory of no ordinary importance, given the 'first-of-its-kind' nature of the referendum and the opposition of the orthodox. Gandhi issues a lengthy statement (see Annexure VI).

But the temple gates are not going to open yet. Legislation is called for, and CR is to get his friend Dr P. Subbaroyan to work at that. Meanwhile, he is following and commenting on Gandhi's thinking on the subject. From Sabarmati's archive, this postcard, which, as the postal cancellations on it show, does the journey from Bombay to Poona in a neat twenty-four hours:

1 January 1933

My dear Bapu,

I see in the press that you have sent 'a very definite suggestion' to the Sanatanists containing some proposals about the Guruvayur temple which 'you believe will satisfy the most exacting Sanatanist' and that 'an emissary conveying the message is already in Guruvayur'. Kindly let me have correct information in this subject addressed to c/o Khadi Vastralaya, Esplanade, Madras

Love,
Raja

Mahatma Gandhi
Yeravada
Poona

58

Gearing up for a major engagement with the question of temple-entry
for Harijans, CR is to work with legislators in Madras and Delhi, with
officialdom, with political and constructive workers. Also, to engage in
polemics with the orthodox and the diehard.

The Congress would have liked him to stay with mainstream politics
rather than take up social reform. But he is clear as to what he should
be doing at the moment—anti-untouchability rather than disobedience.
And Gandhi backs him, with Devadas giving him valuable logistical
support. The two letters below, written within two days of each other,
reveal the scene.

C/o Khadi Vastralaya
Madras
6 January 1933[113]

My dear Bapu,

I have read your great appeal to 'fellow Sanatanists'. I do not know
if it will have moved them all as it did me. But we can all pray that
it may do so. A very orthodox Pandit who has been trying to help
us though not quite with us in this affair told me this morning
that he read your appeal in the Swadesamitran—he does not know
English—and that he was moved to tears. He added, 'I suppose the
original must be more touching than the Tamil I read'. But you do
not want all this; nor did I intend to say this when I began. What I
wished to write about was my anxiety about your health. Such efforts
at expressing one's heart agonies have a serious physical reaction and

---

[113] The original of this letter from CR was written out by Devadas Gandhi, then
in Madras. Devadas has, by a common error at the start of a new year, written down the
year just passed—'32'. It is given here after being corrected to '33'.

I am anxious about it. I wish I could tell you 'please do not repeat the attempts' but what right have I to say so?

I read in the press your proposal to Pandit Panchanan Tarkaratna[114] before I received your card. The Free Press had taken my opinion about it before your card came. The proposal is surely an acid test of the sincerity of the Sanatanists and I am quite glad you presented it to them. The 'Justice' newspaper is furious with you, so also the great Mr. Varadarajulu Naidu. I had to give my opinion to the press on account of the reactions on the part of South Indian Non-Brahmins interested in this reform.

We are carrying on the agitation for the sanction of the bills. We have sent a long cable to London in response to a cable from Bertrand Russell making enquiries. A collection of relevant papers with explanations has been sent by air mail. My interview with the Governor was not bad, but I could see that opponents had primed him with all sorts of difficult propositions.

I intend keeping Devadas here for a little time longer.

Love,
Raja

Trichinopoly
8 January (1933)

My dear Bapu

Devadas and I came here this morning. We leave for Tiruchengodu tomorrow night. After two days there we shall go around to a few places in the south.

---

[114] Panchanan Tarkaratna of Bhatpara, Bengal.

The Madras Mail has an article suggesting that sanction for the Temple Entry Bill should neither be given nor refused and that a committee may be appointed to enquire and report on the strength of the demand and the opposition. A committee of this kind has been appointed in Travancore, it is said, on the advice of Sir C.P. Ramaswami Iyer. Perhaps the 'Madras Mail' article is also inspired. Mr C.S. Ranga Iyer has written to me a letter in which he expresses the fear that government is unwilling to give sanction and may at the most appoint a committee. Without attaching undue importance to these conjectures, I think it may be desirable that you should emphasize the fact the local option contained in Dr Subbaroyan's bill would be far more appropriate and effective for the purpose of gauging and overcoming popular prejudice varying in form and intensity according to the locality.

The customs are so materially different [in] localities that an All India enquiry will land nowhere. Further, an enabling bill provides room for changing times and progress of ideas. Had the proposal been for a mandatory legislation one could understand the appointment of a previous committee. What we want being an enabling measure which contains in itself the provision for a local enquiry each time it is put in operation, a general enquiry now by an All India committee can have no meaning or purpose. We may claim that reformers may be expected to utilise the provisions of the bill when it becomes law only where our propaganda is so successful that the consent of the people of the locality is secured. There can be no rash or uncoordinated interference with custom.

You will have gathered news about the progress of the agitation from the papers. There is plenty of activity on both sides. The other side is indulging in unrestrained libels.

Love to all of you,
Raja

Gandhi's card about Pandit Tarkaratna:

3 January 1933

My dear C.R.,

It was stupid of me not to have discussed with you my proposal to Pandit Panchanan Tarkaratna. Now I have given it to the Press; you will therefore see it earlier than you receive this. I would like to have your opinion on it.

Yours sincerely,

59

Fieldwork remains at the fore. Gandhi advises CR on different matters and CR responds.

8 January 1933

My dear C. R.,

You are silent, but I know that means overwork. Here is a copy of Rao Bahadur Seshu Aiyar's letter. There is much in his suggestions which I like. I have simply sent him an acknowledgment saying that temple-entry propaganda should go side by side with the working of his suggestions wherever such work is feasible.

Yours sincerely

12 January 1933

My dear C.R.,

I have your second letter. I hope that what you have heard is not true, but if it turns out to be true, it would be unfortunate. But I should not take any action upon a mere rumour. Mahadev has just suggested a public statement. I shall see whether such a thing is possible. In any case, I suppose I should know the result in a day or two.

I am glad you like the appeal to the sanatanists. Of course, all such effort is costly, but the cost is worth paying. The deliberate falsehoods that are flung about are the things that shake me and cut me to the marrow. But I have no shadow of a doubt that Truth will conquer.

I expect to meet the sanatanist Shastris about whom Hiralal Nanavati has been writing to me.

I have written a long letter to the Editor of the Justice about his attack on my proposal. He wrote to me sending me three cuttings from his paper and invited my criticism. I gave also on the same question a long interview yesterday to the Associated Press which you will see.

You seem to have forgotten all about Gopala Menon's letter referring to the proposed All-Hindu Conference at Guruvayur. You remember Gopala Menon said that you would attend to it. I therefore sent Gopala Menon a telegram yesterday to see you, because he reminded me that I had done nothing about it. If you want that Conference, you have to advise Acharya Dhruva and Dr. Bhagwandas in good time. In my opinion, Malaviyaji should still be left free.

Yours sincerely

18 January 1933

My dear Bapu,

I have your letters of 8th and 12th Jan. I am going today to Madura with Devadas. Tomorrow we shall be at Tinnevelly, the day after at Nagercoil and on the 21st at Trivandrum. We will reach Calicut on the 23rd.

The A.P.I news today is that sanction for the Bill is likely to be given. I hope it is well-founded.

If your appeal to the Sanatanists was beautiful in one way, your short statement[115] that I read in today's papers in answer to the apprehension about Civil commotions is beautiful in another way. It is perhaps the most splendid performance in controversy that I have seen you do. I suppose you will say that a strict follower of truth does everything easily and well. As long as the Sanatanists do not say

---

[115] Chamanlal Girdhardas Parekh, Chairman, Ahmedabad Mill-owners' Association, was reported to have urged the viceroy not to sanction the introduction of the temple-entry bills, as it would lead to a religious civil war. Gandhi makes the following statement in his interview to Associated Press:

16 January 1933

I am quite sure that Seth Chamanlal could not believe that there was any likelihood of a civil war in the country. As I have said in my appeal to sanatanists, such a thing I hold to be inconceivable. If anybody knows the reformers, I should surely know them. War could take place only if there are two parties to fight one another. Self-styled sanatanists would be simply beating the air if they staged a war. And why should there be a war? The Viceroy gives formal sanction not to a Bill passed but to a Bill that has been introduced, which even when passed ensures absolute freedom from fight.

The fight may come when the matter goes out of the reformers' hands and disappointed and enraged Harijans take the matter in their own hands and fight for their rights against the whole host of caste Hindus. But even that is a remote possibility, so long as reformers are alive to vindicate the honour of sanatana dharma.

The Bill can only pass if it has solid Hindu opinion behind it and not otherwise. I hope, therefore, that nobody will be scared by the telegram to which you have just drawn my attention. (*The Bombay Chronicle*, 17 January 1933)

anything about your proposed compromise and are willing to come forward to accept it, there is no necessity for those interested in the reform to be agitated over your compromise proposal. You have put the Sanatanists to the test; if they fail in the test we cannot lose anything but only gain. My own impression is that the evil is so great that if we succeed in removing this, we should do so once and for all and not by stages so far as the temple is concerned. If the orthodox are able to get over the feeling of pollution they will be doing it in one jump rather than take it by two or three stages. Armchair critics may subject your proposal to many logical dissections, but those who work actually see nothing wrong in your proposal. The disease being a real disease and the seat of the disease being the orthodox mind, your compromise proposal would certainly cure it if accepted, but I suppose a desperate patient will swallow the whole bottle rather than take it in several dozes.

I did not forget about Mr. Gopala Menon's Hindu conference at Guruvayur. Principal Dhruva wires to me that he cannot come till the end of March certainly and that he would prefer to come in the first week of May. This is of no use to the Kerala Conference.

I quite agree with you that Malaviaji should be left free. Malaviaji is convening a conference shortly at Benares of Sanatanist Pandits of all India. I hope that this will not have an unfavourable reaction on the question of sanction. A Conference of this sort convened by Malaviaji may encourage postponement or shelving of the sanction question. If Malaviaji should wire to the Viceroy urging sanction saying that the Bill proposed is only an enabling measure and that the sanction is only to permit discussion in the Council, perhaps then the Conference may not encourage the Viceroy to postpone the question of the Bill on the ground that Malaviaji is taking steps to convert Hindu opinion otherwise than by legislation. I have wired to Malaviaji to this effect and await his reply tomorrow.

I am in communication with Calicut friends regarding their Conference and you need not worry about it.

Your letters are still signed very badly with your left hand. This leaves no room for me to ask how your arms are getting on. It is time for you now to invite the Inspector General to do something more satisfactory to put them right if possible.

All our meetings wherever we go are wonderful demonstrations of how the windows of reason and common sense have been opened to let light into decayed Hinduism. The opposition we meet fills me also with some satisfaction for it proves that Sanatana Dharma is not dead. The movement has made people read sastras and books which they have never read before but were only swearing by. It is a case of the old man that told his sons that treasure was buried in the garden and they dug the garden up and a good crop followed and the treasure was found thereby.

Love,
C. Rajagopalachari

60

Hosted by the devoted Gandhi disciple Gadodia, a merchant in old Delhi, CR gets to work with legislators.

C/o Seth Laxmi Narayan Gadodia
Near Clock Tower, Delhi
11 February 1933

My dear Bapu,

Your letter about C.S. Ranga Iyer. It was no doubt a very bad statement which Mr. Ranga Iyer made in connection with the Khilafat Sankaracharya's telegram. It was all as wrong as bombastic. I do not think, however, that we need to be worried about it, for nobody bothers at all with what Mr. Ranga Iyer says. In spite of this about Mr. Ranga Iyer, he is the only man who has made this business of ours his own. The others are indifferent and are yet doubtful whether it would pay them to take interest in this subject. Ranga Iyer seems to have made up his mind and is therefore more useful than others. It sometimes happens that we do not like a man and there is nothing to be said for him, but he turns out to be more useful than others.

The places that are now available for distribution by Government of India [Joint Committee] are the centre of thought for all M.L.A.s; hence the difficulty in getting them to take a definite attitude in regard to the Bills. It may embarrass the Government, they think, and cost them the seat that they expect in the Joint Committee Selection. Then again there are party jealousies. Sir Hari Singh Gour's party [Nationalist Party] is being depleted and Sir Abdul Rahim's party [Independent Party] strengthened thereby. This means a chance for the latter to become the chief opposition. Some dissident members in Sir Hari Singh Gour's party therefore hesitate to support the Bill or take steps for expediting their passage. I should not worry you with these and other such matters. We are trying to cope with them, though I must confess I sometimes feel very depressed. But then the Gita comes to our assistance:—'Action is thy duty etc' but you have told me that we may interpret this wrongly. That frightens me also.

Devadas caught a chill which caused a little worry but he is alright now after 2 days rest and what may be called a small fast.

Mr. & Mrs. Gadodia are taking very good care of us. Their car is at our disposal almost entirely.

I read your articles for the first number of 'Harijan' of course through the daily newspapers which, as expected, are taking them in advance.

It is remarkable how much less interest is shown in these parts on the question of temple entry than in my own dear South India. I explain it to myself that it is because there is less opposition here and less of temples, with space enough to admit them. We had a fairly good meeting in Delhi yesterday. Mahadeo can read the report of it in the Hindustan Times of Saturday the 11th.

Love,
Raja

Mahatma Gandhi, Central Prison, Poona

61

Ironically, the intrepid no-changer and opponent of Council-entry is busy lobbying legislators and gaining ground experience of legislative floor management in the cause of abolishing untouchability.

C/o Seth Laxmi Narayan Gadodia
Near Clock Tower, Delhi
12 February 1933

My dear Bapu,

There was a ballot yesterday of names of members who had given notice of introduction of Bills. The Untouchability Abolition Bill being ripe with one month's notice for 27th February has been balloted for by 4 members and it occupies the 6th, 11th, 14th and 17th places in the list of 22 such motions. (6th Gaya Prasad Singh, 11th S.C. Mitra, 14th M.C. Rajah and 17th C.S. Ranga Iyer) All these four persons having given notice of the same Bill, their names have all been drawn. Once the Bills for introduction are reached, there will be no difficulty in all of them having a chance because the formal leave for introduction in each case will take only a couple of minutes each.

The real difficulty is the previous business of Bills, which, having reached a further stage beyond introduction, have a priority over Bills for fresh introduction. As to how much of this kind of business has been notified for the next non-official day namely 27th Feb and in what order of priority amongst themselves they have been placed, I shall be able to ascertain definitely tomorrow. In spite of Ganshyamadasji's pessimism, I believe that mere introduction is quite possible on the 27th of Feb without any special favours being secured.

I do not know what reply you have received from the Viceroy in reply to your letter of 1st Feb. Mr Ranga Iyer sent a letter to the Viceroy for publication of Bills which would dispense with the first stage in the Assembly, namely leave for introduction. He has not yet had any reply, though he has been informed by permanent officials that it may be very probably in the negative.

The temple entry bill which was sanctioned in February will not be ripe on a month's notice for 27th Feb and therefore can be introduced in the ordinary course only on the 24th March, hence this has not yet been balloted for. It will be done on the 7th March.

Members of the Assembly are absorbed, some of them in the prospects of being selected to the Joint Committee, some of them in party squabbles and all of them in mutual jealousy as well as fears about what their constituencies might think of them if they should support reform measures. It requires considerable optimism to be able to work among these people. Faced with the issue, they may not vote against us; but they are totally unwilling to take any risk, or any initiative. Even Ramaswamy Mudaliar,[116] Editor of the 'Justice' and leading member of Abdul Rahim's Independent party was not willing to sign a requisition calling upon the Government to allot special additional days for these Bills and give facilities. He raised objections to any plan of hastening the measures and finally said he would have to consult Mr. Abdul Rahim and the members of his party in the Assembly and would take steps to do so. We have secured only 13 signatures so far.

Meanwhile I was disturbed by a telephone message from Mr. Birla last night that Malaviaji had sent down a press statement denouncing legislation and that he had been just persuaded to postpone publication for a time as the legislation has not yet been introduced. I have since read the statement that is lying in the Hindustan Times Office awaiting further instructions from Malaviaji.

---

[116] Sir Arcot Ramasamy Mudaliar (1887–1976) was a lawyer and politician. A senior leader of the Justice Party, he was nominated to the Madras Legislative Council (1920–26) and was a member of the Madras Legislative Assembly (1931–34), losing to S. Satyamurti of the Congress in the 1934 elections. He was a member of the Imperial Legislative Council (1939–41) and a member of Churchill's war cabinet (1942–45). He was India's delegate to the San Francisco Conference and served as the first head of UNESCO.

It is a strong condemnation of the temple entry bill on the ground
that he is opposed to any legislative interference direct or indirect
with temples and urges circulation procedure and objects to any
rushing through or deviation from normal procedure.

The fact seems to be that he has secured the consent of his
Conference of Pandits to his proposal about free Devadarshan on the
condition that he would strenuously oppose any legislation directly
or indirectly dealing with the matter. He is therefore compelled to
issue this statement and he will do so as soon as he can, if in the
meanwhile you are not able to persuade him. I drafted a telegram
to you suggesting that you should invite him at once to confer with
you, but subsequently gave up the idea of wiring and have written
this letter. I believe that Panditji has already written to you. The
publication of such a telegram by Malaviaji is sure to block any
progress in our mission in New Delhi.

Devadas is better. I hope you are keeping fairly well.

Love,
Raja

62

*As CR perseveres, Gandhi keeps a close watch on the fate of the bill
and of the Guruvayur temple-entry question as such. He responds to an
irate letter from an orthodox opponent of change[117] and also tells CR of
a discussion he has had with his fellow prisoner Vallabhbhai Patel on the
work CR is engaged in.*

---

[117] The addressee had written in his article 'The Drive against Untouchability':
'He [Gandhiji] has given up his creed of non-co-operation with Government so far as
untouchability is concerned by accepting special Government favours, and is actively
blessing legislative efforts, once taboo, to facilitate removal of untouchability' (from a
microfilm S.N. 18919). Gandhi's response follows:

13 January 1933

My dear C.R.,

Vallabhbhai had a battle royal with me last night on your behalf. If a person, an utter stranger to him, had chance to be there, from the vehemence of Vallabhbhai's language, he would have concluded that we must be most quarrelsome persons.

He thought that I was doing violent injustice to you, inasmuch as, without consultation with you, I made proposals that might prove to be utterly embarrassing, as had happened on two occasions. The cause of our quarrel was my compromise proposal. He thought that I had no right to publish it without consultation with you, and he was quite sure that though you were too good to mention it to me, you had felt very much embarrassed by it, if not also irritated. I told him that you were too good to conceal your embarrassment from me, if you were really embarrassed, and that would be quite unlike

_____

13 January 1933

Dear Friend,

I have your letter together with your article. I am sorry indeed that there should have been any molestation of you by the audience. I have, as you must be aware, repeatedly written against intolerance, and I shall gladly re-emphasize my warning when the time comes.

As for your article, we must agree to differ. Our conception of sanatana dharma is different. In your impatience you have not even cared to understand my fundamental position. I can only say, 'Read all my statements with a fresh mind, then if you have still doubts, discuss them with Sjt. Rajagopalachariar and if you are not still convinced and would care to do so, come down to Yeravada and I shall gladly give you one hour and try to convince you that the position I take up and the means I adopt to vindicate are both perfectly defensible.'

Yours sincerely,

Sjt. S.T. Ramanuja Iyengar
4 Varadaraja Perumal Coil St.
Trichinopoly

you. I even added that in this particular instance you happened even to like my proposal and that even if it was discovered that you did not like it and that you were really embarrassed, it was impossible for me every time to consult you, or such other colleagues on such occasions.

I went further and argued that work on such lines would become almost impossible. People act together when there is a general agreement between them on fundamentals and [provided] that their deductions from those fundamentals were, as a rule, identical, and that if, at times, they came to different deductions, a timely confession of error would keep their friendship intact, as also the common cause.

Nothing that I could say, however, would conciliate Vallabhbhai. The curfew bell, mutually agreed upon by us, came to the rescue, and put an end to what promised to be an endless discussion. But I retired to bed with a determination that I would refer the matter to you. Your reply, one way or the other, would bring some consolation to your counsel, and you know that it won't make me disconsolate if you agreed with your counsel on both his propositions, namely, that before giving to the world the compromise proposal which I had given to Pandit Panchanan Tarkaratna I should have consulted you, and that it, as a matter of fact, did embarrass you. You would also add to your opinion on these points, your opinion whether on merits you consider my proposal to be sound or otherwise.

A perfect tragedy was enacted here yesterday. Five pandits and their five advisers came to the jail gate yesterday an hour and a half after the appointed time and took two hours and a half in exchanging brief notes with me, the three notes that they exchanged with me taking all the two hours and a half. And, will you believe it, when I tell you that they would not come in and carry on the discussion because I would not remove one word I had added to their draft, the word being an adjective added to the word 'untouchables'. The adjective applied was 'as at present classified'. Of course it altered the whole scope of their discussion. So they went away. Of course it is not our position that there is no untouchability at all in the Shastras. Our position is that there is no untouchability in the Shastras as we practise it today. They were expected to prove that untouchability as at present practised has sanction in the Shastras. It is an impossible task to perform honestly. No text that has yet been cited on their behalf has proved it. The Shastris on our behalf are really very learned men, and also pious men. It is their honest conviction that there is no warrant for the untouchability of the present day in the Shastras. The real untouchability will be there for all time. It is a sound hygienic rule practised all over the world.

Yours sincerely,

12/13 February 1933

My dear C.R.,

I have read your and G.'s appeal to the public. Why do you even so much as mention the fast and its possibility? You surely undermine its spiritual value, if the fast, if it at all comes, is to be a spiritual fast. I do not even know that the fast is a certainty if the Bills do not pass during this session or at all. I think that you should all dismiss it from your consideration altogether and let the public mind work unfettered by it. When it does come it will produce its own effect if it is a spiritual act. If it is the product of a diseased or arrogant mind, it will merely torture the body and excite pity or contempt according to the temperament of the people who may hear of it. Do take this advice as from an expert and act up to it to the fullest extent.

Then you have seriously to consider Pt. Malaviyaji's attitude. He is strongly against the Bills especially if they are not to be circulated. Of course I do not share the view. I shall be writing to him. But you should see him if you can at all spare yourself or send Devdas alone. But on this I have no firm opinion. You will do what appeals to you most. You know the outside atmosphere firsthand. All my knowledge is secondhand and therefore worthless.

I had what must be described in one way as a very unsatisfactory interview with Dr. A. He is irreconcilable. In another way it was satisfactory. I know him better than I did.

Please share the letter with G. and Thakkar Bapa.

Love.
Bapu

Draft Telegram
[13 February 1933]

C.R.

PLEASE DO NOT MENTION POSSIBILITY FAST ANYWHERE ANY ACCOUNT. SUCH MENTION UNBECOMING AND IRRELEVANT. BUT TELL ALL MEMBERS ASSEMBLY ESPECIALLY HINDU MEMBERS THAT FOR INDIA'S HONOUR IT IS NECESSARY CONSIDER UNTOUCHABILITY BILLS THIS SESSION. IF BOMBAY MEETING OF SEPTEMBER WAS REPRESENTATIVE HINDU OPINION HINDU MEMBERS BOUND DELIVER GOODS BY PUSHING FORWARD BILLS. IF HINDU HONOUR MAY ALSO BE REGARDED INDIA'S HONOUR OTHER MEMBERS IN MY OPINION BOUND FACILITATE DISPASSIONATE CONSIDERATION BILLS. AM CONVINCED THAT NONE DESIGNED COERCE SINGLE PERSON OR INTERFERE WITH ANYBODY'S RELIGION. EXISTING POSITION STIFLES CONSCIENCE.

GANDHI

C/o Seth Laxmi Narayan Gadodia
Near Clock Tower, Delhi
16 February 1933

My dear Bapu,

I have your letter of the 13th. I note what you have stated about the fast. I have been trying to forget the fast altogether and I have to make reference to it. It was unfortunate, in the statement issued by Ganshyamdasji and myself, a sentence in the original draft was substituted in reference to Ganshyamadasji's objection to it and the fast came in the amended draft and I did not give sufficient attention to it. This is only an explanation of how the error came to be, not a plea in justification.

Today's [API] news about 27 members having signed to a counter representation as against 15 for special facilities being given, is misleading. More members have signed in a supplementary application for facilities and in the counter representation of '27 members' is inclusive of many non-Hindus secured by the Sanatanists to sign on their side. But I must admit that the Sanatanists have a certain number of people who will combine with them to block the measures.

I feel that my seeing Malaviaji will only make him worse. I am asking Devadas to go with Shankerlal after 3 or 4 days.

What you write about Dr. Ambedkar is quite true.

Love,
Raja

63

Gandhi, meanwhile, is getting advice from many quarters on how to get the bills through. He writes about it in Harijan[118] and sends CR a telegram:

---

[118] Gandhi writes:

A valued friend suggests that I should send personal letters to the members of the Assembly bespeaking their support to the consideration, during the current session, of Sjt. Ranga Iyer's two Bills on untouchability. I hope there is no false pride in me. Having made up my mind, or, as critics would say, deceived myself into the belief, that in spite of my non-co-operation there was nothing wrong in asking the members to do what was right, I would not hesitate, if I was free, to go to them personally and show to them why it was necessary for all the members to allow the Bills to be considered without delay and for the Hindu members to back them for the sake of the purity of their religion. But I am not free and I have found in Sjt. C. Rajagopalachariar a better lobbyist than myself and perhaps better also at the art of wooing obstinate members. He is, therefore, in Delhi as my duly authorized agent to plead my cause. The public know what confidence I have in him as an exponent of and believer in whatever philosophy

25 FEBRUARY 1933

C. RAJAGOPALACHARI

C/O GADODIA, DELHI

SEND RAOBAHADUR RAJAH'S BILL AMENDING SECTION 144 WITH YOUR
OPINION. BAPU

CR reports to him:

C/o Seth Laxmi Narayan Gadodia
Near Clock Tower, Delhi
[25th/28th] February 1933

My dear Bapu,

Your telegram. Herewith M.C. Rajah's Bill amending Section
144 of the Criminal Procedure, drafted to safeguard the rights of
untouchables.

My opinion as a lawyer is against this Bill.

According to the decision of Courts, Magistrates, even under
the existing law, should not issue orders under Section 144 directing
anyone to abstain from the exercise of his lawful rights on the ground
that other people may act contrary to law and create a disturbance.
In all such cases, the courts have laid down the rule that it is the duty
of the Magistrates to protect the exercise of rights and to take steps
against law breakers who may threaten to create a disturbance.

Mr. Rajah's Bill assumes that the action he seeks to protect is in
the exercise of the lawful rights of the so-called untouchables. This
means that the law should first recognise the action as lawful. If this
is assumed there is no necessity for this Bill, as the Magistrates will be

---

there may be in me. Therefore, it would be superfluous, and if it was any other agent,
even discourteous to him, if I was to write directly to the members who, I hope, will
regard Rajagopalachari's appeal to them as much more than a letter to them individually.
(*Harijan*, 18 February 1933)

bound to protect the Harijans in the exercise of their lawful rights. If the Magistrates fail to do this, it is not because of an absence of an enactment of this kind. They do not wish to take responsibility, they do not desire to add to their work. I am not aware that Sect. 144 has been used where the right is clearly and lawfully established in favour of the untouchables. We are aware that though untouchable boys are bound to be admitted in schools and other such public institutions, they are not actually admitted. But that is not due to any order under Section 144.

I do not think that it is right to deprive the Magistracy of all powers to act under Section 144 where there is a real danger to peace and tranquillity. We may disapprove of abuse of powers, but such powers must exist somewhere. This Bill cannot remove the disabilities of Harijans or make it easier, in my opinion, for them to exercise their lawful rights.

I have not yet shown this to Mr. Rajah, but I shall give him a copy after posting this. You may not perhaps condemn the Bill till you give him a hearing.

C. Rajagopalachari

64

Harijan, *the journal Gandhi has just launched, is making waves. Gandhi comments on CR's assessment (sent to another) of the second issue of the journal, apart from sending a word of encouragement to CR:*

25 February 1933

My dear C. R.

Your letter of the 21st. I have heard Vallabhbhai reading your reply to C.P.R. Tastes differ. You consider the second number of *Harijan* excellent except for the denunciation. I consider it excellent certainly for that, if for nothing else. But I agree with your opinion that the thick types for some of the headings look ugly, but things will gradually improve.

I am following your great effort for getting the Bills through. I am not going to shed tears if you do not succeed.

Yours sincerely,

Sjt. C. Rajagopalachariar
C/o Seth L. N. Gadodia
Near Clock Tower, Delhi

CR, meanwhile, reports the latest:

DELHI
28 FEBRUARY 1933

DESPITE GENEROUS DISCIPLINED COOPERATION MAJORITY HOUSE AND CRUEL NEUTRALITY GOVERNMENT ALL BUT ONE HURDLE OVERCOME OBSRUCTION HAD ITS WAY HOUSE ADJOURNED QUARTER AFTER FIVE BILL NOT REACHED NEXT ONLY NONOFFICIAL DAY TWENTYFOURTH.

RAJAGOPALACHARI

Gandhi's reply:

YOUR WIRE SORRY BUT UNRUFFLED WE MUST CARRY ON BAPU

65

Back in Tiruchengodu for a breather, CR tells Gandhi of his predicament and plans.

Gandhi Ashram
Tiruchengodu
14 March 1933

My dear Bapu,

I am leaving for Delhi tomorrow. I wish I could give Papa some more time but it cannot be. She has not been able to induce weight or good health. The bereavement[119] does not explain the physical condition altogether.

I have your letter of 3rd March redirected from Delhi about M.C. Rajah's bill to amend Section 144. I am of the same opinion still. Our untouchability abolition Bill covers the ground sought to be covered by Rajah's bill in respect of Section 144. High Courts have laid down that the Magistrates should endeavour to protect the exercise of lawful rights and make their emergency orders as far as possible against the wrong doers. My legal aesthetics revolts against disfiguring the general law of crimes and criminal procedure with a particular provision for tackling the problem of untouchability.

I would favour a general amending Bill to the effect that Magistrates shall always endeavour when passing orders under 144 to protect the just exercise of lawfully established rights, as against illegal or wanton interference thereof by wrongdoers. This would be reducing to statutory form what is already recognised as law though not always followed. Such a Bill, however, is not to be considered by us now.

The misunderstanding over my legislative efforts is growing. Nothing but the firm conviction that to establish sincerity and good faith by the Harijans this line of action has become essential could have supported me against some very nasty attacks.

Love
Raja

---

[119] Her husband Varadachari's death in June 1932.

66

With Ranga Iyer withdrawing the bill, CR's exercise comes to naught.
But the cause of reform has received a leg-up. It has also served to connect
Gandhi, in jail, with one of his closest colleagues in a programme—anti-
untouchability—that is priority for him.

Gandhi Ashram
Tiruchengodu
11 April 1933

My dear Bapu,

After coming here, I had to leave immediately to attend a quarterly
meeting of the Provincial Board of the Servants of Untouchables
Society at Trichinopoly.

Papa has automatically improved on my arrival. Something is
wrong with Narasimhan[120] and he is lying in bed taking complete
rest. I intend leaving for Madras presently for an examination and
treatment of Papa's teeth and eyes.

I have received a telegram from Sjt. Harbilas Sarda that the
Government has rejected his request for circulation of Bills by
executive order or in the alternative for the allotment of an additional
non-official day in this session. The situation therefore is this:
the temple entry bill will come up for further discussion of the
motion for circulation on the first non-official day in the autumn
session. This cannot be blocked by anything else and is bound to be
completed. If it is passed, it cannot be ready for further progress until
sometime thereafter. The other Bill will have to be balloted for in
order to make any motion thereon even in the autumn session and
can be obstructed. Thus circulation to elicit opinion on the temple
entry Bill does not necessarily mean circulation of the untouchability

---

[120] CR's younger son, C.R. Narasimhan, who had been unwell at the time.

Bill. Though the two Bills are so intimately connected, the fact that Government refuses to give any facility whatever brings about this result.

In refusing to order circulation by executive instruction and refusing to allot half a day extra in this session, Government has definitely decided that the next six months should be merely a blank in regard to the two bills. There could have been no argument against the grant of the request for circulation by executive order which would have meant the utilisation of the next six months for eliciting public opinion without in any manner throwing their weight on the side of reform or giving room for complaint on the part of orthodoxy.

I feel that you should comment on the subject in the 'Harijan' at least for the benefit of those friends outside India who are watching the progress of these legislative proposals. Andrews imagines that Government cannot possibly be against us on this. I hope Vallabhbhai is better.

Love to all of you there,
Raja

67

CR sends to Gandhi an illustration, clearly for use in Harijan.

Gandhi Ashram
Tiruchengodu
23 April 1933

My dear Bapu,

I am sending by separate packet a coloured chart drawn to scale showing Harijan population on the background of other castes,

Muslims, Christians, Sikhs and other religions (Jews and Parsis). Hindus in the chart include Jains and those whose religion is not shown in the census. I have shown a strip drawn to scale giving the proportion of the literate among the Hindus. 'Literate' means the test of the census in some one language and not English.

I hope this chart can be made of some use of in the 'Harijan'. I have excluded Burma in working out the proportions, but both British India and Indian States are included.

Love,
Raja

In his reply of 27 April 1933, Gandhi has some useful comments to make from purely an editor's perspective, and some from a householder's:

My dear C.R.,

I wish that under the coloured chart you had given the figures for the population of the respective castes and divisions and as there is no hurry of publishing the chart, I would like you to give me that information. I could find it myself but I do not know your own figures. They may not be quite what I would find.

In your letter you have said nothing about Narasimhan[120] or Papa. I expect to see Devdas tomorrow.

Yours sincerely,
Sjt. C. Rajagopalachariar

68

Into his fifteenth month in jail, Gandhi announces towards the end of April that he would commence a self-purification fast for twenty-one

days for the greater effectiveness of the anti-untouchability movement.
Rajmohan Gandhi writes very perceptively in The Rajaji Story, *'our*
feeling of suspense, and perhaps even of interest, is likely to flag with each
succeeding fast: we know the story's end'.

He explains how, to Gandhi's contemporaries, his increasing age
increased their anxiety in relation to the fasts in a way we, distanced by
decades, cannot comprehend. Every time he announces a fast, his family
and colleagues fear the worst. This fast is no exception. It is said by
Gandhi's detractors that this is yet another way of getting out of jail. Those
who know Gandhi know better. Jailings have not made him either less
active or less effective. They have only changed—for that spell—the nature
of his activity and his efficacy. But they have taken a toll in terms of health
tones. And as for a fast undertaken within a prison, the ordeal is worse.

Gandhi says this would last for the number of days announced by
him, irrespective of whether he is a prisoner or is outside prison walls.

CR goes to Yeravada and, with Shankerlal Banker, tries every
method to have Gandhi give up the idea of the fast. Mahadev Desai
transcribes the conversation between CR and Gandhi and the Collected
Works *furnishes the text:*

G. Even jurisprudence admits the right of self-destruction. You
will ask me whether Ramatirtha, Ramakrishna, Vivekananda did
this sort of *tapasya*, whether the suicide of Ramatirtha—deliberate
or resulting from a trance—produced any results, whether Jesus
mounting the cross left any impact.

C.R. But Hinduism does not sanction suicide.

G. I don't know. But Mahadev was telling me that there is a practice
of drowning oneself in the Ganga.

C.R. That is to purify oneself with the water of the Ganga. I do
admit that if you are the cause of all these sins you may commit
suicide. Logically it would be your victory, but then you do not
seek such a victory, do you?

G. I want to atone for the sins. Moral ends require moral means.
Cardinal Manning was kept on three biscuits and water. It is easier

to undertake twenty-one days' fast than to die the kind of slow death as Cardinal Manning is said to have died.

A moral reform can be brought about only through *tapashcharya* and self-purification. We should learn from the experience of scientists who have gone through this. My mother and I were born in families where such fasts were an everyday affair. They were a part of their experience. It is probable that my father did not approve of the severe fasts my mother used to undertake but she showed no ill-effects from the fasting and they made us respect her all the more.

C.R. This is only an instance of association of ideas. Can you defend your case by saying that just because your mother fasted you also must? If someone pierces himself with a needle, how will that convince people that it is sinful to regard a person as an untouchable?

G. Then supposing I fast only for a few days? Supposing I don't die at the end of the fast?

C.R. The two things are not related at all. You seem to believe that there is a secret connection between self-mortification and people's convictions. Buddha was the first to raise his voice against such self-mortification.

G. In a true fast the mind and the soul co-operate with the body. Buddha was against purely physical fasting.

C.R. Will you have the strength to think clearly after ten days?

G. On former occasions I did have it. Thoughts become purer during a pure fast even though there may not be any outward sign of that. A co-worker undertook a fast for fifty-five days, still his thoughts have not become pure because his mind was not pure. The very first day he started discussing with me what he would do after the fast.

Even now his mind is not steady. He wrote me a letter in which he described the impurity of his mind. But to a man who has his mind fixed on God or on some noble act things that were obscure at first gradually become clearer and clearer.

C.R. This can be true only to a certain extent.

G. In saying this you tread on dangerous ground. You must accept the conclusion of a scientist. One who is pure, who adheres to truth and wants to cling to it is as much a scientist as a physicist.

C.R. But this is an unnatural situation.

G. It may be unnatural for animals, not for human beings. If you wish to see the unseeable you have to become unseeable.

C.R. Do you wish to see the unseeable?

G. Yes, because I want to serve the Harijans in the best way possible. If untouchability is to be eradicated we must touch the hearts of 160 million people.

C.R. There is a superstition of touching wood to save oneself from ghosts and spirits and God is brought into it. But there must be a limit to such beliefs in the occult.

G. I am not ashamed of the occult element. You seem to say that it is harmful to believe in the occult.

C.R. Yes, if it results in death.

G. You want to have the cake and eat it, too. For the sake of argument I shall grant that fasts which end in death are wrong. Your argument implies that mortification of the flesh can never do good.

C.R. It may sometimes.

G. From the medical point of view?

C.R. No. Even from the spiritual point of view.

G. Then you have lost. If that is the case it should be left to the person who wishes to undertake a fast. I did not undertake this fast of my own free will. I was commanded.

C.R. All right. Can friends advise on this?

G. Certainly.

C.R. If there is an eighty per cent chance of death resulting from this, it is a gamble. You will say that it is a good gamble. I feel that you have been brooding over the same thing in jail and so you have lost your sense of proportion. You have a great fondness for conducting experiments. You are now experimenting with death and you are misguided in it. Can you show me even one person who approves of your step?

G. What could be the value of their opinion? My opinion has greater weight. Andrews does not even know how to lock a room and he is talking about locking up one's life. And how can you claim fully to know God's law?

C.R. I tell you, you should be more cautious. It is possible to get inspiration from God sometimes but not always.

G. Then you accept the possibility of inspiration from God? If you accept this you have lost your case.

C.R. But the inspiration may be wrong in this instance. It is rashness to close one's mind to reason. Sometimes God appears in the form of rashness, sometimes of the wicked, sometimes of the fish and sometimes of a tortoise. I just want you to realize that sometimes even you can be wrong. In this case I want you to realize that.

G. But how can I accept my mistake unless the result shows it? I have decided to undertake the fast in spite of myself. Mahadev will tell you from my letters how my mind has been working.

C.R. You are deliberately suppressing your thoughts.

G. If I accept your argument I should stop working altogether.

C.R. But there can be no such inspiration which is against reason.

G. It may not be against my reason . . .

There is only one aim, that of purification. My own purification as well as my co-workers'. Other effects will also flow from it. I see that impurity can exist in my presence. That means there is impurity in me.

I have not attained complete freedom from unwanted thoughts. Suppose the things I consider impure are proved to be pure, I must still undertake the fast. There are impurities and I feel I am responsible for them.

Moreover, it is a mistake to regard this as a political issue. The main thing is that this movement should be conducted in a purely religious spirit.

Religion is concerned with the inner self. It is a matter of the heart, of faith and of eternal verities. The body has no lasting value. God says that everything that has name and form shall perish. Even the sun is not eternal. Science also proves this.

But our activities are concerned with material things. My fast is for a wholly spiritual purpose. How can I stand in argument with those who are intellectually much superior to me? But when it comes to what the heart says, I am able to hold my own against them because it does not require any knowledge of Sanskrit. It is a blessing that God dwells in the hearts of the poor and my fast is for heart-searching. There certainly is a tradition of undertaking fasts for rains and other material things. . . . You must respect my convictions. You are telling me to dismiss them summarily. You may strive with me, argue with me. It is possible that I am mistaken but you are telling me to accept the possibility as a certainty. I should be a liar if I undertake the fast with the certainty that it would end in my death. So long as you cannot convince me, by quoting my own statements, that I am mistaken you should not undermine my faith.

Nobody can attain to a certitude like God's. But after all, am I not myself the captain of my ship?

———

Then, sometime later, regretting his outburst, he writes:

5 May 1933

My dear C.R.,

You are dearer to me than life itself. I wounded you and Shankerlal deeply yesterday. It is no use my saying 'Forgive me'.

Your forgiveness I have before the asking. But I will do the very thing that I resisted like an ass. I will submit to the examination now and any time you like by any doctor, provided, of course, the Government permit it. I feel that the result of such examination should not be published for fear of political use being made of it. I must say, too, that the medical examination, if it comes, is not likely to affect the commencement of the fast.

More when we meet. This is just to relieve my soul of the impurity that crept in yesterday.

Love to you and Shankerlal,
Bapu

Harijan *reports:*

The next day, however, C. R. came laughing and said 'there was no occasion for the apology, the irritation was more on our side than yours, and we have now decided to have no examination'.

The entreaties having been heard and 'filed away', Gandhi writes in Harijan *on 6 May 1933:*

Chakravarti Rajagopalachari, the keeper of my conscience, sends me a long telegram attacking the very basis of the fast. Add to these the fervent personal appeal, strengthened by a copious flow of tears, of Devdas, my youngest son and valued comrade.

If these typical appeals have left me unmoved, the reader should have no difficulty in perceiving that there must be a force which has overpowered me and prevents me from responding to these and such other appeals.

69

The fast is gone through, Gandhi is released on 8 May 1933. He suspends civil disobedience for a month and asks the Raj to free political

*prisoners and withdraw oppressive ordinances. CR is with Gandhi in
June and another conversation ensues on the post-fast situation.*

Morning, 6 a.m.
2 June 1933

C.R. Is there anything that needs to be done after your statement
on the conclusion of the fast?

G. We should renew the plea I had made earlier for a meeting
with the Viceroy. I will again ask for the Gandhi-Irwin Pact to be
implemented, people to be allowed to collect salt and do peaceful
picketing of foreign-cloth shops and liquor shops.

C.R. They have already sent a reply to your statement. Do you
think we should write anything more?

G. I feel that we should scrupulously keep to the word I gave that
negotiations would be resumed from the point at which they were
broken off.

C.R. But they say we should go to them only after first completely
withdrawing civil disobedience.

G. They can say this only after the negotiations start and the conditions
for settlement are discussed. Where is today the agency that will
withdraw civil disobedience? Who will withdraw it? So there can be
no condition of withdrawal of civil disobedience till the prisoners are
released. I do not at all feel defeated. We just cannot admit having
done something wrong or having committed breach of the Pact.

No settlement is possible on the basis of such a condition. If we
agree to any such condition we would lose the game and will be
ruined. Our claim is that there has been no breach of the Gandhi-
Irwin Pact from our side. If they think otherwise, they can appoint
an enquiry committee. I am ready to abide by the decision of an
impartial enquiry committee. But they are not ready to accept any
such suggestion. I feel this time also we will get the same reply
from the Viceroy as we got on the previous occasion. He would say

that, if we wanted to discuss anything without unconditionally and completely giving up civil disobedience, in his view there was no point in my meeting him. Still I feel it is necessary to write a letter not suggesting a way out but asking for an interview.

C.R. Do you not want to write anything to the Secretary of State?

G. I already know his views. Rangaswami had told me that Hoare had written to him a friendly letter saying that there was nothing in the White Paper that could not be changed and so he should go and see him. So Rangaswami went and saw him. Hoare thinks that it is his job to polish off rough edges and show to the world that he is getting co-operation from all the parties, even from the Moderates and the Congress.

'It would be a good thing if Rangaswami could be persuaded to say something in favour of the reform. It would be equally well if he does not'. That seems to be Hoare's attitude. Moreover, he runs the administration at Simla too. He is behind all this and not the Viceroy. He is carrying on Birkenhead's policy in a more gentle way. I am not saying anything new in this because I returned from London with all this information. And all of them in England—Irwin, Baldwin, Archbishop of Canterbury—are defending his policy.

C.R. Irwin seems to think that there has been so much breach of the Settlement that it cannot be revived and so it is altogether unnecessary to refer to it.

G. We can raise the issue provided the discussion reaches that stage. But even if we meet, ultimately nothing will come out of all that. Birkenhead and [Lord] Reading also said: 'If you do not want war you should accept what the Parliament offers you. Parliament will give reforms gradually. You should be satisfied with that. But at the moment there is no mutual faith or mutual respect at all.'

C.R. This whole chapter has been fully discussed by Sastri. Shall we ask him his opinion today?

G. If you want to see him you may. He will of course not come here. At the annual function of the Servants of India Society he did not say anything special or make his policy known.

C.R. The policy you recommend can be followed only by a few as it is very revolutionary. But it will have no effect on either the Government or the people.

G. I don't care. It is possible what you say is true but I am prepared for it. I am hurt by these pin-pricks. Only those who willingly set out will have to suffer.

C.R. Then the mass struggle comes to an end.

G. That exactly is going to be the key to the whole affair. We have made a mistake in letting the mass struggle go on without any plan. Only when the people have understood a definite plan from the beginning to the end, will a mass struggle come. When responsible persons feel that people are prepared to lose their property and are ready for even greater hardships, they will start the struggle.

C.R. Don't you think that the call for a no-tax campaign in January 1932 was premature?

G. Of course it was. I had told Tandon and others in 1931 that I did not have faith in our strength to carry on a no-tax campaign for attaining swaraj.

C.R. If it was a mistake, should we not rectify it?

G. I will not say that the struggle should be called off even for that purpose.

C.R. Government will not return all the properties even if we withdraw the struggle.

G. Government will not hear of any such thing.

70

The respite from prison and the pause in disobedience gives Gandhi and CR the time to turn their thoughts to 'family'. That is, to Devadas and Lakshmi. It is now the twosome's due, they feel, to become a couple. Their love has been tested by time and has endured the distance and non-

50

MS/12550

Train
3. 6. 33

My dear Ba,

I hope Bapu is steadily getting stronger every day, & before I return to Poona will be able to move about.

Bapu & I had a chat on Friday just before I left. We both felt that the present occasion when you, he, & Jamnalalji are all out, should be availed of for completing the bond between Devdas & Lakshmi. We don't know how long Bapu may be free & available to us, and when a similar chance may, if not utilised now, occur again. So, however hurriedly and quietly it may have to be done, we decided that the wedding may be gone through now at Poona. I hope you will approve of the idea. I had only

51

a minute to say goodbye to you and there was no time for me to explain all this. So I am writing now.

I am bringing Lakshmi & Papa when I go to Poona about 12th June and on your concurrence I hope God will enable Lakshmi to become formally & finally your own child on some auspicious day thereafter.

with loving regards, &c
ever, Yours affectionately
Raja
—

communication enjoined. The time is right, as is the venue, Poona, and the residence of Lady Premlilaben Thackersey,[121] 'Parnakuti', where they are all staying.

Ever the one for form, on returning home, CR pens a formal letter to the mother of 'the boy'.

My dear Ba,

. . . We do not know how long Bapu may be free and available to us, and when a similar chance may, if not utilized now, occur again. So, however hurriedly and quietly it may have to be done, we decided that the wedding may be gone through now . . . I hope you will approve of the idea. I am bringing Lakshmi and Papa when I go to Poona about 12th June and with your concurrence I hope God will enable Lakshmi to become formally and finally your own child on some auspicious day thereafter.

With love and regards,
I am, ever yours affectionately,
Raja

———

The wedding takes place on 16 June 1933. Mahadev Desai has summarized the words spoken by Gandhi on the occasion to Devadas (in Gujarati) and to Lakshmi (in Hindi). Desai records that still weak after the twenty-one-day fast, Gandhi takes over five minutes to gather sufficient strength to speak.

Poona
16 June 1933

You have just heard our familiar hymn of 'The True Vaishnava'. I hope you both will ponder over it, and try to live as the true

---

[121] Premlila V. Thackersey, widow of Sir Vithaldas Thackersey, a prominent businessman.

Vaishnava described by the poet-saint Narasinh Mehta. Devdas, you know my expectations about you. May you fulfil them, and I assure you that if you do so all the objections raised against the match will melt away. Since I reached the age of discretion, I have tried to understand the meaning of dharma and live up to it as best as I could. I do not think that in celebrating this marriage anything has been done against the dictates of dharma. Had it been so, you should not have had my blessings and presence at the ceremony.

You are taking upon yourself a grave responsibility, which is proportionate to the great good fortune that has fallen to your lot. Who knew that your wedding would take place under the roof of the pure-souled Lady Thackersey? Who knew that a man of great learning and spotless character like Lakshman Shastri[122] would be found to act as priest? Perhaps, at some future and convenient date, the ceremony would have taken place at the Ashram. But the fast has brought this about. Let the fruit of what was an essentially religious act be also religious. Let the memory of it inspire you to take every step with a full sense of dharma. You know dharma is Truth, and if you keep it as your pole star, it is sure to protect you. What a piece of good fortune for you that you should have so many friends and elders to bless you on the occasion! May you prove worthy of all these blessings! You have today robbed Rajagopalachari of a cherished gem. May you be worthy of it! May you treasure it! She is real Lakshmi. Guard her, protect her as you would Lakshmi, the goddess of the good and beautiful. May you both live long and tread the path of dharma! May you live for dharma and have the courage to lay down your lives, when the occasion comes, for dharma! Let your life from today be a further dedication to service of the

---

[122] Lakshman Shastri Joshi (1901–94) was a scholar of Sanskrit and literary critic in Marathi. He was a key adviser, from the *shastras'* point of view, in Gandhi's fight against untouchability. The selection of the Poona-based Brahmin scholar Joshi as the person who would solemnize the Devadas–Lakshmi wedding was of significance, in the context of orthodox objections voiced in public and private against that inter-caste marriage.

country, and may you never give yourselves to idle pleasure. This is my blessing and my cherished hope and desire.

Devdas, you have always looked upon Rajagopalachari as a respected elder. From today, he is as good as your father. Tender to him the same loyalty and obedient devotion that you have been tendering to me.

To you, Lakshmi, I need not say much. I believe that Devdas will prove himself a worthy husband to you. Ever since I have seen and known you, I have felt that you have justified your name. Let your marriage strengthen, if possible, the bond of affection that has ever been growing between Rajagopalachari and me. I need not emphasize the unique auspices under which the wedding is being celebrated. It is essentially a religious thing, and may it prove to you both a means for the better performance of your duty! I should have had nothing to do with the marriage, had I not known it to be in consonance with religion, and the fruit of the pure tapasya undergone by both of you in order to gain our sanction and blessings, which you have now amply deserved.

It has been a great effort on my part to say these few words. But I thought it was essential for me to bless you, and warn you of the great responsibility you are taking upon yourselves. May God protect you! Only He protects, for He is the father, mother, and friend, everything rolled into one. Let your life be a dedication to the service of the motherland, and of humanity. May you both ever be humble, and may you both walk in fear of God always!

71

By the end of summer, the Raj's attitude under Willingdon has stiffened further. On 1 August, Gandhi, Kasturba and Mahadev are arrested in Gujarat. Their offence: marching together on foot, in violation of existing orders. On 7 August, CR and sixteen other satyagrahis are arrested in

Tiruchengodu for similar action. All are sentenced to six months' rigorous imprisonment and are sent to Coimbatore Central Jail. CR takes up translating the verses of the Kural into English, and studying Sanskrit.

Devadas and Lakshmi too are in for a surprise. On arriving in Delhi in August to take up work in the Hindustan Times, Devadas is served a notice at Hazrat Nizamuddin station. He refuses to abjure civil disobedience, when asked to do so, and is arrested. Lakshmi is cared for by friends, to CR's great relief.

'God always arranges things better than we can ever hope to do with our limited vision,' he writes to Devadas. And to Lakshmi: 'We should be grateful for the wonderfully devoted and affectionate friends that surround us everywhere.'

By January, Devadas has been released. With Lakshmi, he visits CR in jail. Gandhi, on tour in Travancore, writes on 22 January to Ba to say, among other things:

Devdas and Lakshmi will most probably have gone to Delhi now. They went and met Rajaji.

And to Vallabhbhai Patel on the same day:

They visited Raja. He has not written to me after the visit.

72

Before his release in February 1934, CR gets news of Gandhi's Harijan tour through the south to raise money for a Harijan fund and the devastating earthquake[123] that had hit Bihar, twisting much of that region

---

[123] The 1934 Bihar earthquake, one of the worst earthquakes in modern Indian history, left about 30,000 dead. The 8.4 magnitude earthquake occurred on 15 January

*out of shape. CR sends from his jail a telegram of sympathy to Prasad in
his jail. On emerging from the prison gates, CR goes to Tiruppur where
Gandhi, back from a visit to Bihar, has resumed his Harijan tour. One of
the procedures he has adopted is to auction at these meetings the welcome
addresses that are presented to him. Gandhi asks people to contribute to
the Harijan fund and for the Bihar earthquake relief.*

*From 11 to 14 February, he is in CR's ashram. Addressing a public
meeting attended by 5000 persons at Tiruchengodu on 11 February,
he says:*

Let us say with one voice that Harijans are entitled to the same
privileges and rights as caste Hindus are.

I hope you have not forgotten the sufferers in Bihar. Although
it is so very late, I would gladly give some minutes for collections
for Bihar. And while the volunteers collect money, I propose to sell
these addresses.

In a letter to Kasturba written on 13 February, he says:

Ba,

We are in Rajaji's Ashram today. Nearly 250 persons must have
dined here. The same number slept in the place last night . . .
There was a letter from Devdas. He is quite well.

<hr>

1934 at around 2.13 p.m., with the epicentre located in eastern Nepal. Untouchability
being uppermost on his mind, Gandhi said the earthquake was divine retribution for
the practice of untouchability, evoking derisive responses, including one from Tagore.
Rajendra Prasad, then in jail, was released and set up the Bihar Earthquake Relief
Committee, which was able to raise more funds than the official committee chaired
by the viceroy.

Devadas and Lakshmi at their wedding in
Lady Premlila Thackersey's villa 'Parnakuti',
Poona, 1933.

CR with Devadas, Lakshmi and their children, Simla, 1945. From left to right:
Devadas (with camera), Lakshmi, Rajmohan, Tara (with hand on CR's shoulder),
C.R. Narasimhan and Namagiri holding Gopal. On CR's left, Ramchandra.

The Governor General with Prime Minister Nehru and Deputy Prime Minister Vallabhbhai Patel, Government House, New Delhi, 1948.

CR and Nehru with Military Secretary Maj. Gen. B. Chatterjee (behind them in the centre) and other aides-de-camp, Mughal Gardens, New Delhi, 1948.

Governor General C. Rajagopalachari with Prime Minister Jawaharlal Nehru and, behind him, Minister Satyanarayan Sinha, Parliament House, New Delhi, 1949.

CR taking a stroll in Government House, Simla, 1949.

CR and Namagiri, in his Madras home, 1954.

regained strength. It is an issue to which we must give thought. The time is drawing near for taking a decision. Jawaharlal's explosion is not as frightening as it seems from the flames. He had a right to let off steam, which he has exercised.

───

The orthodox assaults on Gandhi's anti-untouchability campaigns, meanwhile, continue. And, here and there, people retaliate. Pandit Lalnath, a staunch upholder, as he sees himself, of Hindu dharma, is attacked by the reformers and Gandhi promptly undertakes a fast lasting one week to atone. The Pyarelal Papers at Teen Murti yield this letter:

'Congress House'
Mount Road, Madras
14 August 1934

My dear Bapu,

I need hardly write anything about the joy of the safe termination of the fast.

It is unthinkable that you should give up the Congress this year. It will be a greater injury to the institution than anything the Government can conceive. Whatever faults there are, are faults arising out of the constitution which you have framed for it and the defects of human nature that you should certainly have known. You may do anything to reform the institution, but you cannot think of leaving it. If you had never come into it, it would have got on somehow, but having come in and taken it into regions into which it would have never ventured but for your being at the helm, you cannot now disembark and leave it to go crash.

The only penance you can do for the defects which you have noticed and which I respectfully submit you have exaggerated is that you should continue to bear the burden of association as long as you are not rendered physically unfit for it.

The Congress, meanwhile, is moving towards a review of its poli
Councils, with the Mahatma not averse to it and Patel, Prasad a
CR inclined to go along with their leader but Jawaharlal Nehru j
opposed to anything except disobedience. The AICC meets in P
Gandhi present and suspends disobedience and approves the prog
of entering legislatures. Jawaharlal, in prison, writes in his diary
decision has 'bowled him over'.

CR is clear he will not enter the legislature himself, but will
glad to assist the Congress's Parliamentary Board headed by Dr
Ansari. Gandhi toys with the idea of withdrawing from active po
and from the Congress, so as not to pressure the organization wit
influence or presence.

Gandhi's letters (in Gujarati) to Vallabhbhai Patel reveal his
most clearly. He writes to his lieutenant on 19 August:

How can I leave the Congress till you and others permit me
Personally, however, I do feel that there is no other way for m
to be obstructing the growth of the Congress. To cling to th
without faith in it or to fail to act according to one's faith–
pitiable and frightful condition to be in! Is it not your duty
the Congress from it? There may be no harm [in my rema
the Congress] so long as I can think of some means of figh
rot, but what can I do if I cannot think of any way except
the Congress? My doing so will rid it of hypocrisy. If the
of the ordinary Congressman is that no distinction need l
between truth and falsehood, violence and non-violence, khac
jagannathi and muslin, then it is best that he should act acce
But that won't be possible till I leave. These restrictions ca
removed with my consent, for I would never consent to their
If the Congress removes them despite my opposition, would
amount to expelling me? Would it be desirable to let things
far? I want to make you, Raja and others think about all thes

If you can come over, we shall discuss them at leisure.
also have to think what I should do in September or afte

I feel that you should be free at least till the Congress session is over. If you disappear now, the problems and issues that we have raised will tear the Congress into pieces. Your unifying presence is necessary at least till the end of the session.

Love,
Raja

73

Gandhi remains firm of will and commences a distancing from Congress politics, which CR describes to an English observer as 'rather in the nature of a judicial separation than a divorce'. Later in the month CR goes to Sevagram to discuss Gandhi's plans and thinking. Gandhi to Vallabhbhai Patel on 26/27 August 1934:

Bhai Vallabhbhai,

. . . Raja arrived suddenly today and was in a great hurry to return. Since I spent a good deal of time with him I am late with the post . . . shall be able to meet.

I have been discussing with Rajaji my intention of leaving the Congress. He has come specially to discuss that. If possible, he wants to run away on Tuesday.

Clear now that the Congress will contest the 1934 elections to the Central Assembly, CR engages himself fully in the task of getting the Congress a clear majority of the seats being contested. The choice for Congress president is also once again pointing to him, and to Rajendra Prasad. CR steps aside. Gandhi writes to Dr B.C. Roy, who is aggrieved at not being included in the CWC:

You know how I have three times suppressed Rajagopalachari, or rather how Rajagopalachari has allowed himself to be suppressed. Rajagopalachari has certainly gained, and if today he is most useful in the parliamentary struggle in the south, I have no doubt it is due to his self-denial.

——

A letter from CR to Gandhi from the vortex of electioneering, in the Pyarelal Papers:

Madras
28 September 1934

My dear Bapu,

Your letter[124] of 26th. I am confident of at least 80 per cent success for the Congress in the elections in this province and Sardar is not right if he thinks that I feel the Justice Party is winning and therefore ask for postponement of the sessions.

But I accept your judgement and Sardar's, regarding choice of evils. We shall do the best we can, especially as you even go to the length of excusing my absence at the Congress.

As regards your retirement, I am somewhat surprised that Vallabhbhai and Rajen babu have surrendered at the first shot. I think that it is most unfortunate that this feeling has come over you at this inopportune juncture. It is unfortunate for the whole nation. Your retirement from Congress will be a suicidal step that will complete the triumph of the Government over the Congress, and that of the Viceroy over you. An intense and irrecoverable feeling of defeatism will spread over the whole nation, and kill political

---

[124] Not in the *Collected Works*.

hope and enterprise.

I can understand the reasons for the step you propose, but the moment chosen for it is so very inopportune that it becomes all wrong. How I wish you could suffer and carry on, anyhow, for some time longer!

You agreed with me and Andrews that there was something in Smuts's message. Congress success at the polls would have strengthened that something. Your retirement ends the chance for any settlement through you, and with you definitely and legally out of the picture, there is no such thing as an honourable settlement in our time.

If you think that you can retire from the Congress now and keep it and yourself both or either politically important, I think you will be surely disappointed.

This is how I feel. You have closed your letter with a line that I should let you have my opinion. I wrote this knowing that you have made up your mind.

Love,
Raja

———

After a tough campaign against the Justice Party, the Congress wins all eleven seats contested by it in Madras Presidency. Patel wires CR:

You have reason to be proud of your marvellous achievement.

74

CR's work on the Congress's Parliamentary Board entails his trying to widen the organization's support base, in this case, with the Liberals (of the Indian Liberal Party) led by Srinivasa Sastri.

Congress House
Mount Road, Madras
11 January 1935

My dear Bapu,

I telegraphed to Mr. Srinivasa Sastri suggesting his drafting formula for a joint manifesto. He has replied:

'Surely initiative belongs to Congress let me watch and hope'

Chandrashanker[125] writes to me that Mr. Vaze[126] also has said the same thing and that Mr. Sastri has written in reply to Rajendrababu[127] also to the same effect namely that the initiative should come from the Congress. I have now wired to Mr. Sastri as follows:

'Initiative will be mine Rajendrababus I want your assistance framing formula suitable yourself and us then will persuade Congress as such expect success'

Please read the resolution of the Servants of India Society which is printed in page 7 of the 'Servant of India' of January 3rd.
The resolutions winds up thus:

'The Servants of India Society is constrained to record its considered opinion that the scheme embodied in the

---

[125] Chandrashanker Pranshankar Shukla, editor of *Harijanbandhu* and author-compiler of valuable books on Gandhi such as *Gandhiji as We Knew Him* (1945), *Incidents of Gandhiji's Life* (1949) and *Reminiscences of Gandhiji by 48 Contributors* (1951).

[126] S.G. Vaze, vice-president of Servants of India Society, Poona, and editor of the *Servant of India*.

[127] The then Congress president, Rajendra Prasad.

Report[128] is wholly unacceptable and that, on the whole, it will be better to remain under the present constitution than to have the new one.'

It seems to me that this language can be adopted by us without any change of word or phrase in framing the resolution for the Assembly. In that case the Liberals must be taken to have fully agreed and there cannot be anything more to be achieved by way of a joint manifesto. It seems to me there is nothing more to be got out of the Liberal party than what we have got in this resolution of the Servants of India Society and Liberal Federation.

I am reaching Delhi[129] on the 15th morning by Grand Trunk Express.

CR

---

[128] After the third session of the Round Table Conference and the Communal Award of 1932, a series of committees went into the constitutional arrangements for India. A White Paper in 1933 set out a first draft of proposals that were to take the shape of the Government of India Act, 1935, which tried to mediate between conservative opinion in England and political impatience in India. While it brought in federal principles with popular participation at the Centre, and provincial autonomy with elected legislatures in the regions, the fact was that the Centre, still in control of foreign affairs and defence, was irremovable by India's people, and was responsible to the British parliament.

[129] This is for a meeting of the CWC, and for discussions with Gandhi who is also taking the opportunity 'to pass', in Gandhi's words, 'a few days at the Harijan Home for which Shri Ghanshyamdas Birla has donated 20 acres of land costing Rs. 30,000'.

The CWC gives the nation a resolution on the proposed silver jubilee celebrations of King George V, in the drafting of which CR's hand is clearly seen. An excerpt:

The Congress has and can have nothing but good wishes for the personal well-being of His Majesty, but the Congress cannot ignore the fact that the rule in India with which His Majesty is naturally identified has been a positive hindrance to the political, moral and material growth of the nation. It now threatens to culminate in a Constitution which, if enforced, promises to exploit the Nation, to drain her of what she still possesses of wealth and to harden her political subjection as has perhaps never been attempted before.

75

The year 1936 is, for CR, one of intolerable suspense, both politically and personally. The Congress has condemned the Government of India Act of 1935 in its integrated shape, but is not unprepared, under protest, to go along with its provisions pertaining to the regions. And then there is the growing divide between the Muslim League and the Congress over its impact, nationally and in the regions. And though in the elections to be held not before 1937 the Congress expects to do well if it contests them, the path ahead is far from clear.

In his ashram, CR is contemplative, sensitive and—irritated. Stung by what seems to him like undue and uninformed interference in the working of the ashram by the Gandhi Seva Sangh, to which it is affiliated, he writes to the Sangh's president Kishorelal Mashruwala: 'You could run the Ashram directly . . . I should be relieved of the charge.'

Political work—he is still president of the Tamil Nadu Congress Committee (TNCC)—has prevented him from attending one of the Sangh's meetings in Wardha, upon which Gandhi virtually ticks him off: 'You must attend these meetings regularly or not be in these bodies at all'.

CR's response is characteristic. He asks Gandhi to relieve him of membership of the board, of the AICC, the CWC, the Congress's Parliamentary Board, the presidentship of the TNCC and the charge of the ashram. Gandhi and several colleagues are shocked and urge him to stay. Congress President Prasad says, 'We cannot do without you'; Vallabhbhai Patel, Govind Ballabh Pant, Aruna Asaf Ali all implore him to reconsider. Gandhi, on being once again told by CR he will not

---

It is, therefore, impossible for the Working Committee to advise any participation in the forthcoming celebrations. At the same time, the Working Committee has no desire by hostile demonstrations to wound the susceptibilities of Englishmen and others who will want to take part in the celebrations. The Working Committee therefore, advises the general public, including Congressmen who may be members of elected bodies, to be satisfied with mere abstention from the events that may be arranged for celebration.

reconsider, yields. 'You may give up posts of responsibility, but you dare
not give up responsibility so long as there is breath in you.'

And so CR is 'free as a bird', except for membership of the
Parliamentary Board from which Patel, its head, does not let him go.

Dividing his time between the ashram and Madras, where his elder
son Krishnaswami is working for The Hindu *and has found a home*
on Bazlullah Road, CR picks up his pen to write a commentary on the
Gita. And pays a visit, much pressed on him by Gandhi, to Wardha
with Lakshmi, now the mother of two children—a girl, Tara, and a boy,
Rajmohan, named 'amalgamationally' to invoke his grandfathers. Twitted
by Gandhi about 'Raj' preceding 'Mohan', CR says to his sambandhi,
'No, Bapu, the name is yours—Mohan. "Raj" is but an adjective.'

By 1937, the political barometer is rising again. CR writes to Mahadev.
Though the letter is pivoted on khadi, it is so clear that politics flutters in
that fabric.

48, Bazlullah Road
Tyagarayanagar
Madras
29 August 1937

My dear Mahadev,

I think you have been so over-worked with writing for the 'Harijan'
that you have ceased to think clearly or you are also having blood
pressure. I am now somehow very anxious about Bapu's blood
pressure. I was not anxious in former days. But what I observed when
I was last at Wardha adds anxiety to present reports. But anxiety is
a sin as stated in the Sermon on the Mount and before that in the
Bhagavad-Gita.

Tell Bapu that I do not write to him because of his blood pressure.

As for your objections to my claim that Khadi is non-party, if I
admit that it is a party symbol how can I ask the permanent public
service to encourage it? But don't make the mistake of thinking that

because I want to ask the permanent service to wear Khadi, I say that it is not a party symbol. I say this because it is not a party symbol.

The whole party may be bound to wear Khadi, but we do not withdraw appeal for Khadi in respect of those who are either non-party men necessarily or men belonging to an opposite party. We want everybody to wear Khadi as we want everybody to give up untouchability. Is untouchability a party symbol because we ask all Congressmen to discard the practice of untouchability? Both Khadi and untouchability are Congress duties, but not exclusive Congress property. Because men recognised us by our Khadi and beat us, Khadi has become dear to us; but all the same Khadi is not that by which we should be recognised and we alone. When once you admit that we want everybody to wear it, it definitely ceases to be a party symbol. I am afraid if you go on as you are doing, you will presently make reed-pens a party symbol, hand pounded rice also a party symbol, and appeal for it in the name of Congress and Congress only, and not allow Deputy Collectors and Sessions Judges to eat hand pounded rice, but just permit them to eat it if they dare to become Congressmen and not otherwise. But tomorrow morning I have to attend to party meetings and day-after-tomorrow to budgets and I have seven boxfuls of Secretariat files to dispose of tonight. So I shall stop.

Just one word more. With our poor organisation we shall be always short of Khadi, but we cannot stop appealing. It is only when there is great pressure of demand that we produce. Because of the great Congress successes there is a great demand for Khadi now, but that does not mean that I should cease in my endeavours to make Khadi non-party.

You will have a greater surprise presently. I want to make the National Flag non-party! Even those who are not Congressmen may carry the National Flag and hoist it in their house! I suppose you would be shocked. Even Buddha's father had to recognise that Buddha belonged to the whole world. The father's ownership ceases as soon as the child is born.

Tell Bapu that his letter about Hindi Prachar Sabha has reached and been read by me.

Yours affly.

Raja

Just saw Press Telegram indicating improvement in Bapu's health.

76

Patel urges CR in the latter part of 1936 to agree to become Congress president, succeeding Rajendra Prasad. Satyamurti, TNCC president, is enthusiastic about this. CR declines again. CR, endorsing Gandhi, then offers the 'thorny crown' to Jawaharlal Nehru. The offer is accepted and, though differing over many issues with the 'old guard', Nehru appoints Patel, CR and Prasad to his Working Committee.

With the Congress deciding to contest the elections in 1937, CR is asked to enter the fray. He does not want to head TNCC again and supports the re-election of Satyamurti who throws himself into the campaign. With T. Prakasam, Satyamurti gives fifty-eight-year-old CR, who takes up a 'guiding hand' role, yeoman support. In the elections held in 1937, the Congress scores a convincing victory in Madras as indeed it does in the rest of the country. The Congress wins 159 seats, the Justice Party 16, the Muslim League 10. CR himself wins the Madras University constituency handsomely.

The Working Committee meets in Wardha in July to discuss the question of office acceptance under the new act. CR argues in favour. The formation of Congress ministries is approved by the CWC on 7 July 1937.

After a moment of suspense for all, disappointment for many and elation for many more, CR, who had earlier assumed the leadership of the Congress Legislature Party, is chosen by the Congress, including Gandhi, to be the first Congress premier of Madras. S. Satyamurti, the stalwart of the Congress in the legislatures, both at the Centre and in Madras, steps poignantly aside. The moment is his, the office is CR's. To widespread dismay, Satyamurti is not even included in the cabinet.

The ministries are to last until the outbreak of the Second World War. The one in Madras led by CR proves to be exemplary. Decades later, a British historian is to record: 'If Mr C. Rajagopalachari of Madras was the most distinguished figure among Congress Premiers, he had worthy colleagues in Pandit G.B. Pant of the United Provinces and Mr B.G. Kher of Bombay.'

The letter that follows is written by Premier Rajagopalachari to the Mahatma, a circumstance that could scarce have been imagined when their acquaintance began. It deals with the subject of Hindustani being taught in Madras. CR's government has introduced the subject for study from standards six to eight in 125 schools. Failure in the subject at examinations will not block promotion, but study of the subject is intra-curricular. 'It is chutney on the leaf,' CR explains the scheme, 'taste it or leave it.' But E.V. Ramaswami Naicker and the Justice Party attack the scheme. And Gandhi writes to CR about it.

24 December 1938

My dear C.R.,

Sir Radhakrishnan was here yesterday. He said that anti-Hindi agitation was on the increase. He had suggested to you that you should accept a conscience clause, exempting those children from learning Hindi whose parents stated in writing that they had a conscientious objection to their children learning Hindi. I suppose you remember that such a suggestion was made in Harijan in the initial stages of the agitation. I think that it is not too late to give effect to it.

It should not matter to you even though the concession may be interpreted as concession to unreasonable agitation. You will do what appears to you to be best.

What about separation of Andhra as a separate province? You had made some statement that you were moving in the matter. Are you? How are you keeping otherwise?

Love.
Yours,
Bapu

CR responds:

Bazlullah Road
Tyagarayanagar
Madras
28 December 1938

My dear Bapu,

Your letter of 24th just reached my hands. Radhakrishnan[130] scribbled a note to me after meeting you and he had indicated your mind in this matter.

This agitation is a mere symptom of the disease. The castes are there and the caste hatred is there. Political ambitions frustrated make the leadership. All this you know. But the point is that I am thoroughly convinced that if Hindi did not come in handy, it would have been the toddy tappers, or the schoolmasters or the non-Brahmin tobacco-merchants or something else. Like the scientists that discovered truths and gave weapons to the warmongers you have given 'Satyagraha' to the world, to the curers of social and

---

[130] Sarvepalli Radhakrishnan (1888–1975), philosopher-statesman, the first vice-president of India (1952–62) and, succeeding President Rajendra Prasad, the second President of India (1962–67).

political diseases, as well as the mischief-makers. We cannot help or even regret it, any more than we can blame science for the poison gas or the bombs.

You know very well, I believe, that there is no real 'compulsion' in the scheme, though our opponents have given that name to it. There is no penalty involved. A boy may not pass or get any marks and it will not affect his promotion. The only feature about it is that it is intra curricular and not outside hours. As the Director of Public Instruction Mysore recently explained, making an important subject like this 'optional' means making it an alternative to some other important subject, which is not desirable. As regards the 'Conscience' clause (which is a misnomer for the kind of objection raised), my objection to it is not pride or prestige—I know this is not an honest man's objection—it is the grave apprehension I have, that in the surrounding circumstances and difficulties of our so-called self-government, the step will add to the mischief of the direct action method which is being sought to be applied against every step of the government or any of its administrative departments. This will just be used immediately to incite parties to resort to this method for everything, if they want to force the Govt to accept their demand.

I am prepared to fight it out, and that is the true test of Satyagraha. The people, that is, the common folk, do not want me to yield. There are some easy going politicians, specially the Brahmins, who want me to yield or do anything to get rid of the trouble and have cheap power through me as they imagine. They would ask me just in the same way to give up temple entry, to give up prohibition, and to give up tenancy reform and in fact to give up anything but Government.

I think giving anything like victory to Ramaswami Naicker now would be fatal to the progress of self-government and make Swaraj an impossibility in our land of castes and 'minorities'. My patience has not been tired out, and I shall be ready to give up government if I fail, but I do not wish to yield to the misuse of Satyagraha.

Bear with me,

Love,
Raja

77

Congress ministries resign after intense cogitation and consultation. CR's ministry, hugely popular and equally respected, has done twenty-seven months in office. Gandhi issues the following statement to the World Press news agency:

23 OCTOBER 1939

IN ANSWER TO (YOUR) INQUIRY (I MAY SAY) THE CONGRESS HAS DEMANDED NO CONSTITUTIONAL CHANGE DURING WAR. ITS DEMAND IS FOR DECLARATION THAT BRITAIN'S WAR AIMS NECESSARILY INCLUDE INDIA'S INDEPENDENCE ACCORDING TO THE CHARTER FRAMED BY HER ELECTED REPRESENTATIVES AFTER WAR. THIS DECLARATION SHOULD BE ACTED UP TO DURING WAR TO THE UTMOST EXTENT POSSIBLE.

THE MINORITIES QUESTION IS A BOGEY. NOT THAT IT DOES NOT EXIST BUT ITS PROPER SOLUTION CAN ONLY COME OUT OF THE PROPOSED CONSTITUENT ASSEMBLY. THE BURDEN OF SOLVING THE TANGLE RESTS NOT ON BRITAIN BUT ON THE CONSTITUENT ASSEMBLY. ACCORDING TO INDIAN OPINION HINDU–MUSLIM QUESTION IS THE DIRECT PRODUCT OF BRITISH RULE. THE LEAST THE CONGRESS COULD DO WAS TO WITHDRAW THE CONGRESS MINISTERS FROM PROVINCIAL ADMINISTRATIONS.

FURTHER ACTION WILL WHOLLY DEPEND UPON BRITAIN'S HANDLING OF THE CRISIS. THE CONGRESS HAS LEFT THE DOOR OPEN TO BRITAIN TO MEND THE MISTAKE.

Harijan, 28 October 1939

———

CR writes:

48, Bazlullah Road
Tyagarayanagar
Madras
28 October 1939

My dear Mahadev,

I tendered resignation of our Ministry at 2 p.m. yesterday. I did not think it necessary to wait for any further instructions from your end because I knew there would be considerable delay in getting at the necessary papers at Wardha, and for me at the same time to find any responsible person at the 'phone at Wardha, while you were necessarily busy talking at Segaon. I did not consider it advisable further to postpone the business when there was nothing really substantial to consider as new matter. Of course, if a further genuine invitation comes to Bapu to help reconsideration of the whole policy in regard to the Central Government, the position may be different, but we could not possibly postpone action awaiting such a call.

The Governor is going to see a number of persons to consider whether a new Government could be formed under the Government of India Act before taking the step to use the powers of proclamation to suspend the provisions. This ceremony may be completed on Monday.

Now that I am freer than I was before I should like to convey to Bapu my thoughts in regard to further national action. Whatever may be the motives and the deft exploitation by the British people of the Hindu-Muslim cleft, the fact must be recognised that today the ablest and most disinterested leaders of the Muslim community have led their entire people to feel that they stand apart and must continue to stand apart from the Hindu population. It is not flatterers and office seekers, but a man like Jinnah that have made up the Muslim mind in this direction, and we cannot afford to deceive ourselves by proceeding on the assumption that the Muslim leaders are the tools of the British. The British may use them, but the decision is their own, and cannot be brushed aside as merely a corollary of British wickedness.

The problem, therefore, is whether any national programme of resistance directed against the British can be effective in dissolving this opposition of the Musalmans or will succeed in drawing them into it. I feel very strongly that any hope of that kind is vain. Any resistance on our part and any modicum of success in that programme will only widen the cleft. We may secure even cent per cent success in the programme against the British, but it cannot solve the problem as against the Muslim leaders and their solid following, unless indeed we envisage complete anarchy and civil war left entirely to ourselves by the rest of the world.

If we take it for granted that we must secure the willing consent of the Musalmans for a partnership in self-government, it seems to me that civil resistance against the British by one community from which the other community religiously keeps out will only increase the differences and the hatred, even as office acceptance has tended to bring about. Any sacrifice, whatever may be its grandeur, on the part of one community definitely known to be undergone with the object of gaining political power will only amount to a yajna performed by some sect for the purpose of securing power which the other community interprets to be a domination and oppression exercised against it. The whole business will seem to the Musalmans like Indrajit's Tapas to get weapons to defeat Rama, Asuric Tapas as in Gita XVI if they thought in terms of the Gita!

We must, therefore, it seems to me, devise a programme which will rouse not the jealousy or the fear, but the immediate appreciation of the Musalmans. I do not know what kind of programme can at all be invented for this and whether it can be combined with any action against the British either as a mechanical mixture or as a chemical combination. I feel that it would be a futile sacrifice, more or less like animal sacrifice, to carry on a programme of suffering which is bound to be from the outset taken as a subtle invention of the devil directed against the Musalman community.

Yours affectionately,
Raja

Gandhi responds:

Segaon
Wardha
30 October 1939

My dear C.R.,

Yours to Mahadev of 28th was duly read by me. I agree with every word of what you say. I had anticipated you as you will see from Harijan. Keep well. We—Rajendra Prasad and I—are off to Delhi, I hope, only for a few hours.

Love.
Bapu

Shri C. Rajagopalachari
48 Bazulullah Road
Thyagarayanagar
Madras

78

The 'National Government' idea is talked of, and Congress–League parleys dwell on it, cautiously one day, optimistically another. As Rajmohan Gandhi says in The Rajaji Story, *'He had greatly enjoyed his Premiership, and it was obvious that if a settlement with the Raj led to a national government, CR would have a key position in it.' But such a settlement is nowhere in sight. And when at Gandhi's instance the programme of 'individual satyagraha' is launched, Vinoba Bhave— chosen by Gandhi to be the first satyagrahi—is the first to be arrested under War Regulations, followed by Nehru, who is arrested even before he could utter an unlawful phrase, then Patel and, not much later, by CR. Arrested from his Bazlullah Road home on 3 December 1940, he is awarded one year. 'No one will rejoice more,' the sentencing magistrate Abbas Ali declares in open court, 'if peace is declared and Rajaji returns from jail and occupies the high position he held with such distinction.'*

Taken first to his familiar Vellore jail, then to Trichy, the now sixty-two-year-old CR tries to readjust to being His Majesty's guest. He holds classes on the Gita, the Kural and Shakespeare. Satyamurti is among his fellow prisoners.

A letter to Mahadev from Trichy jail describes the prison scene.

21 February 1941
Trichinopoly

My dear Mahadev,

Narasimhan to whom I am writing my periodical permitted letter will send this on to you. Please tell Bapu my love, I got his sweet little note sent through Narasimhan. Evergreens are precious and stand all the 'delays' of prison correspondence. I am quite happy, tell him. I am spinning and reading and completely avoid thinking of politics. I read with a good company of scholars and others, every day some Valmiki, some Kural, some Bhagavad Gita and some Tamil holy Vaishnavite books. 82 beautiful chapters of Valmiki are over.

So also 30 chapters of Kural, and a few hundreds of verses of the Alwars (Tamil saintly Vaishnavites). The Gita has been done once rapidly and again taken up for reading with Shankara and Ramanuja: What a lot of hard nuts one finds! The simple faith of good men formed in the Alwars' writings is like honey. But what avails it to a hard heart like what I have!

I have re-read a few plays, Shakespeare, with some young boys. What a great man this ancient giant was!

My late colleague Harijan minister Muniswami Pillay is working hard spreading the practice of the charkha among us. He is propagandist, saint and engineer combined. He is my next bed and looks after me like a mother. So also some others including Dr Rajan and Bapineedu. Satyamurti is well, but does not get as much sleep as he should. I was glad to learn from Kripalani that Bapu was happy and fit.

Love to you and the gang there.

Raja

79

His prison term over, with a two-month remission, in October 1941, CR meets Gandhi in Sevagram. Their perceptions differ. CR is for suspending the campaign and 'giving Britain another chance'. Not so, Gandhi. Britain will offer nothing worthwhile to India, he says. Nehru and Patel are with the leader. Besides, for the Mahatma, the issue of ahimsa versus the war is not theoretical.

'We keep our face turned steadily in the direction of ahimsa,' says CR in Lucknow, 'but . . . the defence of India is a case to be treated as an exception.' After Pearl Harbor, CR seems to have a point. Meeting at Bardoli, the CWC says the Congress will offer Britain its cooperation to the Allies if India's freedom is declared. But CR is not for that condition. He is almost becoming a war leader. After the Wardha meeting of the

AICC where he speaks for seventy-five minutes, arguing for cooperation with the defence effort, Gandhi says: 'I have said for some years and say it now that not Rajaji but Jawaharlal will be my successor.'

CR's interest in the establishment of a national administration at the Centre in this hour of battle leads him to concede the Muslim League's claim over 'certain areas' and to seek the League's support for a popular government in Madras. CR's colleagues are astonished and some of them, like Patel, furious. Gandhi is not. 'I am wholly opposed to him,' he says, 'but I hold Rajaji has acted in a wholly Constitutional manner.'

CR meets Jinnah and gives Gandhi a report in Sevagram, following up a conversation with this written account:

Sevagram
2 February 1942

My dear Bapu,

I have already given you an account of the conversations I had with Mr Jinnah last week. I write this in order that you may have the matter in a more precise form. It is needless to say that Mr. Jinnah has not authorised me to put anything in writing on his behalf.

Mr. Jinnah appreciated the object of my visit viz., that though I had no authority for any kind of negotiation nor any message from any one to be conveyed to him, I went to him in my individual capacity to know from him first-hand whether the stand I took in regard to the solution of the Congress–League differences was one which in Mr. Jinnah's opinion could settle the problem and evoke a useful response from his side, and therefore I could legitimately press it on the Congress for acceptance.

As a result of the talks, I am satisfied that Mr Jinnah is genuinely desirous of a Congress League settlement and would welcome negotiations for that purpose. But I believe there is no useful purpose to be served by meeting him if the principle of the claim for separation of Muslim areas is not accepted.

I explained my proposal in precise terms to him viz., that the Congress should accede to the right of separate sovereignty to areas wherein the majority of the population are Muslims subject to the following:

1. The present provincial boundaries are not to be the basis, but contiguous districts wherein the population is a Muslim majority are to be marked out.
2. After the war is over, the wishes of the people of these areas are to be ascertained and given effect to in this regard.
3. The Congress does not by this acceptance of the right of separation give up the right of dissuading the people concerned against the separation, but definitely accepts it, should the same be persisted in and the verdict is given by the inhabitants in favour of separation.
4. The voting should be of all the people in these areas and not only of the Muslims.

If this position of mine is accepted by Gandhiji, he will ask the League Working Committee to reconsider its own resolution on the subject, adopted during the Cripps negotiation. If a Congress-League settlement is reached on this basis, Mr. Jinnah and the League will join in a united demand for Independence and elimination of all British authority after the war and for a provisional Government of India in the interim period along the lines taken up by the Congress.

As regards the States, I did not have any talks with him on the subject, but Mr. Jinnah is of opinion that the problem of the States had better not be taken up for solution now, as it would hold up everything.

I do not see that for the interim Provisional Government of India, the problem of the States needs to be solved. But I believe that Mr. Jinnah would not object if other things are settled, to a general policy that we should both cooperate in the demand for Constitutional forms of government in States.

Mr. Jinnah is positive that after separation as contemplated by him both Indias should bind themselves to defend each other against all aggression from outside.

Yours sincerely,
C. Rajagopalachari

80

Answering a reader's question, Gandhi writes in Harijan:

QUESTION BOX

The Difference

Q. You have repeated in your interview to the Press in Bombay what you have said often that nothing can prevent the Muslims from having what they want unless the objecters would fight over the issue. What is the difference between you and Shri Rajagopalachari's attitude?

A. Though he has quoted me in his support I see the same difference between him and me that there is between chalk and cheese. He yields the right of secession now to buy unity in the hope of keeping away the Japanese. I consider the vivisection of India to be a sin. My statement amounts to the enunciation of the proposition that I cannot prevent my neighbour from committing a sin. Shri Rajagopalachari would be party in the sin, if the neighbour chooses to commit it. I cannot be party. What is more, I am firmly of opinion that there is no unity whilst the third party is there to prevent it. It created the artificial division and it keeps it up. In its presence both Hindus and Muslims and for that matter all seemingly conflicting or disgruntled interests and elements will look to it for support and will get it.

Their interest is greater than the independence of their country.
No one need throw my other statement in my face, viz., that there
is no independence without unity. I do not withdraw a word of it.
It is an obvious truth. From its contemplation I have discovered the
formula of inviting the British power to withdraw. Their withdrawal
does not by itself bring independence. It may induce unity or it
may lead to chaos. There is also the risk of another power filling
in the vacancy if it is there. If, however, the withdrawal is orderly
and voluntary the British not only gain a moral height but secure
the ungrudging friendship of a great nation. I wish all conflicting
elements and interests will make a combined effort to rid India of
foreign domination. If they do not, any understanding with them
will be like a house built on sand. Fear of the Japanese occupation
of India has blinded C. R. to the obvious truth. Independence
sheds all fear—fear of the Japanese, of anarchy, and of the wrath of
the British lion.

Sevagram, 18 May 1942

*The criticism comes at a time when CR is also being targeted by the
blinkered nationalists. At Madurai, while addressing a big meeting,
violent disturbers throw a missile at him.* The Hindu *reports: 'He
jumped into the crowd of hostile demonstrators and declared "You want to
attack me? Come on, here I am."'*

Gandhi writes him the following letter:

Sevagram
Wardha
23 May 1942

My dear C.R.,

So Laxmi has passed first class! This is mere introduction.

Though we differ as poles asunder, my heart goes out to you in
your stand against hooliganism at your meetings.

I found in Bombay it was no use my making any attempt to
see Q.A.[131] Moreover he was not there. You know you are to
come here almost monthly to rest here and be free from the care
of attending meetings.

Love.

Bapu

—⁓—

*CR responds, blending the political with the personal. It is written
by a devotee who has given his heart to the Master, not his powers of
reasoning. Nor the autonomy of political action.*

As at 48, Bazlullah Road
Tyagarayanagar
Madras
29 May 1942

My dear Bapu,

By the same post that brought the Harijan from which you hurled
chalk and cheese and sin against me came your sweet letter brimful
of love that is eternal. I am in the train moving back towards Madras.
I have to do Erode and Salem having finished Coimbatore last night
and then reach Madras on 31st. After Madura there have been no
incidents anywhere.

Lakshmi's first class[132] is a good thing if only because it gave you
a kind of thrill and pleasure. I particularly liked the high percentage

---

[131] Quaid-e-Azam M.A. Jinnah.

[132] His daughter, a mother of three children now, had just passed her Intermediate
(or tenth standard) exam.

of marks she got in Sanskrit. It is good for the children to discuss their mother's passing exams!

We are 'poles asunder' you say. Not so, I feel. You will come to me one day! I know your mode of thought and understand what you mean by 'sin' and such phrases, but it is for the ordinary people a phrase that increases confusion and protects and fosters prejudice.

Some people think I quote you to get moral strength for myself. I do so to controvert, and treating it like scripture. I do not give you the right to explain it away. I want you to think of the joint family basis which you have expressly laid down. However, keep back your consent—give me your love always.

Raja

Gandhi replies:

My dear CR,

Yours. Nothing will delight me more than to come near to you than you to me. It seems to me that the time has come for you to come here and convert me before you go further with your own propaganda. It is ugly to find ourselves talking at each other. I suggest that we talk to each other. It would be a great tragedy if you cannot convert your best friends whose love you don't doubt.

Love,
Bapu

20 May 1942

Chi. Lakshmi,

You have passed in the first division. I am glad. Keep up the progress.

Blessings from
Bapu

81

Gandhi writes in Harijan:

There is no doubt that Rajaji is handling a cause which has isolated him from his colleagues. But his worst enemy will not accuse him of any selfish motive behind the extraordinary energy with which he has thrown himself into the controversy of which he is the author. It reflects the greatest credit on him. He is entitled to a respectful hearing. His motive is lofty. It is a noble thing to strive for Hindu-Muslim unity, equally noble to strive to ward off the Japanese intrusion. In his opinion the two are intertwined.

Hooliganism is no answer to his argument. The disturbances at his meetings are a sign of great intolerance. Evolution of democracy is not possible if we are not prepared to hear the other side. We shut the doors of reason when we refuse to listen to our opponents or having listened make fun of them. If intolerance becomes a habit, we run the risk of missing the truth. Whilst with the limits that nature has put upon our understanding we must act fearlessly according to the light vouchsafed to us, we must always keep an open mind and be ever ready to find that what we believed to be truth was, after all, untruth. This openness of mind strengthens the truth in us and removes the dross from it, if there is any. I plead therefore with all who are disturbing Rajaji's meetings not to do so but to give him a patient and respectful hearing to which he is entitled.

The reader knows that I hold Rajaji to be in the wrong. He is creating a false atmosphere. He does not believe in Pakistan nor do the nationalist Muslims and others who concede the right of separation or secession. They and Rajaji say that that is the way to wean the Muslim League from the demand for separation. I am surprised that many Muslims rejoice over a concession of doubtful value. I see nothing but seeds of further quarrel in it. It should be enough to state the proposition that nothing can prevent the Muslim League from having it if the Muslims really want it. They will take it by the vote or the sword unless they will submit to arbitration. But all this can only happen when the British Power is entirely withdrawn and the Japanese menace has abated. Till then there is neither Pakistan nor Hindustan or any other 'stan'. It is today Englishtan and may be tomorrow Japanistan, if we do not take care. If all who consider India to be their home now and for ever will pull their full weight to deliver it from the present and the impending peril, and when both the perils are finally removed, it will be time to talk of Pakistan and other 'stan's and to come to an amicable decision or fight. No third party will or should decide our fate. It should be reason or the sword.

Rajaji's method leads us to the blind alley unless his admirable and patriotic persistence opens a way unknown to him or any of us.

Whatever the fate of different opinions, my plea is for mutual toleration and respect.

Sevagram, 24 May 1942
Harijan, 31 May 1942

Meanwhile, a khadi issue intervenes.

Madras
8 June 1942

My dear Bapu,

I was shocked to receive a letter from Ramanathan this morning in these terms. I have sent herewith an unexpurgated copy. I do not wish the AISA to lose Ramanathan. Jajuji cannot find a better man for the job here. I am sad over this development. I had hope that Muniswami Pillay might be good enough for full charge later on. But meanwhile I had hoped that Ramanathan would be given all encouragement and that he would be made to feel that he is fully trusted and liked, as he should be. It will be a tragedy if this misunderstanding must end in his resignation. I have not replied to him.

Love,
Raja

All India Spinners Association
Tirupur, 7th June 1942

My dear Sir,

Your tour programme is not announced in the papers. I take it you are not going to Andhra immediately, as you proposed. I am very sorry to inform you that I shall have to resign from the A.I.S.A. I have not done so yet because I feel I should take your permission before doing so. Because you insisted upon my taking up this job, I did so with pleasure. During the year and a half that I have again spent in Khadi Service I have done a few things of which I do feel proud. The entire cadre of Khadi service has been reshuffled and a lot of new blood let in. Account keeping and inspection are as perfect as may be expected in any such organisation. I have built up a workshop which you so kindly declared open, which is unique of its kind in all India. Village centres have been reorganised and will be able to stimulate production almost without limit. I am blowing my own trumpet because I feel sad at heart at the thought that my very success seems to have excited envy and disgust at the headquarters instead of elation and sympathy. I cannot get on with Mr. Jaju who is poisoning Bapu's mind against me. Mr. Jaju has employed Mr.

R. Ramaswami, to go about the province, creating factions
and writing malicious reports against me which Mr. Jaju not
only takes as gospel truth without even asking what I have
to say, but he reads out these falsehoods to Bapu who has
written to me that he is disturbed at my conduct. I do not
wish to write more of my woes and worry you, because you
are already worried enough. But I have told you enough to
let you know that I cannot get on in the A.I.S.A. I shall send
the resignation after hearing from you.

Yours sincerely,
(sd.) S. Ramanathan

82

*Satyamurti causes and figures in another exchange preserved among
Pyarelal's Gandhi Papers at Teen Murti. Satyamurti's letters (see
Annexure VII) had been dictated by him to his daughter, Lakshmi (later,
Lakshmi Krishnamurti).*

Sevagram
Wardha
C.P.
6/7 June 1942

My dear C.R.,

Here is a typical letter from Satyamurti—you will know what weight
to give to it.

Love.
Bapu

7 June 1942

This was overlooked yesterday. Meanwhile I have your two letters. You will come when you can. Your argument makes no appeal to any of us. Surely they are not all blinded by my reactions. Anyway you have to reason with them. I am glad the depression is leaving you.

Love.
Bapu

———

Madras
10 June 1942

My dear Bapu,

I am returning Satyamurti's letters as they should be among your permanent papers.

These letters undoubtedly make me angry. But I do not regret whatever charity I was capable of and showed towards this man. These fresh experiences in the possible variations of human character are painful. I am not a very good man, but I dislike this experience. He is working hard to save you from me. You can guess what he must be doing or wish to do here.

Thank you for reiterating to him your belief in my patriotism! What I claim is that it is truer, even in an objective sense, than you would allow! I see no hope in your ideas as to what has to be done now. I see no plan of any value in the Congress timetable. What I say would, if you only accepted it, produce immediate fruit and strength to the nation. But I cannot make you accept it!

Love,
Raja

83

In July of 1942, K. Kamaraj Nadar, the thirty-nine-year-old
president of the TNCC asks CR to show cause within fifteen days
why disciplinary action should not be taken against him for carrying on
propaganda against Congress resolutions. Gandhi too advises CR to sever
connections with the Congress and carry on his campaign from outside
'with all zeal and ability'. He adds that Patel wants CR to vacate his
seat in the Assembly as well.

CR writes a spirited reply to Kamaraj 'as one who knows the value
of discipline as well as the need for liberty of thought in a national
organisation'.

But he resigns, of course, sending this wire to Gandhi.

Sevagram
Wardhaganj
8 July 1942

Gandhiji

Please give Maulanasahib[133] this I resign hereby Congress. Am also
resigning assembly membership

Rajagopalachari

84

This entry is of a CR letter that is unavailable—an absent presence—
which must have been sent immediately after the telegram. Its contents
and its impact can be divined from the reply it receives.

---

[133] Maulana Azad, Congress president at the time.

Sevagram
20 July 1942

My dear C.R.,

I was about to write to you when your letter came.

Of course I understand and appreciate the exquisite consideration running through your letter. I invite you all four to come here and pass out your love and argument to wean me from what appears to be an error. Any way your monthly visit is due. You can come any day you like.

What I wanted to write to you about was this. Why don't you form a league with Muslim friends to propagate your idea of settlement. Have you seen Q.A.'s reply to my note? So you accept the definition of Pakistan? What is the common idea about Independence? Surely you should have a common understanding over fundamentals before you come to an agreement.

Let not your fear of the Japs betray you into a worse state of things. But more of this when you come.

Love to you all,
Bapu

85

Quit India follows shortly thereafter, with CR completely out of it. Gandhi is arrested along with the entire Working Committee. With Kasturba by his side, Gandhi fasts in his Aga Khan Palace Prison in Poona for three weeks from 10 February 1943 in response to the charge made against him by the Raj that he had condoned if not actually organized violence and that he was secretly plotting with the Japanese. Family are selectively allowed to meet Gandhi, as is CR.

He meets him for four days, talking 'both seriously and lightly', as
CR informs the press.

During these conversations emerges the outline of what comes to be
called the Rajaji Formula for a settlement between the Congress and the
League. CR writes it down for Gandhi to read. Gandhi does so and
signifies his assent.

CR follows up on it, meeting Jinnah in Bombay.

Meanwhile, Kasturba Gandhi's health is failing. She succumbs
to her illness, a prisoner of the British government, on 21 February
1944. CR is in Madras. Pyarelal has preserved the letter CR writes
to Gandhi:

> 48, Bazlullah Road
> Tyagarayanagar
> Madras
> 25 February 1944

My dear Bapu,

I have not found the nerve to say anything publicly about it, but I
wrote to Devadas a letter which I hope he has got.

Ba has found final release. If there be any truth in the Hindu
Dharma she has lived up to it and fulfilled her earthly trial. You
have been nearly as foolish as Harishchandra and she has not lagged
behind Chandramati! There is no life-story in our generation where
woman has stood her trial so much in the manner of our Hindu
public and traditions as Ba has triumphantly done. The loss of dear
ones is common in the world and it is foolish for me to try my hand
at consolation with one like you. I am glad Harilal and Manu were
there with Devadas at the time of the final fading away. I learnt the
news at 2:30 the same night.

> Love,
> C.R.

86

*March 1946 sees important political developments. Elections are once again
in the air. The intrepid Satyamurti is no more. CR, out of the Congress,
is again asked to re-enter the electoral fray. Patel wants him back. But
the equation with Kamaraj, twenty-five years younger than him, and as
many times more powerful within the party, is not easy. Gandhi travels
southwards and, when in Madras, hears of rumour mills insinuating that
CR has arranged the visit to reinstall himself as premier. Disgusted, CR
says he will have none of election politics. Gandhi uses the word 'clique' to
dispel the whisper campaign. The word is controversial. Gandhi writes:*

About Rajaji

I have read Shri Kamaraja Nadar's Press message. I am sorry.

I can easily be silent, but the cause may suffer. He says he is my
follower. In that case he should have referred to me before rushing to
the Press and certainly before resigning. I have intentionally described
myself as a Bhangi. In the man–made social ladder I want to be at
the bottom. I would like Shri Kamraj to cease to be a Nadar and
to become a Bhangi with me and then in all humility withdraw his
resignation. Whatever it is legally or not, the Provincial and Working
Committees alone can decide. Morally it is perfectly possible, if he
himself feels he has hurt himself and the cause by resigning. Then
he will rejoin the difficult post (if it is legally possible) as a strong
man. He was weak in resigning. He says he prevented four others
from following him. It was well that they did not resign.

Why worry about the use of the word 'clique'? In spite of all
my love for the English language, it is a foreign tongue for me and
I am as likely as not to make mistakes in using it. Of course, I have
used the word 'clique' deliberately. I must not withdraw it. This is its
dictionary meaning: 'small exclusive party'. I know that there is such
a clique in Tamil Nadu against Rajaji. I am unable definitely to name
one single person in it. No one need wear the cap unless it fits him.

There are many cliques in the Congress organization as even in the best managed organizations in the world. The fewer their number the better the organization.

Were I not challenged at the time that I was touring in the South, I would have been silent.

I must admit that I did not talk to those who were with me in that special train. I was buried in my work which was divided between meetings at frequent stoppages and writing whilst the train was in motion. And let the public know that those who are physically nearest to me have to be so forbearing that they would not come near me and interfere with my work. Such has been the usage during my stormy life. My own children thus get the least of me. Aruna Asaf Ali came for two days to see me fresh from her hiding place and was so forbearing that she had of me only as much as she could during my walks.

Sevagram, 15 February 1946
Harijan, 24 February 1946

But there is banter as well.

Poona
5 March 1946

My dear C. R.,

I must write this in what has become as good as your mother tongue. I have written to you more than once in Hindustani and, when you wanted top lines, I gave you them. I have developed a dislike for writing to an Indian in any but the national language. So I write to Sastriar and Bidhan in Hindustani.

So much for the preface.

Why do you worry about events? Do your duty, never think of results: Let things take their course. It is enough, you and I have acted right.

Of course I was bound to write about you what I felt. I would never have excused myself, if, when challenged, I had kept silent. It gave us all an insight into man's thoughtlessness. You must, therefore, cheer up and get well quickly. Tell me when you are coming.

While I was closing this, I got your love letter. Do write to me in Tamil. *Anbu* I knew. What is *udan*?[134]

Bapu

11 March 1946

My dear C. R.,

It is just 6.15 a. m. I am to be off to Bombay by 7.30 a. m.

If we discover a mistake, must we continue it? We began making love in English—a mistake. Must it express itself only by repeating the initial mistake? You have cake and eat it also.

Love is love under a variety of garbs—even when the lovers are dumb. Probably it is fullest when it is speechless. I had thought, under its gentle unfelt compulsion, you will easily glide into Hindustani and thus put the necessary finishing touch to your service of Hindustani. But let it be as you will, not I.

I do not like your despondence. You have to be thoroughly well. Why not come to me? I hope to return in five or six days.

This tamasha will vanish leaving the water of life cleaner for the agitation. If it does not, what then?

Anbudan.
Bapu

---

[134] *Anbudan* means 'with love'.

Madras
19 March 1946

My dear Bapu,

Srinivasa Aiyangar's daughter is . . .

I am doing my best to correct the stomach. I am not giving it up. I have not yet succeeded. These internal membrane troubles elude the skill of even naturopathists. You have to adopt a diet that reduces vital supply and the vicious circle goes round. But why need I explain all this to you? You know all about it. However I am trying to overcome my troubles.

I have no ideas of going to Poona. I presume you will shortly move to Delhi for another chapter of nature-cure! I think all parties are in a more chastened mood this time and we may see something come out of it.

The temple entry legislation you know has been the subject of contest in courts, (the Madura temple opening being the cause of action). Our legislation has been contested on the ground of being ultra vires of the Government. All the courts so far have affirmed our power as exercised when we were in office. It is now before the Federal Court and Sir Alladi has just returned after arguing it for us. He says he has done well and the decision in our favour will be confirmed. But one does not know until judgement is given. I understand the 'orthodox' representatives.

Saw Zafrullah in his house and represented to him it was oppression of minorities. The Federal Court consists of an English Lawyer, Sir Patrick Spence, Sir Zafrullah and Varadacharya (of Madras Bar). The last is a sanatanist. It would be a terrible thing if things were upset after nine years of working. . . .

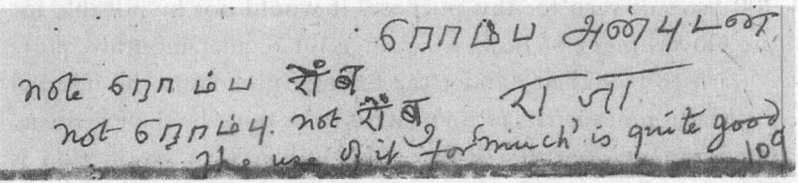

87

CR is inducted into the interim government headed by Jawaharlal Nehru. In 1919, when CR first wrote to the Mahatma, he could not have thought that he would be writing this kind of a letter to him, on a monogrammed letterhead, two decades later. The letter, seemingly 'functional', is of more than ordinary value. It shows how CR and a Congress minister at the Centre could demur from the Mahatma, the Father of the Nation, 'without fear or favour'.

Member of Council, Industries and Supplies
New Delhi
5 March 1947

My dear Bapu,

My telegram to Mr. Satish Chandra Das Gupta dated 24th February was as follows:

'Some mills propose gifting yarn to Gandhiji for relief in Noakhali areas stop Please state if you could take delivery and arrange distribution stop Also specify counts of yarn which would be appreciated'

Your telegram about 1900 bales per month came as a surprise. It is unlikely that we shall be able to secure more than about 100 to 200 bales of yarn for this purpose. It would not be possible for the Government of India to arrange for regular monthly quota of yarn to Noakhali. Under the existing procedure the internal distribution of yarn in a Province has to be done by the Provincial Government. Bengal's share of the Indian yarn production is placed at the disposal of the Bengal Government. They would probably resent any attempt to earmark a portion of this quota for distribution in Noakhali through other than Government agency.

It would also be impracticable to arrange for a quota outside Bengal's share since this could only come out of the share of some other Province and there is great shortage of yarn.

C. Rajagopalachari

88

The last to belong in this series is a letter Pyarelal writes on 29 January 1948 to CR at the Government House, Calcutta, address. The letter has a haunting sentence: 'Bapu is O.K. in every respect.' Like the first, it is best reproduced in facsimile as well.

Birla House
New Delhi
29 January 1948

Revered Rajaji,

So the fast like other natural portents has come and gone and so must I be too—the casual witness of the scene. I shall be leaving here on the evening of the 31st by the Delhi Express so as to reach Calcutta on the morning of Feb.2. I shall be in Calcutta on the 2nd and 3rd and leave for Noakhali on the night of the 3rd. by the Dacca Express.

More when we meet. Bapu is O.K. in every respect. He is due to leave for Wardha on the 1st and expects to return here on the 13th or 14th after observing Jamnalalji's death anniversary on the 12th at Wardha.

With best regards to you and Papa and love to Narasimhan,

Yours sincerely,
Pyarelal

Birla House, 2195
New Delhi, 29.1.48.

Revered Rajaji,

So the fast like other natural portents
has come and gone and so must I be too - the
casual witness of the scene. I shall be leaving
here on the evening of the 31st by the Delhi
Express so as to reach Calcutta on the morning
of Feb.2. I shall be in Calcutta on the 2nd
and 3rd and leave for Noakhali on the night
of the 3rd. by the Dacca Express.

More when we meet. Bapu is O.K. in
every respect. He is due to leave for
Wardha on the 1st and expects to return here
on the 13th or 14th after observing Jamnalalji's death anniversary on the 12th at
Wardha.

With best regards to you and Papa
and love to Narasimhan,

Yours sincerely,

Pyarelal

Shri C.Rajagopalachariar,
Government House,
Calcutta.

Devadas watches CR trying to get his camera to focus, circa 1945.

CR to Devadas Gandhi

1

*Devadas Gandhi was four months shy of twenty when he received the
following letter from fifty-two-year-old CR, the third known letter from
future father-in-law to would-be son-in-law. It reflects the deep personal
bond already established between the two at, clearly, the Mahatma's
instance and the most natural and 'intended' enthusiasm of the two.*

*Politics figures in the letter, both national and regional, as do
individual politicians. But, more significantly, the kind of affectionate
concern that comes from an elder in the family towards someone wanting
and needing to learn. Devadas has been ill with a condition that is
obviously none too serious but sufficient to cause CR to worry.*

Venkata Vilas
Luz Church Road
Mylapore
Madras
12 January 1920

My dear Devadas

I had time to write to you the day before yesterday and yesterday,
during the long and tedious (though physically it had all that could
be desired) journey from Calcutta. But I have been hesitating as the
operation involved so much of suppression of feelings longing to find
expression. But to find expression is no less difficult than to suppress.
The affection you have bestowed on me is a priceless gift with which
God has most unexpectedly chosen to brighten my life. But I shall not
lay bare things which are most beautiful when embedded in the heart.

I read with avidity, Bapu's beautiful evidence before the Hunter Committee.

I have written and spoken to friends in Salem, Madura and Berhampore about Young India. I hope orders will be placed soon, and before long the required number will be made up.

I hope you will be able to persuade Bapuji to take some rest now. He needs it very much, and what is more at once. Even if a long period of rest is out of question, a fortnight's stay in the Ashram without visitors may do a deal of good.

Satyamurti and others are going on in an incorrigible manner. It is a pity that Kasturi Rangayangar has failed to see eye to eye with Bapu of late. But all will come out right in the end as truth must triumph.

Public spirit among so-called educated classes has gone back to Pre Satyagraha days' standard, as far as appearances go. But I am hopeful the common people who have been deeply affected by Satyagraha and Bapuji's life will pull the leaders back to the right road.

You should keep me informed of your daily life and movements. I shall take the earliest opportunity to meet you. I think this is a psychological time for a great and strenuous push for Hindi in Madras. I do not selfishly suggest this to induce you to come here, but give it as a fact for careful consideration in the public interest.

I hope you have recovered your complexion, and the proper angles of your face, and that handkerchiefs have been discarded.

Yours affectionately,
C.R

2

A second letter is written on the same day, this time more of a 'cover' letter, to send to Devadas a parcel of books in English. There is nothing from the Mahatma to suggest a request from the father to CR to widen Devadas's reading, something the father was unable to attend to. Nor is there any letter available to show that Devadas asked for the consignment. Be that as it may, CR has taken it upon himself to fill the unoccupied (and non-existent) boxes or shelves of Devadas's library with CR's own preferred reading—a not untypical example of the older man's generosity with his own intellectual repertory.

Venkata Vilas
Luz Church Road
Mylapore
Madras
12 January 1920

My dear Devadas

I am sending you a parcel of books, to be read at your leisure. Twenty-three in number. Thomson's Indian History and Hutton's new readings from Indian history may be read first. After reading the primer on Rome, you may read the book on Roman civilization. Read also the book on English History as soon as possible. You will find the Geography of Asia interesting though scrappy. The literature books may be read whenever you like. Greece primer may be read along with Hawthorne's Tanglewood Tales. You will find all the primers on scientific subjects very easy and useful reading.

Yours sincerely,
C. Rajagopalachar

3

The 'distance education' regime continues, covering handwriting skills and spelling care, with emphasis on cultivating a writing style. The instruction is accompanied in classic CR style with a barb thrown in the direction of prevalent political writing styles.

Venkata Vilas
Luz Church Road
Mylapore, Madras
15 January 1920

My dear Devadas

. . . I have not been able to send you as many books as I had desired to. The English prose books have not been selected with any particular idea except that these are a few among the best books of the world. The poetical selections may be kept up for years as you cannot read more than one or two songs a week. But I want you to go through the science primers with zest and let me know what you think of them. The English and Indian histories and the small books on Rome and Greece will be very interesting, besides making you obtain an idea of modern, simple, English style. The style of Congress speeches and newspaper leaders may mislead you into a heavy pedantic style. But I see no signs of it, as your letters are written in just the language which you ought to develop. I may inform you that very few college youths succeed in attaining the simplicity and correct expression you have unconsciously reached. As for the handwriting you should not be nervous about it. It is good enough. It is getting quite legible. If you remember that the last one two letters in a word have the same right to be legible as the rest, and may be of the same size, the beauty of appearance will come in by constant writing.

The spelling of a few words needs a little attention if you do not mind. 'Absence' is right, not 'abscence'. How do you like the 'Common Faults' book that I have sent?

I have written a third rate schoolmaster's letter. But you will read into the words all the affection that is in me.

Yours affectionately,
C.R

4

*Now comes what is perhaps the first 'peek' into CR's own family
circumstances, in the shape of a description of his father's illness and the
responsibilities cast on a man who has family to look after and a national
struggle to serve, in addition to minding the intellectual development of a
preoccupied Master's son. Perhaps the most interesting feature of the letter
is its portrayal of CR's first recorded foray into the world of trade unions,
on a Gandhian gait.*

Venkata Vilas
Luz Church Road
Mylapore, Madras
4 February 1920

My dear Devadas

Your very nice letter of 28 Jan reached duly i.e. on the 5th day
(Hindu calculation). It is so unsatisfactory to have to write letters
under such conditions. But ours is a big country of which we are
proud. Friendships made with full knowledge of the size of the
motherland must cheerfully accept the natural consequences of
that size! Correspondence must crawl across huge distances and
warmth of affection cannot avail to increase the pace. There is a
very interesting essay of Charles Lamb on this subject of distant
correspondents which you may look up when you next go to the
Ashram, or earlier if you can get at Lamb's Essays of Elia which,
by the way, is one of the best books of the world, and of which I
was very fond.

I am sorry to tell you my father has had a relapse. On Sunday, I
spent a very anxious night. His suffering was intense and I had to be
looking on. I am glad to tell you that in spite of all this, my mind has
not yet rebelled against God's will, as it did some years ago (which
looks like yesterday) when I had to see great anguish suffered by a
dear one and I had similarly to look on unable to relieve or share

the physical pain. The symptoms are now better, but in a case of this sort, they say repeated attacks may be expected.

You will be interested to know that I had another illustration of the success of the law of Satyagraha. The Aluminium Company workmen had a grievance. They demanded a bonus for 1919 which the Directors refused and so they wanted to strike. I placed the question before a full meeting of the workmen and strongly urged the inadvisability of striking over such a question. I pictured to them in vivid colours how they were going to feel after two weeks of endurance. The men recorded their votes by secret ballot: I thought I would thereby eliminate the influence of the more violent spirits. But the vote was almost unanimous for a strike. I accepted the decision but asked them (1) not to go on strike straightaway, but give due notice of it to the employers, (2) to continue to work efficiently and honestly as before till the expiry of the period of notice and (3) to avoid action, speech or thought born out of hostility to the employers. I asked them to bear in mind the key of right conduct viz., during the precious interval when the employers had notice of the strike, they should endeavour to make the Managing Director feel unwilling to part with their services. They followed the directions implicitly and the result was remarkable. The Company stuck no doubt to their refusal to give a bonus for a bad year, but they offered at once to increase the scale of wages permanently by 25 per cent. What the men had asked was a bonus of a month's wages. They had an increase already last July in the scale of wages. But now they were offered a fresh addition which will in one year amount to thrice the bonus asked. Besides, the directors have promised to work out a regular scheme for profit-sharing in the future, which will take effect from this year forward. I am not proud of this achievement personally, but I am proud of it for the sake of Satyagraha.

The controversy between Mr Tilak and Bapuji has gone into all the papers. But no one comments. I expect however the Indian Social Reformer will not let it go. This pseudo—old world—politics of lying and diplomacy must be fought out and disposed off finally during Bapu's lifetime, so that we may at least have a fresh start. Never mind if the world goes wrong again.

I am sorry to learn about the illnesses at the Ashram. I hope your mother is better now. I have a letter from Mr Patwardhan that Mr Mahadev is quite out of danger, and that the typhoid is a non-virulent type. He does not say anything about your mother [on 31 January].

You will be glad to know that in Tinnevelly, where a friend of mine is in the Committee of the College, 30 boys in the lower secondary forms have taken Hindustani as 2nd language (about 25 of them being Hindu boys). My friend also is a Hindu, but stands thoroughly for Urdu script, which all the boys have got through and are answering question papers in. I will send you a sample of the work of these boys to be shown to Bapu.

Mr Patwardhan's report is 'Madras subscribers for Y. India are increasing, but not as fast as the Punjab'.

Yours affectionately,
C.R

5

This letter written on the eve of CR's first jail sentence is invaluable for the reference it has to CR's daughters and Gandhi's superscription (see corresponding entry in CR's letters to Gandhi) on it, anticipating future events like a water diviner's twig pulled towards its find.

Vellore
15 December 1921

My dear Devadas

I am just served with summons to take my trial today at 4 pm for disobedience of an order under Sec.144. I suppose I shall be able to stand jail life all right. At any rate I believe I ought to get better in health.

My boys are all at Salem and my daughters are at Rangoon. I wonder if you might find the latter's address useful some time or other. Namagiri and Lakshmi are my daughters' names and they are at 36, Forty-Fifth Street, Rangoon.

I have left some money with my elder brother at Salem who is looking after my own and my deceased brother's children. It will carry on for some time. But if when I am in prison for this civil disobedience case govt. puts up a case under Sec.124A also, and they give me a longer term, and if our own people do not respond to the call as we want, and Swaraj does not come in soon, my brother will have to be helped with more funds. But this need not bother you or Bapuji now. I feel today as young as yourself and so buoyant. I am not sure where Mahadev will be during the Congress session. Tell him my love.

Yours affly
C. Rajagopalachari

6

This letter comes after an interval, when CR is back at the centre stage of national politics and positioned at the very heart of Gandhi's engagements with the communal question through his by now practised method of fasting.

Delhi
26 September 1924

My dear Devadas

I scrawled a few lines on a postcard for you on the way. But you can guess that I have been missing you at every spot here. You would have brightened everything here. I told Bapu that you would be coming during the last week. 'That is right', he said quite warmly. I agree that you would be most useful there. But why not be useful all through. There is no choice between now and then. You could be here right through. Mahadev is very sad that you are not here. I believe you would be very serviceable to Bapu if you came here and stay on. But you have become so 'kattar' these days. Is that the word for 'obstinate'?

Well, I saw Bapu. I felt I could crush him in an embrace. I never felt the blood boil in passionate affection such as when I saw him yesterday lying on his bed. But of course all demonstration was ever and is impossible for me. I kept as cold an exterior as ever.

He was beautiful.

He smiled and talked just as if he had been taking his milk and fruits every meal every day. His voice was weak, but not quite as weak as one might expect. He has stood the fast very well. I have now really no fears. It will be a great strain but there need be none of the worst fears. What is more, I put it to him that he was certain he would stand the strain. He replied, 'Absolutely and what is more the doctors too think so'. 'Then', I said, 'on that basis we have no objection to what you are doing. But if at any time, the doctors feel that that certainty is gone and there is danger, how can we allow you to commit suicide?' He said 'Then there is time to consider'. I was so overjoyed at this mental relaxation of the decision and left it there. Mahadev was with me and felt likewise. I don't remember the words but have given the substance. It is curious how I have completely lost memory of the words but the thing was so deeply impressed on my mind.

I had a talk with Doctor Ansari. He has assured me that there is no danger. They have obtained word from him that the doctors should be the sole masters of the enema and leave him no choice in their action, in respect of that, while they may not interfere with his penance as regards eating and drinking. This is the greatest security we have against fatal risks.

Bapu is being removed today to a nice garden house outside the city.

Good oil massage is being given and he is taking good quantity of water.

His facial symptoms are most satisfactory as far as an anxious layman can judge.

Well, I must tell you something about politics too. I am afraid I am a changed man now as regards the Mussulman leaders. I don't like them at all. I see no change of heart in them. They have not realized the least bit the psychology of the fast—that Bapu is in deepest grief over the ingratitude of the Mussulmans and the sufferings of the Hindus and the indifference and heartlessness of the Mussulman leaders, and gropes with untarnished faith still towards God crying for light and help in his great anguish. I see no change whatever in the hardened hearts of the Mussulman leaders.

I shall return I fear from Delhi with altered mind in regard to the most essential things. All of us who have stood by the way shown by Bapu feel so fearfully hopeless now.

One thing is clear, that a long period of suspension of all Swaraj activities is before us.

With deepest love
CR

7

With Gandhi's creating space in national politics for the Swaraj Party, its different strategies and varying tactics of struggle against the Raj, CR takes an open-ended sabbath from the cause to start his own replica of Sabarmati. Gandhi has let him do so because he knows CR will not change his decision easily and, in any case, the ashram will recharge the batteries of his 'southern warrior'.

Pudupalayam
24 January 1925

My dear Devadas

I am very busy here arranging to have the ashram opened as early as possible. I expect to get it started on or about the 2nd February. I see that nothing begins unless we begin it somehow and then work at it.

Now, I am not writing this letter merely to keep you informed. I want you to come here for the opening day. I know what a lot of dislocation of other things it means, but I do hope you will see why I ask this so specifically and agree. I want this institution to grow, and flourish. If you come with a special message from Bapu which is to not be published but only read by you at the opening, it will be a spiritual encouragement of the greatest value.

I leave it to you to fix the exact day. But I want it to be in the first week of February. You can time your other engagements to suit and you can go back immediately.

Do wire to me 'agreed' arriving such and such a day.

Postal address
C. Rajagopalachar
Gandhi Ashram
Tiruchengodu

Telegraphic address
Rajagopalachar
Gandhiashram
Tiruchengodu (Salem)

Railway station
(S.I.R between Salem and Erode)
Sankaridrug

The village is 12 miles from the station, beautiful road with conveyances.

Yours affly,

C.R

8

CR places asterisks after the opening lines of his letter to make Devadas pause and turn to its enclosure which, alas, is unavailable to me. It has to be the most important letter Gandhi ever wrote to CR. Perhaps, encouraged by this compilation its possessor will share its contents with the interested public.

Gandhi Ashram

Tiruchengodu

23 July 1925

Dearest Devadas

Look at this letter from Bapu. Read it before proceeding with my letter.

★ ★ ★

What do you think! Can I bear the great weight of his love. I send it to you for I must share such joys and sorrows with you.

Return the letter. If I had a little palace and furniture and album or cabinet, I would have a place befittingly to treasure such a letter. However let me have it.

I have replied that I approve of all that he has done. The truth is my fits of opposition are temporary outbursts of Adam. My soul has been surrendered long ago and I can't but agree.

When will you come here? What a fond question! When I know you don't care for me.

Deepest love,

Yours,

C.R

My love to Pyarelal. How is the poor fellow? Are you still cruel to him or have you learnt to be mentor without hurting the sensitive nature which God has given him?

9

From prisoner to prisoner, this letter goes to a Devadas who is, by now, CR's son-in-law-to-be. Devadas is in Gorakhpur jail, of which the most important inmate is Jawaharlal Nehru. Imprisonment, apart from the physical torments it must bring, also carries agonies of the isolated mind about the condition of loved ones, as this letter shows. Also, as in the case of an intellectually and culturally honed mind, an involvement in matters of consciously cultivated objectivity such as books.

Central Jail

Vellore

2 June 1932

Sjt Devadas Gandhi
District Jail
Gorakhpur U.P.

My dear Devadas,

Lakshmi forwarded your letter to me. I have just got it. This letter of mine too will take pretty long to reach you, what with the intervals imposed on our correspondence and distance. All the same it was a pleasure to receive a letter from you.

You appreciate the advantage of being alone instead of in the midst of company not of your own choice. Quite true, but my agreeing with you involves an opinion about my present company here! Everything has its complications. That is the truth and law of the world.

I hope you are having enough fresh air and exercise. Are you keeping fairly well? I tremble to think of what the weather must be over there now. I came in with a weight of 103 lbs and stood at that for four months. I have now shot up to 110 lbs! I am very well; though I have ever to be on the defensive as regards the attacks of giddiness.

My present term ends with 9 July. Yours of course is a long way off yet in that way. But it makes no real difference, I suppose.

Lakshmi will be soon going away from Bellary to Coimbatore. She is very well. Her letters to me are like sunshine. I heard from Narasimhan that you had written to him. His condition is improving though I think we can't take these reports as much, until the arrest of the trouble is definitely achieved. He says he does not read much. He is now walking over a mile daily under doctors' orders. He began with a furlong.

Papa's case is causing me worry. Dr Rajan took a 'Skiogram' (or whatever you call the X-ray picture). He read it one way—negatively and I was glad. Shortly after that I got a contrary report from the Mysore Sanatorium doctor to whom it was submitted for interpretation. I am trying to secure a third opinion. Old methods are being lost before new methods are well reduced to possession.

Is Jawaharlalji very ill, i.e. anything seriously wrong, or only some temporary trouble? I wonder if you have any news about him.

Sanskrit grammar is too beautiful for mortals like me, but I have all the same done the first book of Hitopadesa and I am now doing Panchatantram starting at the 4th book. I have a friend to help who is a good teacher. I have coped with some chapters of the Gita by myself. Hindi is making good progress in the jail. Almost every one is at it. Some are gurgling away at Urdu too.

I am writing nothing. Somehow I haven't found the inspiration to do anything that way.

Thanks for 'The Wet Parade'. I notice that it is an autograph presentation copy. But I have read the book already—one of the first books I got in jail this time. It is a fine novelization of all that has to be said on American Prohibition. Chapter after chapter moves up in deliberate order, just clothing up all the Prohibition 'points'. Too much of set purpose and 'according to programme'; but a good and exhaustive treatment of the subject, to satisfy those already committed and make them feel armed and strengthened. You may remember Mathooradas gave me once a book of Zola's to read. It is incomparably superior, but that book deals with Alcohol rather than Prohibition. Sinclair's book is a powerful indictment of corruption in American politics—might frighten one in regard to political prospects in India.

A really high class English author is so superior to mere propaganda writers like Upton Sinclair. Soon after finishing 'The Wet Parade', I got a book of short stories of Hardy's. The contrast was so great. The delicate touch of real art is so different from the propagandist style. Hardy has a short story called 'The Son's Veto' that reminded me of the episode on 'The Wet Parade', the incident of Roger Chilcote and Anita—all the difference between raw manure and the fruit made out of it. The substance is the same, but the composition and flavour are different.

Miss Peterson sent me a nice little copy of Thomas à Kempis's 'Imitation of Christ'. It is a truly beautiful book. There is so much of it that is so near to the Gita. One may even imagine that Thomas à Kempis had read the Gita somehow and used it.

What a tragedy for Vallabhbhai's son. The little grandson will now have only Vallabhbhai to play with. I fear Dahyabhai is utterly disconsolate. Truly in life we are in the midst of death.

I hope Bapu is keeping really well. He has found time to write letters to Narasimhan and ask him for a doctor's report about his condition. Wonderful man—the biggest house-holder among us all. When you write to him, convey my love, as well as to Mahadev and to Vallabhbhai.

So also write to Ba and give my affectionate regards.

Well, this is a long letter, but what have I really told you?

May you and Lakshmi want nothing and be happy all the days of your life!

With love always,
Raja

10

Another letter from CR immediately after his release from jail brings to Devadas news of the sudden death of CR's son-in-law, S. Varadachari. Gandhi's letters and 'instructions' to Devadas and to Kasturba over this (see the Collected Works*) reflect the leader's close involvement in his colleagues' life cycles.*

9 July 1932

My dear Devadas,

I hope my letters to you have not been intercepted. Papa is a widow! I received the news in prison on the 28th. I was released on expiry of my term this morning and am proceeding straight to Tiruchengode where Papa and Lakshmi are waiting for me, as if the grief would be less on seeing their father!

It is not only a question of strength and fortitude. It has become all too dark for me.

Are you quite well now?

Yours affectionately,
Raja

Bapu wrote I understand once to me. But the letter must have been intercepted. I didn't get it.

Enclosure in letter to Mrs Kamala Nehru

45

Dehra Dun Gaol
30.5.33

M8/12545

My dear Devadas,

Thank you for your telegram informing me of the ending of Bapu's great fast. It has been a wonderful thing, the way Bapu has faced and conquered this trial. 'Man doth not yield himself to the angels or even unto death save by the weakness of his feeble will' says an ancient writing, and Bapu has shown how a mighty will can hold together a frail body and bend it to a desired purpose.

I am writing to you after a long time, nearly two years it must be. I have long wanted to tell you how happy I was to learn of your engagement to Lakshmi. I have hardly spoken to her but she struck me, whenever I saw her, as a very dignified and charming girl. You are fortunate and deserve congratulation — and so does she!

In a fortnight or so in January 1932 Bernard Alexhore was with me in Naini Prison. He told me much that was interesting about Bapu's stay in England and especially about the doings of the members of his party. He has gone and got married now, I understand, and has retired to his ancestral haunts in Ceylon.

Love

Yours affly

Jawaharlal

Devadas Gandhi
Parna kuti
Poona

11

Devadas was arrested almost immediately after the Devadas–Lakshmi
wedding in 1933. As was CR. Another letter from prisoner to prisoner.

Censored
-sd/- Superintendent
Coimbatore
11 January 1934

My dear Devadas,

Your telegrams from Multan, & Itarsi, & the telegram from
Ghanshyamdasji, all reached today. I replied to you to Wardha, and
to Ghanshyamdasji to Bombay as directed by him. The last wire
has not reached him at Bombay but has been posted to Delhi from
Bombay—this is the Telegraph Office information received here:
'owing to addressee not being in Bombay and having left for Delhi.'
This is how things will happen in spite of meticulous care—man
proposes but the Telegraph messenger disposes. The message was
to thank him for his kind offer and to say that you will decide after
seeing Bapu and me.

I hope you are keeping fit in spite of your 'hard labour' and
privations as A Class Prisoner which earned for you 45 days
remission. What a fraud! Lakshmi must be in thrills of emotion
finding you again whole and sound. I did not imagine she would
be so intensely fond of her husband.

I got your letter of 29 Dec written from jail forwarded to me by
Lakshmi. You are pleased naturally with my progress in Sanskrit.
But I am not so simple as to imagine that I will be at any time
anything more than a baby in it. Yet I do feel satisfied with this baby's
knowledge, because I had not hoped to attain even that much.

Some nasty and careless official must have interfered with Lakshmi's letter to you (of 7 Nov.) & forgotten to replace my letter enclosed with it, & so you have lost it altogether . . .

I still feel that Lakshmi should not go away now. It may be a father's foolishness. But there it is. Still I shall leave it to you to decide the question finally. I think you had better come & see me. I have fixed it up with the authorities here. You may come any day and send a note to the supdt who will be in office everyday between 9 & 10 in the morning. It is best you come unaccompanied by non-family friends for the subject matter of the talk is a purely family affair & time should be saved. Don't make up your mind but keep it open until you talk to me. My feeling is that you should see Bapu before seeing me, not only that I may have the advantage of his opinion, but for propriety, & the joy of it.

Love
Raja

12

Nearly two decades after he cast his lot with the Mahatma and plunged into the freedom struggle, without the faintest clue on when or whether it will succeed, CR is at the helm of Congress's bid for a legislative success in provincial elections held under the Government of India Act, 1935. Satyamurti is the campaign's turbine and CR its sharpest rotor blade. The Biblical 'fall' described in this letter refers to a self-abnegating Gandhian's positioning on the doors of a 'first-ever' electoral stake and that most unattractive aspect thereof—the raising of election funds. Also, as it turns out, at the turnstile of high office.

He has also moved from being—for Devadas— 'Rajagopalachar' to 'Raja' to the entirely homey 'Anna'. Anna literally means 'elder brother' but is used in some Tamil homes, particularly Tamil Aiyangar ones, for 'father'.

49 Bazlulla Road
Tyagarayanagar
Madras
21 January 1937

My dear Devadas,

I am glad I have not got any communication from you or Ghanshyamdasji making fun of my sudden fall.

I have been rushed into it & I have hardly 4 weeks to win all the elections in Tamil Nad, Kerala and Andhra & a bit of Karnatak. Andhra is in a bad state. Still I hope we shall have a majority clear & entirely Congress in this Province. We have to work for cent per cent success for Tamil Nad to get a majority for the Congress in Madras. We have a fair chance for 85 percent & I should not be surprised if we get 90%.

We have had to put up numerous candidates who require financial help for minimum normal expenses. I have been rushed into this, and see little time for accomplishing the necessary collections. Those who were in it before me have done nothing in this direction!

So, I thought of an SOS to you. You must see Ghanshyamdasji at once and tell him this is an urgent personal call from me. If he wishes to be useful in this crisis, he must put aside all his objections, such as can be & send me a very liberal cheque. I hope you can speak to him and induce him to do this.

Vallabhbhai I know has fleeced everyone & he says it is too late for *anything* to be sent from Central collections to this province. We have got *no help whatsoever* from them. Local collections have for several reasons failed you can understand.

Please let the cheque be made payable to me or Mr K. Srinivasan (Hindu). I wanted at first to telegraph but desisted. I have to go out on a tour programme for weaker constituencies & have no time to remain in Madras for over two or three days.

Telegraph: Rajagopalachari—Bazlulla—Madras Tyagarayanagar—
Is there anyone else there whom you can approach at once and raise something decent privately? I intend distributing this help privately & personally to the most important and deserving cases. Some anti-Congress leaders of importance have to be defeated by poor well tried Congressmen.

Yours affly
Anna

13

Only CR can combine editorial fastidiousness with electoral exhilaration as this letter, written in the wake of Congress's success in the polls, shows.

49, Bazlulla Road
Tyagarayanagar
Madras
20 February 1937

My dear Devadas,

Today is the second half polling day all over Madras Presidency. The new edition Gita, two copies reached me today. I have just opened the copies and looked at the get up. You cannot say that alignment of the pages, especially introductory form is very good, some how Newspaper Offices cannot produce books neatly. Perhaps the mistake is only in the cutting of the paper.

There are signs of greater hurry in this edition, than in the first, here and there. All the same I am grateful to you, for having undertaken and finished this job in addition to the tremendous burden already on your shoulders.

Love to Lakshmi & the little ones.

Yours affectionately,
Anna

Sjt. Devadas Gandhi
C/o The 'Hindustan Times'
Delhi.

14

By the time this letter is written, CR has held his first public office with acclaimed success, that of premier, Madras Presidency, and vacated it with unconcealed regret, at the call of Congress's boycott following the outbreak of the Second World War.

49, Bazlulla Road
Tyagarayanagar
Madras
1 March 1940

My dear Devadas,

I have your most interesting report of the important conversation. (By the way, how extraordinarily well you write these days!)

I have told Maulana and he has agreed to give the interview. He has also been told by me he should give it soon. But how one can get him to *do* it is beyond me. I have told him, & he has agreed, to emphasise the evil of separate electorates. Bapu nicely flattered him on the basis of your letter, saying that the world press has been much impressed by his election. This has whetted his appetite to be famous & you may get the interview.

As for politics, the expected has been done.

I am going back via Calcutta as I came. Narasimhan is not well at all. I am glad to learn that Lakshmi and the kiddies are all well.

I got your telegram also. How & on what am I to write for you? I fear I cannot get anything out of my brain now.

Love
Anna

I reach Madras on 4th morning.

15

CR's unhappiness with the Congress's opposition to the war effort takes many forms, including public opposition to the resistance and warnings about Axis intents. His opposition to 'Quit India' wins him wide intellectual support but wider political berating. He is criticized, even vilified, but remains unaffected. With Gandhi and the entire Congress leadership jailed and resistance to the war effort being forcibly put down, Devadas asks CR to at least criticize the Raj's suppression of the Congress. CR replies as follows:

48, Bazlulla Road
Tyagarayanagar
Madras
15 January 1943

My dear Devadas,

I can understand your agony. But there is no way out of it. We must suffer what has been deliberately sown for us to reap.

My voice you want me to raise against the oppressions and injustices of repression. Of what avail is my voice? Who am I? How shall I do it? Shall I write to the press which cannot publish things where accuracy is not vouched for. Shall I whine writing to the authorities? Shall I hope for mercy that way? Shall I make speeches on the subject, which cannot go on for any appreciable length of time?

You seem to think that because I have not been locked up I possess an influence which others have lost. It is wrong.

Errors have led us into the inescapable shame & suffering. We make it all worse by public efforts at escaping from it.

If you find any one willing to give an authentic account of any cases of oppression and it is first hand evidence of one who has seen or suffered, why not give it to one of the members of the Assembly which will soon meet in Delhi? I don't set great store by it. But it may be done in the absence of any other remedy. I am no doubt disgusting you. But I am no less disgusted at how people are behaving like parrots without any common sense. All hopes of work and helping the people in prison to get out of the mess is at an end so far as I am concerned. The Cawnpore heroes have done it. Rajah Maheshwar Dayal Seth had an offer which should have been accepted at once. It was rejected & Dr Mookerjee played to the gallery instead of doing the right things as he promised. We must lie in the bed made for us.

The children are well. Narasimhan is in raptures over Mohan's quickness & quickness of grasp.

Love, Anna

16

Written in the same vein, this letter starts with a reference to the distinguished head of the establishment of the Madras newspaper,

The Hindu, *which was critical of CR's role, and goes on to make perceptive comments on the political stances of M.A. Jinnah and others.*

49, Bazlullah Road
Tyagaraya Nagar
Madras
5 February 1943

My dear Devadas,

. . . I read your letter to Narasimhan—therein you repeat what you wrote to me also—your drift apart from Mr K. Srinivasan. You seem to think I am particularly interested in Mr Srinivasan. I am what I am, think what I think, do what I do, not because of Mr Srinivasan, nor even in spite of him! I don't even meet him as often as you apparently think I do. His views are in many matters wholly different from mine, & where they coincide, it is not a result of consultation.

There you are, & therefore do not go on writing to me to make him think this or that, or encourage in yourself any notion of conspiracy between him & me!

Then for Jinnah! You say people there (Bombay) or (let it be elsewhere) feel my support of him is being somewhat 'overdone' by me. They are at perfect liberty to hold that view. I hold the opinions I hold, not to oblige Mr Jinnah or to support him. Let us not support him, and let us get our objective (if indeed we can claim to have any!). I shall be happy if I see it done within my lifetime. We are successfully ruining all chances—almost—of national freedom and progress.

Abdul Latif—his motives are bad, & his interpretations of motives are also wrong—but he has hit it off more truly than the others. I don't want to oblige anybody, where we could achieve our purpose without such obliging. But I do not want the country to be devastated by the present British administration and the people to suffer all that they are suffering. I do not want the communal blackmailing that the Muslims outside the Pakistan area want to continue—and this is what Abdul Latif & others want & which the Hindu Mahasabha helps to maintain with suicidal folly. I want this country to be freed from the present arrogant domination. But a slave mentality has seized hold of our best people, worse than the slave mentality against which Bapu preached, a mentality from which reason has been excommunicated and a parrot-psychology installed and which has rendered the most fruit-fail world crisis, a barren event for India.

The net result—as I see it—is that everybody whom we consider precious for the nation will continue in prison till the end of the war and for some time thereafter & this country is in for a fresh period of exploitation.

I am very sad. My bitterness is not I know good. But you should understand how I am really feeling.

Yours affectionately,
Anna

17

*With the war staggering towards a denouement, Gandhi released after
a breakdown of his health following Kasturba's death and his fast, CR
writes this in a somewhat different rasa.*

Bajajwadi, Wardha
30 November 1944

My dear Devadas,

Ghanshyamdasji's telegram as well as letter were duly received by me on my return from Nagpur. I also enclosed the papers enclosed with your letter to Bapu.

Bapu is well. But he is very weak, i.e., he is, in general physical strength, poorer than he was a month ago I believe. Otherwise he is, I found, quite cheerful and 'alert'. There is no cause for alarm on account of what has been called an 'accident'. He had taken castor oil and it had caused nausea, & when he rose to a standing posture from the warm water bath, he felt 'swimming', & as he was silent at the time he could not call for the required leaning assistance, & he had to lean on something or the other at the place where he stood which yielded & so he came down. He soon recovered. This was all.

I have had nice chats with him and I have been insisting on a thirty days 'fast from *all* work' (not food). He has agreed and has promised to take it with all the rigour of ceremonial and pledged abstention which he applies to good food. This will set him up. All those around him have approved of it. A change of place will involve travel, mental worry and new work at new places. So I advised same place but strict bar & lock against all letters, advice, interviews etc. So this will be done (I hope so).

Then about my going to Delhi, I have read your letter and all the relevant things and talked it over with Bapu also. I feel it would be a great strain on my physical frame now to travel so far & the winter is very unpleasant to me. I am sure you know how glad I would be to see you all and be with you for a couple of weeks. But the cold is disagreeable to my internals. My circulation cannot stand it & I suffer. Then the work is not promising. I fully understand all that you have written about the Govt's mind. There is nothing in it but what there has been all the time.

When Sapru calls me I shall be at his disposal. I should not see Government men now in the interval. It will lead to complications and misunderstandings.

My own conviction is that there can be no agreement with Jinnah under present conditions. We must start with the Federal Centre under the Govt of India Act of 1935 and pledge ourselves to accept any agreed solution to replace the relevant part of the constitution of

1935. This is what the Sapru Committee[1] should start with. This will put more minds in a mood to accept proposals that are just and fair. Both sides (or all sides) will then be anxious to agree. Now having nothing to lose, they are all impossible. I don't think Bapu realizes this as yet. I don't think 'Congress' realizes this. They are still believers in the potency of the 'negative' and the patriotism of 'NO'. I shall if opportunity is given to me strongly advise the Sapru Committee on these lines, whatever be the scope of limitations of their 'reference'.

I hope Ghanshyamdasji won't be upset because I have not responded to his request to go to Delhi. It is just possible he may not realize how weak I am in general health now.

I am just carrying on. I don't wish to strain it too far and you know that in my case I must look after myself. There is not a band of anxious attendants around me as in Bapu's case, and I should not stand it even if I could have it!

Yours affectionately
Anna

18

The transfer of power no longer a distant goal but an imminent prospect, the Congress is putting together a list of its leaders for public responsibility. Is CR, the 'Quit India' opponent, going to be in it? Congress President Maulana Azad is to have a say, though Gandhi's views will obviously matter the most.

---

[1] When the Gandhi–Jinnah talks came to naught, the Sapru Committee was appointed in November 1944 to examine the communal issue within a judicial framework. Sir Tej Bahadur Sapru's committee of twenty-nine members, representing various communal groups, submitted proposals to the viceroy, Lord Wavell, to break the political impasse, but in vain.

60 Bazlullah Road
Tyagarayanagar
Madras,
22 March 1946

My dear Devadas,

I hope you are under no mistaken notion that I shall be in Delhi now. The natural corollary of events now is that I shall not be there—because the scheme of official conferences cannot include me and because Maulana would like to avoid complications by starting invitations. I am not an independent wise-acre now, as Sir Tej & others of that ilk. It is only Bapu that could feel the need for having me by his side, and that is hardly likely to be considered now. He lives from minute to minute these days. His mental strength cannot cope with preparatory strain. So in all probability the breakdown will take place without me near by to watch it this time!

Every one is anxious for a settlement, but the combined diplomatic capacity is poor and so I fear the result will be negative in spite of all the favourable circumstances now gathered together . . .

Yours affly
Anna

19

This telegram shows the quickening of speculation and action.

Stamp: 5 April 1946

X BF TENKASI 5-20 DEVADAS GANDHI HINDUSTAN TIMES NEW DELHI

PLEASE CONTACT MAULANA WIRE MADRAS IF HE WANTS ME AS REUTERS INFORM RAJAGOPALACHARI

20

With the Labour government's announcement that Britain will relinquish power, power is all but transferred. Appropriately, the following is written from aboard a levitating flight.

Plane
13 August 1946
Nagpur to Madras

My dear Devadas,

. . . Well, the great struggle is over. I believe you are pleased. The names are still unsettled. What last minute changes and decisions will be made I can't tell. But the main task is over. I must say the Labour Government has shown courage & firmness. The old man Pethick Lawrence is a brick. Even on Sunday Bapu was suspicious and cold. But his distrusts & doubts have been nobly disproved & the reply from the Viceroy on the 12th was received with just & unanimous appreciation. I saw Bapu on 12th night to say goodbye. It was late & he was in bed within curtains. He was also glad and appreciated everything.

Love
Anna

21

CR is to join the Congress–League ministry. Sir Akbar Hydari of the Indian Civil Service, for whom CR has high regard, wants CR to move into his Lutyens bungalow, on Clive Road, New Delhi, a prospect CR obviously is pleased about for an unexpected aesthetic reason.

60 Bazlullah Road
Tyagarayanagar
Madras
[April 1946]

. . . Sir Akbar Hydari had wanted me & I have agreed to take up
the house he has been in, if things should shape as they have done.
I see a Hindu report from Delhi that all my colleagues have fixed
up their houses! This led me to write to you this. I would prefer
to take Hydari's house if available. I suppose one place is as good as
another. But I like the Ajanta painting which old Hydari had got
and put up there & which young Hydari agreed to leave for me.
You can try & get at him.

Yours affly,
Anna

22

With the collapse of the interim ministry and Partition slicing the
culmination of struggle at the moment of its success, the governorship of
the truncated and, therefore, volatile new state of West Bengal becomes
important. N. Gopalaswami Iyengar is sounded for the position and
declines. CR is appointed to it. The state does not exactly warm up
to the appointment of one who was volubly opposed to Deshbandhu
Chittaranjan Das in the 1920s and to Netaji Subhas Bose in the 1930s
and early 1940s. But once positioned there, CR wins the heart of Bengal
and—more important—its far-from-uncritical mind.

Rajmohan Gandhi writes in his biography of CR:

Until 1912 viceroys and governor-generals had ruled India from
Calcutta's government house, the edifice that CR accompanied
by retiring Governor Burrows, entered; it had housed governors

*of (undivided) Bengal from 1912. Till the middle of the night
he would be the guest of the Burrows; then until his departure
at dawn, the Briton would be Rajaji's guest. At 8 a.m. the
Union Jack would be lowered and the Indian tricolour unfurled
by CR would fly over the mansion. At 1 a.m. on Friday,
15 August (Bengal at the time was an hour ahead of IST) in
the throne room of Government House, he was sworn in. By
now, in the darkness outside Government House, large crowds
had collected and were shouting 'Jai Hind', 'Vande Mataram'
and 'Gandhiji ki Jai'. Fireworks lit the night sky. The curfew
which for nearly a year had emptied Calcutta's streets in the
late hours was completely ignored . . . as dawn broke a huge
crowd pressed against the gates of Government House. Soon the
gates were flung open and the masses flooded in. Thirty seconds
before 8 a.m., by when he had seen Burrows and his wife into
a sea-plane, CR mounted a specially erected pavilion in the
Government House lawns. At the first boom of a 17-gun salute
fired from Fort William, he unfurled the flag. This was, to quote
the* Statesman, *the signal for a 'wild outburst of joy which swept
Government House and its environs for hours together.' At least
20,000 people swarmed into Government House, at last the
property of India and Indians, many pushing their way into the
rooms, handling the portraits, and dancing on the sofas . . . CR
greeted the revellers from the pavilion and later from a window in
the building, when the crowd gave lusty cries of 'Rajaji-ki-jai' . . .
but the reality of partition was stabbing rejoicing hearts. CR
sought to fight it with a wish. In an address to the West Bengal
Assembly on the day of liberty, he hoped that the bars of division
would 'ere long melt away' and that 'the two free states will come
together once again into a wise and lasting union'. Would CR be
able to befriend Bengal? He would certainly try . . .* [2]

[2] Rajmohan Gandhi, *The Rajaji Story, 1937–1972* (Delhi: Bharatiya Vidya Bhavan, 1984), p. 142.

Government House
Calcutta
9 January 1948

My dear Devadas,

. . . I was out on a short tour in Murshidabad & Nadia districts. It is all a wonderful experience for me. It is remarkable how good the people here are and how they shower affection on me. It is like water to a parched throat. The sweet conservative culture that is preserved and taught to the little ones in these middle class Bengal homes is truly wonderful. I have been making I think some of my best speeches but alas there is no one to report! If only The Hindu could be got to be published at Calcutta!

You need not tell me—I know as I can infer from what is going on—what terribly bad complications we have got entangled in. Alas that India on attainment of Freedom is orphaned in civic guidance. God has been cruel; but he knows what is just retribution.

Love to Lakshmi & all the kids,

Yours affectionately,
Anna

Papa has been distributing more Sports prizes. Ramu would have liked my speech to the Mohan Bagan Sports Club people if he had been present. Unfortunately, it is not reported & so he cannot read it.

23

Rajmohan Gandhi writes:

> *To regard Government House as home required effort . . . a full month after moving he wrote to Burrows: 'I am still trying to familiarize myself with your late residence.' . . . It was not a home*

*designed to encourage self-reliance. Skilled servants were needed
at every turn: to shut the massive windows, bring down the huge
velvet curtains, remove the heavy embroidered bed-covers, work
the geysers or locate the right switch for the right lamp. The large
number of attendants bothered CR. He wrote to Devadas: 'Papa
and I and all of us much prefer the Clive Road house. You may
not understand, but No. 1 Clive Road was a more spacious place
than this. I feel like am living in a cage here with people all round
peeping through the bars.*[3]

CR and West Bengal were meant for each other at the state's birth.

On 13 January 1948, Gandhi starts yet another—his last—fast
in New Delhi to seek redress for the wrongs suffered by Muslims in
the national capital. When he gathered that the Government of India
was holding back Rs 55 crore due to be paid to Pakistan as part of the
settlement of the cash balance on Partition, he made the giving of that
amount a precondition to the breaking of his fast.

CR had almost on every previous fast undertaken by the Mahatma
asked for it not to be undertaken, or given up. Not so this time. 'The
only sane man today is Gandhi,' he says. 'I have wrangled with
Gandhiji on similar occasions in the past. But this time I confess I am
not inclined to wrangle.'

Written less than a fortnight before the Mahatma's assassination, this
letter has a distinct 'It is going to happen'-ness to it.

Government House
Calcutta
17 January 1948

My dear Devadas,

Yes your letter to Bapu & his reply reached my hands & I have
read them.

---

[3] Ibid., p. 145.

God has humbled us in many ways. He alone can extricate us from the mouth of the crocodile to which Bapu refers as if it all happened in fact. The Elephant story is not an answer to your arguments, but only an explanation of his own state of mind. I feel more depressed after reading your despatch than I felt this morning after reading the papers.

I hope Jawaharlalji will do something and get Bapu to give up his fast. No one else can do it now. I feel I can do nothing. Delhi is so different. When I was there last I felt there was an opaque screen between me & the people, so different from what I feel here.

Love
Anna

24

Rajmohan Gandhi's biography describes the fateful day, 30 January 1948, thus:

January 30. It was just before six in the evening. CR was about to leave for a meeting. The phone near the portico of Government House rang. (ADC) Singaravelu took it and heard: 'This is the PTI. Please inform the Governor that Mahatma Gandhi has been assassinated.' Singaravelu shouted out the news. CR heard it as he emerged on his way to the car, from a lift. Shocked, but in full control, he asked Singaravelu to put in a call to Mountbatten. The Governor General would be able to confirm—or correct—the word. Before the call came through, Narasimhan heard the AIR announce the murder and rushed to tell his father. The Governor General, reached while about to leave for Birla House, where Gandhi had been felled, said the news was true. CR said to Mountbatten: 'Look after Jawahar'.[4]

---

[4] Ibid., p. 154.

*PTI rings again, for a message. 'We have been robbed,' CR says, 'of
our greatest possession by a senseless lunatic. May God help India.' He
flies to Delhi the next morning.*

*In one of his most moving speeches, CR said: 'Mahatmaji was very
dear to me, but I do not grieve for him. No man can find a death so
glorious. He was walking to join and lead a prayer; he was going to speak
to his Ram. He was a few minutes late and so he was walking fast . . .
How many of you would not like to die when running to pray?'*

*Five months later, Devadas, with Lakshmi accompanying him, goes
to London for a Reuters meeting. CR and Namagiri take care of the
children while the two are away. CR writes to Devadas the following
from the Governor's Himalayan residence.*

Government House
Darjeeling
14 May 1948

My dear Devadas,

I hope you both will have arrived safe and without damage to
nerves by the time this goes to you. All the children are well &
jolly. Gopu has been perfectly civil. He is a miniature gentleman at
table and a model for everybody. He is, of course, cheerful & well.
Ponies—football—and everything in order.

Whomsover you see convey my greetings if they happen to be
my friends. In particular Krishna Menon, Pethick-Lawrence, Sir
Stafford Cripps, & his younger parliamentary gang—Rev Herbert
Anderson whom you *must* see some time—Agatha Dorothy Hogg.
It would be grand if you see Wavell & Linlithgow.

Papa is very busy as usual but fairly calm. Gopu has taken very
well to her. Even if he gets up in the middle of the night he does
not fuss but gets her to attend quietly.

I am sorry I caused you a deal of annoyance by trying to undo
arrangements and it is a great joy to me that you left according to
plan with Lakshmi & all is well.

We should be back in Calcutta on 1 June. I shall be in Delhi from 2 to 5 June & back to Calcutta again. Will leave for Delhi again 20th if present arrangements stand.

Love
Anna

25

On 1 April 1948 Prime Minister Nehru sends a courier to Calcutta with a letter for CR: 'You know that Lord Mountbatten is leaving his office about the 22nd June. We have to find a successor for him, and inevitably our eyes turn to you . . . I hope you will agree. Your presence in Delhi will be a great help to all of us, and especially to me.' CR replies: 'It is very pleasant to be told . . . that my presence at Delhi will be of great help to you all. This proposal has been threatening to come for some time past.'

He asks for time to think it over. He is to agree to what is a 'first'— the first time an Indian is to become Governor General of India. But, never the one for smooth beginnings or neat endings, CR is not to be India's first President.

Darjeeling
20 May 1948

My dear Devadas

. . . I hope you will both have a fine and instructive time of it in Great Britain.

I wish I were young!

As Delhi is getting nearer and nearer my misgivings are getting more and more serious. Nothing but the remarkable volume of good wishes from all over the world can help me.

Anna

CR with grandson Gopal in Government House, New Delhi, 1948.

CR to Gopalkrishna Gandhi

1

My dear Gopu,

I saw your excellently written letter to Periamma[1] and so got all the news.

Congratulations on your great and rapid progress.

Your dear grandfather,
Anna in his room.[2]

2

25 April 1956

My dear Gopu,

Your nice letter came some days ago. I am glad you are all so eagerly looking forward to a great experience.[3] I wish you all sound health

---

[1] 'Periamma' is the Tamil form of address for the mother's older sister, in this case, CR's elder daughter, Namagiri.

[2] In a letter to my aunt Namagiri, I had asked her how 'Anna in his room' was, CR being then imprinted in my ten-year-old mind as the grandfather who rarely left his room and, in fact, the 'easy chair' on which he generally sat.

[3] My sister, Tara, my eldest brother, Rajmohan, and I accompanied my parents in the summer of 1956 on a visit to England, Scotland and Europe.

and joy and a safe and speedy return. I shall not be going to Bombay to see you off, but imagine I am there on the pier when you look back on the crowd as your boat leaves. Love travels far. This is for everybody including Tara.[4]

Your affectionate
Anna

3

5 September 1957

My dear Gopu,

I saw your letter to Indira.[5] You write very well and truly.

But you should not let yourself go sad. Appa[6] is not in his body but he lives in your memory. He has acquired in your memory a fine holy and beautiful body like that of a god. Why should you be so sad? You have to look after your Amma, Mohan,[7] Ramu,[8] and so many others.

And remember many others have faced the death of their fathers and grown up. Indira herself to whom you wrote lost her father when she was younger than you or about that, and her brothers all four of them shared that fate, and they were tiny boys and Sudarshan[9] was just a baby.

So, do not be sad.

I am glad to note what fine and correct English you write.

---

[4] Tara Gandhi Bhattacharjee, born 1934.

[5] Indira Ananthanarayana née Ramaswami, CR's granddaughter and daughter of C.R. Ramaswami.

[6] Devadas Gandhi had died on 3 August 1957, after a heart attack, his first and fatal one.

[7] Rajmohan, born 1935.

[8] Ramchandra, 1937–2007.

[9] CR's youngest grandson, son of C.R. Ramaswami.

Do not be afraid of arithmetic or anything else. If you get someone to explain, it will be all easy.

God bless you. Love from all here.

Anna

4

16 October 1958

My dear Gopu,

I was able to look into your postcard to Periamma and was glad to read it. I am cheered up to know that you are having a 'kolu'[10] which indicates that Amma is cheerful as she should be. God bless her. These days I am constantly thinking of her. You should know that Amma is as dear to me as Gopu is dear to Amma. Love to all of you.

Anna

5

20 May 1959

My dear Gopu,

Congratulations on your promotion to the 10th class. It was a pleasure to read your letter written in such excellent English containing such good all round news. Garhmukhteshwar was a place where much cruelty was practiced during the Hindu–Muslim riot days. But the

---

[10] A Navaratri display of icons, toys and decoratives, traditional to Tamil Nadu.

Ganga flows there to wash out all sins. Let us have your Pathankot[11] letter. I am well. Ramabhadran[12] is doing grand.

Love,
Anna.

6

3 February 1960

My dear Gopu,

Periamma showed me your letter. I was glad to read it and was amused by the cutting also. It is all good. I shall spend the greater part of the coming week in Bangalore. Your hand writing is quite good so far. But if you write in a hurry it is likely to get spoiled. Do not get into the wrong habit of writing as if you were in a great hurry. A good legible handwriting is as necessary as clean clothes. Shape each letter properly and fully. That is the secret.

Love, Anna

7

23 January 1961

My dear Gopu,

Periamma was thrilled when she noted that you were introduced to the British Queen[13] at Rajghat, in an atmosphere of sacred memories about your grandfather.

---

[11] I was going to Pathankot to join up in a Bhoodan visit of Vinoba Bhave.

[12] CR's great-grandson, son of Janaki and S. Govindarajan.

[13] Queen Elizabeth II and Prince Philip visited India for the first time from 21 January to 1 February 1961 and later from 16 to 26 February 1961.

I was thinking how glad your father would have been had he been alive to see it. But he is watching you all in spirit. Be good, diligent and cheerful and look forward to be a successful young man to look after your mother when she will grow old and needs to be looked after.

My blessings
Anna

8

3 July 1961

My dear Gopu,

I was glad to get your letter telling us you have been admitted into the Honours BA course in St. Stephen's College.[14] All good luck to you. The volume of Burke you have taken with you will be good additional reading for you. Remember Burke was a writer of the glory years of the eighteenth century like Goldsmith and Johnson. A large body of very great English writers came after them. The 18th century writers were great forerunners of the great literature of England.

Anna

9

15 July 1961

My dear Gopu

Tell Amma that Sri Santanam brought and gave us the beautiful fruits and that I thoroughly enjoyed the peaches and the unpretentious

---

[14] St Stephen's College, Delhi.

looking but really very good mangoes. The pears are waiting to get properly ripe. The peaches were really first class.

I should like to know when you actually join and begin to work in the university. You should make a point to choose and read whatever English books you come across in the library. You should read at least a dozen of Shakespeare's plays if not all of them. Read books for pleasure and only use Oxford Dictionary to help. Never mind if parts go un-understood. At present you should read the New Testament Authorized Version as soon as you can.

I have great hopes about you and your English course.

Love from everybody here

Yours affectionately
Anna

10

18 July 1961

My dear Gopu,

I am gathering a number of Shakespeare's plays for you and will send them in a parcel shortly. These are all annotated books and secondhand. You may or may not use the notes and introductions. But read all the plays as if they were detective stories read for amusement. This is the best preparation for Literature Honours.

Love, Anna

Finished all the fruits sent by Amma

11

21 July 1961

My dear Gopu,

I was very glad to get your letter. I am delighted you have started English literature in earnest. Bacon (16th century) is the wisest among all the English writers and Lamb is the sweetest soul among all. Lamb, among the finest figures in English prose, was all his life working in the East India company office as a 'writer and account keeper'. Isn't it funny? Lamb belonged to the eighteenth century, same as Clive.

I have secured about a dozen plays for you, I shall send them soon.

I have identified the variety as 'langra' alright. An awfully sweet variety.

Love Anna

12

24 July 1961

My dear Gopu,

The Kalki agent in Delhi will arrange to deliver to you a parcel of books containing 11 plays of Shakespeare with annotations. I hope you will find time to read these plays of Shakespeare more or less for pleasure. It will serve your purpose very well if you do so.

I am also sending by registered post a book of all Shakespeare's historical plays with a glossary at the end. The type is good and you ought to read these plays in the order of publication in the book. This will give you a concrete story of the Kings of England from John to Henry the Eighth. This will be more useful to you than much reading of history books. Quiller-Couch otherwise known as 'Q' has written a very good book on these historical plays of Shakespeare. You may find it in your own library to read, after you have amused yourself with these plays.

I have given you, I think, one year's work!

Yours affectionately
C. Rajagopalachari[15]

13

5 August 1961

My dear Gopu,

Amma must have by now gone through another anniversary of Appa's leaving you all sadly and so suddenly and unexpectedly.

My blessings and prayers to you all. I got a complete separate letter from Tara from Bhatpara,[16] besides the one she wrote to Periamma. I hope you are taking good care of your eyes—reading only in the correct position never doing it lying down or bending the head down too much. You have much non-detailed reading to do. Goldsmith, Addison, Pope, Johnson, Dryden, Milton, Shakespeare, Scott, Dickens, Thackeray, Tennyson etc.

---

[15] A rare example of a letter typed to dictation ending, in the manner of typed 'official' letters, with the writer's full signature.

[16] My sister Tara was married to the Santiniketan-based agronomist Jyotiprasad Bhattacharjee, originally of Bhatpara, North 24 Parganas, West Bengal.

Don't forget to read the New Testament and some parts of the Old Testament. Without it you can never fully appreciate English literature.

Love
Anna

14

28 September 1961

My dear Gopu,

The anniversary of Ramu's[17] marriage has passed without a letter of congratulations from me but not without my silent blessings.

If it is possible for your professor to get at Dr. Johnson's criticism of Milton (which was printed as an introduction to an old edition of Paradise Lost) I hope you will get it and read it. No student of English literature should fail to read that classic of criticism. You will there find Johnson's style as well as rich thought about English poetry.

A student of English literature has a great deal to read. The Bible, Shakespeare, Milton are indispensible reading. Love to Tara and Jyoti and Sukanya[18] and Amma.

Yours affectionately
Anna

---

[17] My brother Ramchandra married Indu Chawla in September 1960.

[18] Sukanya Bharat-Ram née Bhattacharjee, born to Tara and Jyotiprasad Bhattacharjee in September 1961.

When is Ramu[19] coming over?
Everybody here is well including Cheenu.[20]

15

26 October 1961

My dear Gopu,

It was very sweet of you to share your first earnings with Papa.[21]

I have had talks with Jyoti here about everyone in Delhi.

I hope you are putting forth your full effort to master English literature. Read the original books whenever possible. I am sure you will come out with high honours in your B.A. As regards your profession when you have done with M.A, I feel you are cut out for Law and you must take your B.L degree. Then it is an option for you to settle down in I.A.S or enter the bar and become a great lawyer.

My blessings and love
Anna

16

22 September 1962

My dear Gopu

It has been now decided, I have to embark at once for Washington.[22] There is no time to go to Delhi. I take the plane at Madras on

---

[19] Ramchandra Gandhi was migrating from a teaching assignment at Pilani, Rajasthan, to the philosophy department of St Stephen's College, Delhi.

[20] CR's grandson and eldest son of C.R. Ramaswami, C.R. Srinivasan.

[21] I had sent to my aunt a portion of an honorarium I had received for an article I wrote for the *Statesman*, New Delhi.

[22] Responding to an appeal from the Gandhi Peace Foundation, of which Prime

Tuesday 25th and at Bombay the same midnight for New York via London. The plan is to reach Washington on Thursday night. We halt at London for one day. We see President Kennedy on Friday noon. I am sorry this last minute arrangement has become necessary and I have missed the pleasure of seeing you all before going. Please give my love to Ramu and Amma and Tara.

Yours affectionately
Anna

17

New York
8 October 1962

My dear Gopu,

I am keeping wonderfully well here in America. I have seen some of the most important persons in all America. I gave good talks to them all. God has helped me to keep good health and to do my work well. Everyone I think who heard me including all the big bureaucrats were impressed and their conscience is not easy. But God keeps to himself results. I write to tell you and Amma and everyone else my program.

Minister Nehru was an executive committee member, CR with R.R. Diwakar and B. Shiva Rao went to London and Washington to urge their governments to end nuclear weapons testing. B.K. Nehru, then ambassador of India in Washington, writes in his memoirs (see Rajmohan Gandhi, *The Rajaji Story, 1937–1972*, p. 311):

> I have had the good fortune of being present when great men have argued their points of view with each other in many parts of the world. But I had seldom seen a case presented with such lucidity of argument, such economy of speech, such felicity of language, such gentleness of manner, and such command of facts as Rajaji displayed that day. It was interesting to watch President Kennedy's reactions, for he too was a great admirer of style. One could almost see his eyes open wider and wider in wonder and admiration of the frail little man who was making this masterly presentation.

Leaving New York 12th Oct
Arrive at London 13th Oct
Depart for Rome 18th Oct
Depart from Rome for Bombay 21st Oct
Arrive Bombay 22nd morning
Leave Bombay for Delhi on 23rd evening
Fly to Madras on 25th Oct.

Hope Tara, Jyoti and Ramu and little Sukanya are all in good health and happy.

I had today wonderful talks at lunch with New York Times editorial staff and a very good meeting with the Council on Foreign Relations, with Mr. Dean, American delegate in Geneva at the head and a number of big guns around the table.

Write to Papa that I am very well. A Class officials of the Indian U.N delegation here in New York are acting as honorary cooks without any assistants whatsoever and producing excellent food for me, with exemplary devotion. The food I have been getting here is A1.

God bless you
Anna

18

8 November 1965

My dear Gopu,

I have your letter of Nov 5. It was just received. It has crossed my letter to you. My pleasure and Periamma's are no less than yours in the visit[23] we enjoyed. It was a great time though the four days passed so swiftly.

---

[23] My mother and I had spent four days in Madras.

Your hand writing ought not to be allowed gradually to become illegible as I fear it is. Do take the pains to form the letters each one of them distinctly. It takes a little more time, but it does not much matter. A clear nice legible handwriting is a great possession. You have it now. I want you to value it and nurse it well.

Thanks for the cutting.

Amma knows how greatly I am re-generated by being with her even for a little time. I hope she looks after her health and that Tara and her little family are as well, all of them, as when I was there. God bless all of you.

Anna

19

Madras
10 November 1965

My dear Gopu,

I have gone through 224 pages of Anthony Trollope's Autobiography. It is more than half the book. It is a book you *must* read. I feel you should not graduate in English Literature without going through this self-story of a most conscientious English novelist belonging to the great days of English fiction, I hope your college library has this most readable work. Chapters 12, 13 and 14 are chapters you should read if you are not ready for a full-scale go-through.

I am reading a beautifully printed Oxford Univ. Press edition of 1950—good large type—borrowed by Monica Felton from the British Council Madras and, against rules, sub-lent to me.

Love to all of you. I am in good health tell Amma. I wish she and all of you should enjoy the health I am by God's grace enjoying—although my eyes are not as good as they should be, but that cannot be helped at 87 and when you were young you had been heavily myopic, from reading-age up to 13, without the help of spectacles!

Tell Amma that Periamma is devoting all her time and energy and brains to make me comfortable and keep me in good health.

Love to all,
Anna

20

Madras
24 February 1967

My dear Gopu,

I have your letter of February 21 enclosing cuttings. I had your letter about Mahabharata date also. Thank you. I enclose cuttings returned.

I believe we (Swatantra and D.M.K) are winning all or nearly all the seats (M.P. and local Assembly) of Madras city.

Yours affectionately,

This was written four days ago but by a mistake was left unposted. I am now in a position to tell you what you already know, Congress has lost all the city MP and Assembly seats to the United Front. Congress is in a debacle in the state.

Love
Anna

21

My dear Gopu,

You will get this quite close to your interview date. The 'yoga' of interviews is to be straight, free and easy, not caring for results, and carrying on as in private conversation. Offer a prayer to Bhagawan before going to the interview. Of course Amma will pray for you and so will I.

God bless you
Anna

22

My dear Gopu,

We got the message sent by Chandrachudan[24] informing us that Amma and you will arrive on 26th Tuesday owing to postponement of the medical examination.

Your letter giving the full story of your interview was an excellent report and gave me the whole picture. I can understand your dissatisfaction. One can't deal with all sorts of queries which

---

[24] R. Chandrachudan, Devadas Gandhi's secretary and devoted associate in the *Hindustan Times* of many years, and later in the New Delhi bureau of *The Hindu*. He died at the age of ninety-seven in December 2009.

it is easy enough for the members of the board to ferret out of their lore. But for which no examinee can prepare.

Babbit[25] was no leader of any movement obscure or important. Babbit is a character in one of Sinclair Lewis's novels (American novelist). He delineated the middle class ambition of success in money making which prevailed in America. Babbitry is the name that vulgarity acquired through Sinclair Lewis' novel.

I wonder what humanistic movement in English Literature was intended. Perhaps the novels of Dickens and Hardy may have been intended by the question. However it is all finished and we need not further worry about it.

Love
Anna

23

Madras
23 March 1968

My dear Gopu,

According to Chandrachudan's message we expect you to arrive at 1.30 pm on Tuesday 26th.

Your own estimate coincides with my feeling about it from your reports. Both in the written tests and in the interview your performances have been moderate and we should deem it lucky if

---

[25] Babbit, Babbitry and the humanistic traditions of English literature were part of questions posed to me during the interview, on the basis that I had read English literature. I was unable to even begin to answer these questions, a failure I had ruefully reported to CR. He, of course, knew the answers, or almost.

you come out within the number to be recruited. I should also not be surprised if you come off very well. It depends on the performances of others, too and does not rest on your own.

We need not worry about it.

If there is any change in your return flight, send a telegram. Otherwise, we await your arrival on 26th.

Anna

Narasimhan Mama has involved himself in a stiff election contest in Salem. He will be in Salem till April 10.

24

Madras
9 August 1968

My dear Gopu,

Amma brought the three beautiful Mussoorie group[26] pictures and showed them to me. It was an infinite pleasure to see the happy faces of the young administrators gathered together. The pleasure would have been complete if I could bring myself to foresee a happy and successful administration. But you know my grief on this subject. I am flourishing on a sodium free diet having substituted 'K Salt' for Common Salt. 'K' stands for Potassium.

I find it is quite easy to carry on and it has eliminated the missing

---

[26] The results of the All India Services Examinations and the connected interviews appeared on 22 April 1968, placing me in a rather middling position among the successful candidates. I joined up as a probationer at the National Academy of Administration, Mussoorie, later that summer.

beat in my pulse. We are all well and trust you will take all care of yourself. The photos show you in very good health.

God bless you,

Love,
Anna

The first part of my prediction that Nixon would be the Republican choice has come true.

25

Naoroji Road
Chetput
Madras-31
8 December 1970

My dear Gopu,

It was a pleasant surprise to see Amma here today. She has told me how hard you have been working. It was very good of you to call us on the phone to receive my blessings to you. Take care of your health while you work hard.

Yours affectionately,

Sri Gopalkrishna Gandhi
Assistant Collector
Sub-Collector's Bungalow
Tindivanam

Annexure I

The Realities

It is possible that the reader is being disturbed by the bewildering changes he may be noticing at present in the *Young India* writings. I can assure him that they are not changes but they are a distinct advance in the direction we are going or should go. They are natural corollaries to the principles we profess.

If we will remember that non-violence is more important than non-co-operation and that the latter without the former is a sin, what I am at present developing in these pages will be as clear as daylight.

The difficulty, however, is that the reader does not know much of what is going on behind the scenes. I am restraining myself partly on purpose and partly because I cannot do otherwise. It is difficult to pass on decisions from moment to moment and from day to day to the fellow-workers. I must simply trust that as they are in my opinion the necessary corollary to the main principle, they will be as plain to the reader as they are to me.

The fact is, action must vary with every varying circumstance. It is not inconsistent, if it springs from the same source. What must be however apparent to everyone is that our differences are increasing. Each group is making of its programme a matter of principle. Each sincerely believes that its programme will bring us nearer to the common goal. So long as there is a body of people in the country—and it is a large if not a growing body—so long will there be parties prosecuting the Councils programme. Our non-co-operation therefore has taken the form of non-co-operation in practice with one another instead of the Government. Without wishing it we are weakening one another and to that extent helping the system we are all seeking to destroy. Let us recognize its chief characteristic.

It is parasitical and derives nutrition from the fungi of national life. Our non-co-operation was meant to be a living, active, non-violent force matched against the essential violence of the system. Unfortunately the non-co-operation never became actively non-violent. We satisfied ourselves with physical non-violence of the weak and helpless. Having failed to produce the immediate effect of destroying the system, it has recoiled upon us with double strength and now bids fair to destroy us, if we do not take care betimes. I, for one, am therefore determined not to participate in the domestic wrangle but would even invite all concerned to do likewise. If we cannot actively help, we must not hinder. I am just as keen a believer as ever in the five boycotts. But I clearly see, as I did not at the time of the A.l.C.C. meeting, that whilst we maintain them in our own persons, there is no atmosphere for working them. There is too much distrust in the air. Every action is suspected and misinterpreted. And whilst we carry on a war of explanation and counter-explanation, the enemy at the door is rejoicing and consolidating his forces. We must avoid this almost at any cost.

I have therefore suggested that we should find out the lowest common measure among all the political parties and invite them all to co-operate on the Congress platform for achieving that common measure. This is the work of internal development without which there will be no effective external political pressure. The politicians who put the external work before the internal, or who think (which is the same thing) that the internal is too slow for them, should have the greatest freedom to develop their strength, but in my opinion, this should be outside the Congress platform. The Congress must progressively represent the masses. They are as yet untouched by politics. They have no political consciousness of the type our politicians desire.

Their politics are confined to bread and salt—I dare not say butter, for millions do not know the taste of ghee or even oil. Their politics are confined to communal adjustments. It is right however to say that we the politicians do represent the masses in opposition to the Government. But if we begin to use them before they are ready, we shall cease to represent them. We must first come in living touch with them by working for them and in their midst. We must share their sorrows, understand their difficulties and anticipate their wants. With the pariahs we must be pariahs and see how we feel to clean the closets of the upper classes and have the remains of their table thrown at us.

We must see how we like being in the boxes, miscalled houses, of the labourers of Bombay. We must identify ourselves with the villagers who toil under the hot sun beating on their bent backs and see how we would like to drink water from the pool in which the villagers bathe, wash their clothes and pots and in which their cattle drink and roll.

Then and not till then shall we truly represent the masses and they will, as surely as I am writing this, respond to every call. 'We cannot all do this, and if we are to do this, good-bye to swaraj for a thousand years and more,' some will say. I shall sympathize with the objection. But I do claim that some of us at least will have to go through the agony and out of it only will a nation full, vigorous and free be born. I suggest to all that they should give their mental co-operation and that they should mentally identify themselves with the masses, and as a visible and tangible token thereof, they should earnestly spin for at least thirty minutes per day in their name and for their sake. It will be a mighty prayer from the intelligentsia among the Hindus, Mussalmans, Parsis, Christians and others of India, rising up to heaven for their, that is, India's deliverance. I see no way of removing the Hindu–Muslim tension, which is becoming daily tenser, save by all the parties coming together on the Congress platform and devising the best method of solving a problem which seems to defy solution and to dash to pieces all the fond hope, we had of securing a national freedom that is broad-based upon mutual trust and mutual help. If for no other reason, let us, at least for the sake of achieving unity, give up the internecine political strife.

Here is my proposal to that end:

1. The Congress should suspend all the boycotts except that of foreign cloth till the session of 1925.
2. The Congress should, subject to (1), remove the boycott of Empire goods.
3. The Congress should confine its activity solely to the propaganda of hand-spinning and hand-spun khaddar, the achievement of Hindu-Muslim unity, and in addition, its Hindu members' activity to the removal of untouchability.
4. The Congress should carry on the existing national educational institutions; and if possible, open more and keep them independent of Government control or influence.
5. The four-anna franchise should be abolished and in its place the qualification for membership should be spinning by every member for half an hour per day and delivery to the Congress from month to month of at least 2,000 yards of self-spun yarn, cotton being supplied where the member is too poor to afford it.

It is necessary to say a word about the proposed radical change in the Congress constitution. I may be pardoned for saying that I am the principal author of the Congress constitution. It was intended to be the most democratic in the world, and if successfully worked, to bring swaraj without more. But it was not so worked. We had not sufficient honest and able workers. It must be confessed that it has broken down in the sense in which it was intended. We never had even one crore of members on the roll. At the present moment probably our nominal roll does not exceed two lakhs for all India. And the vast majority of these too are as a rule not interested in our proceedings save for paying four annas and voting. But what we need is an effective, swift moving, cohesive, responsive organization containing intelligent, industrious national workers. Even if we are a few only, we should give a better account of ourselves than a cumbrous and slow body with no mind of its own. The only boycott proposed to be retained is that of foreign-cloth and if we are to make it successful, we can only do so by making the Congress for a time predominantly a spinners' association. It will be a great triumph and a great demonstration, if we succeed in one constructive item of a striking magnitude. I hold that the only possible thing of the kind is hand-spinning and hand-spun khaddar. If we are to make of khaddar a national success, the spinning-wheel is the only thing. If we are permanently to interest the masses in the national welfare of the country, the spinning-wheel is the only medium. If we are to banish pauperism from the land, the spinning-wheel again is the only remedy.

The implications of my proposals are that

(a) the Swarajists should be free to organize themselves without any opposition from the Congress or No-changers;

(b) the members of other political bodies should be invited and induced to join the Congress;

(c) the No-changers should be precluded from carrying on any propaganda either direct or indirect against Council-entry;

(d) those who do not personally believe in any of the four boycotts will be free, without any disgrace whatsoever, to act as if they did not exist. Thus non-co-operating lawyers will be free to resume practice if they chose and title-holders, school-masters, etc., will be free to join the Congress and be eligible to the executive. The scheme enables all the political parties to work unitedly for the internal development. The Congress presents a suitable opportunity for a conference of all political parties and outside the Congress to frame a swaraj scheme acceptable to all and for presentation to the Government. Personally I am of opinion that time has not arrived for any such presentation. I believe that it would increase our internal strength beyond expectation if we could all simply unite to make the foregoing constructive programme a success. But a large number of those who have hitherto led the country think otherwise. In any event a swaraj scheme for the sake of ourselves is a necessity. As the reader will remember, I am in this matter a complete convert to Babu Bhagwandas's view. I would therefore join any such conference, if my presence was required, and assist at framing the scheme. The reason for insisting on this matter being treated as an activity outside the Congress is to keep the Congress purely for internal development for full one year. When we have achieved a measure of success commensurate with the task before us, the Congress may function for outside political activity.

What if the proposal is not accepted and it is found difficult to bring together all parties on the Congress platform and to heal the breach between the Swarajists and ourselves? My answer is simple. If the whole fight is for 'capturing' the Congress, I must refuse to enter upon it. I would advise all who think with me to do likewise. I would advise handing the Congress over to the Swarajists on their terms and leave the Swarajists to work the Councils programme unhampered by any counter-propaganda. I would engage the No-changers purely on the constructive programme and advise them to seek such help from the other parties as they can give. Those who depend for national regeneration solely on the constructive programme may be expected to lead in the matter of self-sacrifice. Not one of the things we hold dear can be achieved by trying to retain power in the Congress in opposition to the Swarajists. We must hold it on their sufferance. Both parties will be guilty of corrupting the simple people who worship the name 'Congress', if they are made at our bidding to engage in a suicidal tug-of-war. Power that comes from service faithfully rendered ennobles. Power that is sought in the name of service and can only be obtained by a majority of votes is a delusion and a snare to be avoided, especially at the present moment.

Whether I have convinced the reader of the soundness of my proposal or not my mind is made up. It hurts me to think that those with whom I have hitherto worked hand in glove should be working in a seemingly opposite direction.

What I have sketched above is not conditions of surrender. Mine is an unconditional surrender. I would guide the Congress next year only if all parties wish me to. I am trying to see daylight out of this impenetrable darkness. I seem to see it dimly. But I may be still wrong. All I know is that there is no fight left in me. This is much for a born fighter to say. I have fought my dearest ones. But I fight out of love. I should fight the Swarajists too out of love. But I must, I see, first prove my love. I thought I had proved it. I see I was wrong. I am therefore retracing my steps. I ask everyone to help me to do so and to reunite the two wings on a common platform. The Congress must, for sometime to come at least, remain largely a homogeneous body.

Young India, 11 September 1924

Annexure II

CR's introduction to Mahadev Desai's Gujarati translation of John Morley's classic, *On Compromise*

John Morley was one of England's great seekers after truth. He was by nature endowed with a truly religious spirit. But he was one of those philosophers who held that man cannot know anything about the things beyond. He did not accept any revelation or religion. Yet as I said above, he was full of the true spirit of religion. If all of us could be as pure and lofty in spirit as John Morley it may not matter whether we professed any religion or not. John Morley's reverential attitude towards the Unknown, his respect for Truth, and his ideal of service to humanity made him as truly religious as any one who believed in God.

His revolt against superstitious beliefs and practices was very strong. He condemned the ceremonies and forms imposed by the current church of England as serving to perpetuate error and the enslavement of the human mind. He was of opinion that spiritualised agnosticism was the only right attitude which men should have in regards to the Eternal mystery. This book, however, does not deal with this question, or any other particular theory of religion or politics. It deals with the general question of how far we should allow other people's opinions and practices to affect our thought, our speech, and our action when our own convictions lead us in the opposite direction, that is to say, how far we may set aside truth on account of society's opposition to new ideas.

Morley keenly felt that Idealism and the spirit of Truth had declined in England. He deplored the tendency to speak and act quite contrary to one's own convictions. He felt that too many men failed to take interest in the larger questions of life and confined their cares to the immediate and so-called practical phases of life. He deplored that men had not the courage to think freely and to express their minds fearlessly. They deferred to public opinion and the errors of other people even in the formulation and expression of opinion as distinguished from action. Men shrank from conclusions and went through life pretending to hold beliefs which they had really rejected. The famous book of which this is a translation was written by him as a protest against these evils and to urge men to think, speak and act according to their own convictions.

Courage and great sacrifice are needed to discard the opinions and practices of men among whom we live, but this is the only way to progress. If we want Truth to replace error in the transactions of men, if we have any faith in Truth and its potency, individuals must reduce to a minimum the restrictions imposed on account of other people's erroneous beliefs and susceptibilities. The individual revolt is the very stuff of social evolution. Time brings in improvements, not spontaneously but only through human effort. If out of deference to the ignorance or prejudices of the majority individuals suppress themselves, no human progress is possible, and evolution would be a dream.

A study of this book will show that Morley does not want that man should refuse to recognise any restraints on account of current beliefs and practices. Other people's opinions are facts of which we should take due cognizance as of other important facts. Feelings should be duly respected, though not pampered. Rights of other people should be rigorously respected. When, how, and in what matters at a given moment, one should propagate one's views when they differ from those of the vast majority of people, and when it may be better for progress to preserve a wise silence are matters for careful consideration and judgment. Social or family life should not be embittered by constant disputations or by vain flaunting of disbelief. But dissimulation and untruth in the name of expediency are never permissible, being fatally inexpedient in the larger and ultimate interests of Society.

Though Morley did not write this book to refute the Divine Existence or to support any particular theory of religion or of politics, but deals therein only with the general question of the nonconfirmist's duty of acting in accordance with his convictions whatever they may be, Morley's agnosticism and his opposition to Anglican Christianity furnish him with profuse illustrations for his general plea. They are no more than illustrations; and the argument for truthful and unrestricted thought and expression and for reducing to a minimum the restraints imposed on action in pursuance of individual conviction, would remain just the same, if instead of being an agnostic, Morley had been a devout and orthodox Christian or Vedantist. In spite of this, we cannot ignore the natural and cumulative psychological effect of illustrations. Not withstanding his great logical care in stating the case hypothetically in all his concrete reasoning, the bias of agnosticism cannot be avoided by a writer of the school of Morley. And lofty Agnosticism tends to degenerate into shallow materialism so far as the hasty and youthful reader is concerned. It is well therefore to warn readers that it is neither author's nor translator's object to spread religious Disbelief. Both author and translator though they belong to different schools of religious thought want that truth should be emancipated, that thought and expression should boldly follow the lines of our convictions, and that there should be no plea of expediency or compromise, except when we seek to enforce our opinions in positive action; and even there, accommodation is permissible only in those cases where the assent of others is essential for the realisation of opinion; and then, too, only such provisional accommodation as keeps the final goal of truth in unclouded view. The individual should ever be on the watch against the temptation of personal ease and selfish comfort resulting from confirmity with current error, and not allow such a temptation to speak in terms of a deference for other people's opinions.

The master key for solving all questions of conflict is Non-violence in the widest sense of the term. A perusal of the last chapter will show the remarkable identity of thought in this respect between this Western philosopher and our own greater reformer, Mahatma Gandhi.

No one is more competent to translate this book written in the cause of Truth than Sjt. Mahadeo Desai. He has earned by his loving and faithful service the unbounded confidence of the great and illustrious devotee of truth who is the pride of India, who has combined in himself the most rigorous regard for principles and the qualities of a great and successful man of action. Mahatmaji's friend and companion, Sjt. Mahadeo Desai, needs no introduction to the Gujarati world, which should be thankful to him for this translation of Morley's famous work.

Our problems of progress and emancipation in this country are urgent and various. Thousands of known and unknown men and women find themselves in conflicts wherein their newly found ideals and aspirations entangle them. This book will certainly encourage and help such persons.

C. Rajagopalachari

Pudupalayam, 26 May 1925

Annexure III

CR's memorandum of September 1931

As a result of the campaign, a number of shops were not taken up by renters at the recent auction sales of toddy shop-licenses and for many shops the bids were so low that the Government have not accepted them. From information received so far, in spite of the efforts of all arms of Government, and two or three auctions, out of 9000 toddy shops in the Madras presidency, nearly 3000 are still unsold. Licenses have been sold to fetch somewhere near Rs. 50 lakhs per annum in place of one and a half crore rupees per annum recovered from toddy shop rentals every year before this.

30 percent of the shops in Tamil Nadu have not yet been assigned to licensees. Secret tenders and bargains are going on between officials and prospective renters over these shops. Even the toddy shops that have been assigned have been accepted for much lower rentals, than last year's.

The shops that have been sold off so far have been given away for annual rentals totalling about Rs. 35 lakhs, that is to say, less than half of what the toddy shop licenses in Tamil Nadu were sold for in the previous years.

The tree tax on trees marked for toddy ordinarily fetched about an equal amount to the shop rentals. It may be expected that licensees this year will not risk leasing as many trees as usual and will not therefore have as many trees marked as in former years. The tree tax receipts also, therefore, must fall in proportion to the fall in rentals. It may not be an over-estimate on these data to say that the total excise revenue will be affected so far as Tamil Nadu is concerned to the extent of from 75 lakhs to one crore under toddy alone.

Taking certain typical districts, out of 560 toddy shops in Coimbatore, as many as 260 remain yet unsold. So also in North Arcot, out of 400 odd shops, more than 200 are yet unsold. In South Arcot out of nearly 300 shops, more than a hundred are still undisposed of. In Ramnad district almost all the shops have been disposed of, but have fetched only 2 lakhs annual rental as against an average of 4 lakhs of previous years.

These results do not by any means represent uniform work in the districts. They are the spread-out over the whole area of very good and persistent effort in some places and the resulting general atmosphere.

The auction barometer, for instance in Rajapalaiyam area, shows that whereas the average toddy shop rentals for the previous three years in that taluk exceeded Rs. 58000 per annum, this year the bids came to a total of only Rs. 17800. Only ten of the ninety-one toddy shops in Dharapuram taluk could be sold. In Udumalpet taluk there were no bids whatever for 16 out of 21 shops.

I have exhibited these figures showing the fall in Government revenue because it is a measure of the liquor dealer's estimate of his future business, i.e., the effect of our work. They are shrewd men though they are gamblers. They are able to sense the feeling in the country. I therefore take their bids as a reliable trade measure of the degree of success we have attained in our work. Let no one imagine that hectic activities during the auction sales will produce any effect on the hardened liquor dealer. It is only when he is convinced that people have been impressed by our work and will not drink that he will refrain from bidding or stake only a low figure. Seeing all this, one may justifiably feel proud of the work done by the volunteers of our province for the good of the poorest among poor people. We have not done as well as we wanted. But our seeming failures are not a shame. The shame is all on the other side, which by force of entrenched authority, keeps up an evil traffic when the people have made it clear beyond all doubt that they do not want it.

Annexure IV

C.R.'s statement issued to the press on 29 November 1932

The situation regarding Guruvayur Temple may be summarized thus:

With all deference I have to say that advanced age and frail health render it extremely difficult if not impossible for the Zamorin to tackle a problem of this kind. He was pleased to receive me on Saturday last. He said it would not be possible for him to discuss the vexed question. But even if he had not so warned me, it was obvious to me that it was no use inflicting a discussion on him. He seemed as if he had made up his mind not to worry himself. From this point of view, the situation is very grave.

The workers of the anti-untouchability campaign in Kerala are thoroughly alive to the seriousness of the situation. I am glad to assure all those outside Kerala who are anxious about impending fasts that Kerala workers are displaying utmost energy and enthusiasm and have initiated a thorough going referendum in Ponani Taluka, which is expected to be completed by 20th December. The Taluka has been selected as a sample area for ascertainment of Kerala Hindu Savarna opinion. It is impossible for a non-official agency to undertake and complete a house to house visit and referendum in the whole district, not to speak of the whole of Kerala. Guruvayur Temple is in Ponani Taluka. Hindu public feeling is the same in this Taluka as in other talukas. If at all, vested interests in combination with the temple are naturally stronger in this Taluka than elsewhere, and the results of a referendum here, if in favour of throwing the temple open, can be taken as conclusive of Hindu opinion.

The area is difficult in regard to communications, but Kerala Untouchability League Workers have bravely undertaken the task. It is hoped the public will render every possible help to complete the work in time. Workers are taking books of forms specially prepared for the referendum to every house. Everyone whether in favour or against our demand should deem it his or her duty to record that opinion to enable a just solution to the problem in accordance with public opinion. Untouchability is a crime in our opinion. But even if one may not subscribe to this, it is a civic duty to give one's opinion openly on this urgent occasion. We hope therefore that the public will render every assistance to workers who have undertaken to elicit and record public opinion in an indisputable manner.

As far as I can see, the Zamorin will not commit himself, whether he will abide by the result of the referendum. This being his attitude at present does not however mean that when we have an impartial record of public opinion, he can ignore it. His difficulty so far has been his legal inability as trustee to act on his own opinion. When the referendum gives a clear result, he will be bound as a trustee to move the law if he feels doubts, and cannot sit quiet over such an expression of the public demand. It would have been most satisfactory if the Zamorin could agree beforehand to abide by the result of the referendum and come forward to help in the taking of votes, by deputing men of his choice to cooperate with us. But even if he does not wish to commit himself thus, our work will proceed independently and will have its own value with an impartial public.

The custom of untouchability having prevailed in its worst form in Kerala, the reaction also is very strong. It is remarkable how some of the most orthodox families are showing the greatest enthusiasm for reform.

Both Kelappan and Mahatmaji are men who do not count the cost, but will keep their word, and sacred vows. If the work done before the end of December does not justify a postponement of the fast they have undertaken, sure as Fate, they will both take it up on Second January and then the nation will have no time to deal with the situation. When public opinion is recorded properly, we will have to deal with the law and the Zamorin. If reasonably satisfactory procedure is available other than the final sacrifice they have decided upon, neither Kelappan nor Mahatmaji will refuse to give us a chance. But if men and women display indifference we cannot blame Mahatmaji or Kelappan if they launch on their fast. I appeal, therefore, for immediate vigorous action on the part of everyone before it becomes too late. What I have seen over the last five days fills me with hope.

Annexure V

Gandhi's letter to K. Kelappan:

23 November 1932

My dear Kelappan,

I have your letter. I wish you would write daily and give me a full report of progress from day to day. Of course you will cheerfully resume your fast if it becomes necessary. But we must strain every nerve to prevent its resumption.

Do not for one moment imagine that I promised to fast with you because of anything you had said in your telegrams. I know that you would be better pleased if I did not join you. But with me it was a point of honour that I should join you if the fast which was suspended upon my advice had to be resumed. After all, you should have no difficulty in believing me when I tell you that at least during the days of the fast, all my acts were prompted by the inner voice. All the movements of a life of perfect surrender to God are so directed, and it is my perpetual endeavour to make my life one of perfect surrender. Therefore I would like you not to expend your energy in dissuading me from the fast if it becomes necessary, but devote every ounce of your energy to organizing public opinion so that the temple is opened to the Harijans before the due date. I have read your letter to the Zamorin. I think that it is quite all right. It would have been better if you had omitted all reference to the Vaidiks and Tantriks. Your position with regard to them was already known.

I had long conversations with Sadashiv Rao. He told me all about you. I have given him my views fully but in order to make assurance doubly sure I reduce them to writing.

Our claim is that the proposed fast can never savour of coercion because it is based on the assumption that the vast majority of the temple-going savarnas are in favour of temple-entry. If this cannot be proved up to the hilt, there is no case for fasting by us. Fasting with the knowledge that savarnas are opposed to temple-entry by Harijans would undoubtedly amount to coercion. If we make that painful discovery, it would not mean that we cease to agitate for temple-entry by avarnas, but the movement will then have to take a different turn. I can even conceive the possibility of a fast in such an event, but that could only be in an unmistakably different setting. In order to demonstrate to all concerned the fact that we have the majority of temple-goers on our side, there should be a methodical taking of a referendum of temple-goers, say within a ten-mile radius. And in order to have the thing absolutely above the board, signatures should be taken at public meetings in the presence of witnesses known to the signatories with their full names, addresses and occupations, together with age and sex. It is being suggested that whilst many people have been in favour of Harijans entering temples, they may be afraid owing to pressure from their landlords or otherwise to say so openly. I should say that even in that case we must be declared to have lost. Whatever the cause of abstention may be, if we do not get the majority of votes we must be declared to have lost the battle so far as the proposed fast is concerned.

Needless to say that there should be no coercion of any kind on our part during the taking of the referendum. On the contrary every endeavour should be made to carry on the referendum with the co-operation and goodwill of the opponents. The points of difference between the so-called orthodox party and the reformers should be reduced to a minimum. The orthodox party can have nothing to say against the reformers so long as they do not resort to any coercion. If they are assured that there will be no attempt whatsoever made either on the part of the reformers or Harijans to force entry, there would be no opposition by the orthodox, and even if there is, it is bound to fall flat. Real non-violence can never beget violence. Too much emphasis cannot be laid upon the point that the removal of untouchability, apart from the political side of it, which is settled, is a wholly religious matter.

Question was put to me whether sympathizers of temple-entry may start fasting a few days before the second of January, in order, I suppose, to force the issue. This must not be done on any account whatsoever. Nor, if the fast begins, can anyone join us in the fasting out of sympathy.

Fasting by you, if it comes, must not take place on the public road. It must be in a house or a hut. There can be no public exhibition of you, whilst you are under fast.

Urmila Devi, the widowed sister of the late Deshabandhu Das, will be leaving here on the 27th by the Madras Express. She will be accompanied by her son. She is being sent there in response to Gopala Menon's suggestion that a sister from the North may be sent. She has a weak heart, she must not therefore be rushed too much. She leads an austere life of a Hindu widow. She is an accomplished English scholar and has been doing public work for years in Bengal. I could not think of a fitter woman for work to be sent from the North. Urmila Devi can address men as well as women. She must be taken to the homes of the orthodox and she must be taken to Harijan quarters. I do not know where it is proposed to house [her]. [If] no other arrangement has already been made, I suggest the Gujarati house where I was taken during the last tour. She should be provided with a mosquito curtain if [there] are mosquitoes at all. She should be provided with a commode wherever possible. She is a pure vegetarian.

You must keep yourself in perfect order. There should be no loss of confidence and no work under a nervous strain. We can but work with zeal and honesty. The result lies in God's hands. Purest instruments alone should lead the movement. Give me a list of all the active workers. I suggest that Malaviyaji be not worried to go to Kerala. He is too weak and he has his hands otherwise absolutely full. You should even telegraph to him saying that if he sends his blessings and messengers it would be deeply appreciated, but Kerala would spare him the trouble of undertaking the long journey whilst he is occupied in national work of the highest importance.

Annexure VI

Gandhi's statement to the press after winning the referendum for temple-entry

30 December 1932

I had full consultation with Mr. C. Rajagopalachari, Mr. K. Madhavan Nair and Mr. Kelappan, who have come to Poona to confer with me. They have placed the results of the Guruvayur referendum before me. The referendum was taken of the Ponnani Taluk where the temple is situated.

Never perhaps was a referendum taken with such scrupulous care or with such scientific precision before this. Rarely to my knowledge, have 73 per cent of the eligible voters voted.

In order to find out the truth, voting was confined only to those who were actual temple-goers, that is to say, those who were not entitled to enter the Guruvayur Temple and those who would not, such as the Arya Samajists, were excluded from the voters' list. I had intended without thinking of all implications actually to find out by some method of examination, who were actual temple-goers, but I have found it to be utterly impracticable. It was enough to announce that only those should vote who believed in temple-going, who had faith in temple-worship as an integral part of the Hindu religion and who were entitled to enter the Guruvayur Temple.

The total population entitled to the temple-entry being approximately 65,000, the outside estimate of adults may be taken as 30,000. As a matter of fact, 27,465 adult men and women were actually visited for receiving their votes. Of these 55 per cent were in favour of temple-entry; nine per cent against, eight per cent were neutrals, and 27 per cent abstained.

It should be remembered that the referendum was taken amidst adverse influences. The Zamorin would not co-operate, and I am sorry to have to say, even cast aspersions upon the workers and the procedure they followed. The Ponnani Taluk is the stronghold of orthodoxy and yet there was a decisive majority in favour of admission of the untouchables to that shrine now made famous throughout the length and breadth of the land.

The figures were also instructive, as showing that both men and women had no hesitation in spite of the contemplated fast, of expressing their dissent. I would also draw a fair deduction from the neutrals and non-co-operators. They could not at all, if they had chosen to give their decision, be regarded as against the temple-entry of the Harijans. It would not be a bad or unfair guess to make, if I suggested that a fourth of these, at least, were probably for temple-entry. The percentage of the voters favouring temple-entry would then be sixty-five per cent of the total eligible voters. If they be excluded altogether from the referendum, the majority would be 77 per cent. Turn the figures as we may, the unchallengeable conclusion is that a decisive majority of eligible voters are in favour of the entry by the Harijans. . . .

Hinduism teaches that when evils and corruption are beyond control by ordinary means, human endeavour is supplemented by *tapasya* or penance which, in its extreme form, means fasting either conditional or unconditional. Therefore it is no new thing. But for the influence, supposed or real, I enjoy among the masses, perhaps no notice would be taken of it.

My conviction is that Hinduism has fallen from the purity and vitality it once had. Its very scriptures are evidence of the continuous progress and adaptability to circumstances that arose from time to time. Though it has retained unimpaired the claim to divine inspiration for the scriptures as a body, it did not hesitate to introduce new reforms and make changes. Hence it is that we have in Hinduism not only Vedas, but all later writings claiming authority. But a time came, when this healthy growth or evolution was arrested, and instead of the written word being used as an aid to the search for light from within, it was held to be all-sufficing, whether it accorded with longings and strivings of the spirit within or not. The descendants of those who wrestled with God Himself and drew from Him some of the imperishable things one finds in Vedas and later writings, felt too exhausted for further effort, either to wring out new meaning from an old verse or mantra or produce a new mantra. They felt that they had done with God and that God had finished His work, after inspiring the last verse of the latest Shastra. And so one finds an army of interpreters seeking to reconcile, often irreconcilable texts, unmindful as to whether they answer the pressing needs of the age or whether they can stand the light of searching examination. And even penances took mere outward form, instead of being an expression of the inward agonizing struggle. I may be wrong in my diagnosis, but such being my case and finding the Hindu society irresponsive to the central call of Hinduism, that is, progressive realization of unity of all life, not as a philosophical doctrine but as a solid fact of life, I thought that by continuous effort to live my religion as I understood it, I had the fitness for doing penance by way of fasting and that I had such a call from within. . . .

It would be a betrayal of trust and a betrayal of the Harijans if, in any shape or form, I slackened my effort or gave up altogether the intention of fasting in connection with the removal of untouchability.

I would like the voiceless and helpless Harijans to feel that thousands of Hindu reformers, as zealous of Hindu religion and scriptures on which it is based, as any Hindu calling himself a sanatanist can be, are prepared, no less than I am, to sacrifice their lives, if need be, in an attempt to remove untouchability, root and branch. There can be no rest, therefore, for me or those who, by word of mouth or show of hands, silently endorsed the resolution, until untouchability becomes a thing of the past. It would be only out of the ashes of untouchability that Hinduism can revive, and thus be purified and become a vital and vitalizing force in the world.

Annexure VII

Two letters by S. Satyamurti to Gandhi:

Camp: 'Shivanadi'
Kodai Kanal
28 May 1942

My dear Mahatmaji,

Yes you have more than anticipated me. I am duly grateful. The country has reason to be. But Rajaji goes on arguing still, though vanquished. Drastic action must be taken against him. He is setting a bad example. He has no right to carry on this propaganda against the Congress in these critical times. At any rate he must resign the leadership of the Madras Legislature Congress Party unless he persuades the majority of the Party to rebel. He will not succeed. He knows it, that is why he has not yet summoned a meeting of the Party. He must be made to. If you agree, I suggest you advise the Congress Parliamentary Committee and the Working Committee to act promptly and effectively.

I was present at the last meeting of the Working Committee. I know the differences between the Sardar and Rajen Babu on the one hand and the Maulana Saheb and Pandit Jawahar Lal on the other.

They are fundamental, but I respectfully suggest, that Congress unity is more fundamental. You and the Maulana can bring about that unity. A divided Congress today will be a national tragedy.

Lakshmi is writing this letter for me as I am weak. This altitude tries my heart. I am therefore getting down in a few days. I hope to be better then.

With kind regards,
Yours very sincerely,
S. Satyamurti

Camp: Sivanadi
Kodai kanal
2 June 1942

My dear Mahatmaji,

You will have received my last letter. I have read your latest article on Rajaji's propaganda. I agree with almost every word of what you say in that article. But there are two words that disturb me. You describe Rajaji's persistence as 'admirable and patriotic'. I demur. What is there admirable and patriotic in seeking and getting the help of anti-Congress elements (e.g.) the Justice Party, the Muslim League, the Friends of the Soviet Union whose only concern is Russia, students and labourers inspired by Sri M.N. Roy and his ilk and others, with a view to 'convert' the Congress?

I have followed his propaganda closely and I am convinced that his attempt is not to convert the Congress so much as to weaken and destroy if possible its influence on the people. I am quoting from his own speeches. 'The greatest danger to the Congress is its tendency to become secret and authoritarian'. 'The 120 members of the A.I.C.C. who voted against him did not think for themselves'. 'Congress who differ from him are not serious about resisting the Japanese menace'. 'The Congress has done nothing all these years to try to achieve Congress–Muslim unity'. 'Congressmen who differ from him do so because they are not serious about the freedom of the country'. 'You should forget the Congress as an organisation and think of the people.'

Again, what is there patriotic in his persistence in a propaganda which merely supplies arguments to Col. Amery, Sir S. Cripps, Mr Jinnah and other enemies of India's integrity and freedom? He is only repeating what they have been saying all these years.

I shouldn't have bothered you with this letter but for the fact that these two words may encourage him to go and encourage others to follow him. What do you think will be the position of the Congress if leading Congressmen start this kind of propaganda? I have ventured to share these thoughts with you in the full confidence that they will receive attention at your hands.

My heart is giving me trouble here. So we get down on the 5th and reach Courtallam on the 6th.

My address there is c/o the Post Master, Courtallam, via Tenkasi, S.I. Rly.

I shall be glad to hear from you there. I hope you and Mrs. Gandhi are well. My wife and Lakshmi are.

Yours very sincerely,
S. Satyamurti

Gandhi's reply:

6 June 1942

What you say is right, but you cannot deny his patriotism because he errs grievously. All I do by using those adjectives is to free him of an unworthy motive or ambition. I do hope your heart trouble is over and that you will be fully restored.

Yours,
MK Gandhi

Suggested Reading

Copley, A.R.H. *The Political Career of C. Rajagopalachari 1937–1954: A Moralist in Politics.* Delhi: Macmillan, 1978.

Felton, Monica. *I Meet Rajaji.* New Delhi: Katha, 2003.

Gandhi, Rajmohan. *Rajaji: A Life.* New Delhi: Penguin, 1997.

Gandhi, Rajmohan. *The Rajaji Story: 1937–1972.* Bombay: Bharatiya Vidya Bhavan, 1984.

Gandhi, Rajmohan. *The Rajaji Story: A Warrior from the South.* Madras: Bharathan Publications, 1978.

Srinivasan, Vasanthi. *Gandhi's Conscience-Keeper: C. Rajagopalachari and Indian Politics.* New Delhi: Permanent Black, 2009.

Suggested Reading

Index

172, 175, 177, 184, 190, 200, 234,
290, 303
arrest and imprisonment, 148, 199,
259, 265
letters from
CR, 247–62, 265–84
Jawaharlal Nehru, 263–64
marriage with Lakshmi, 3–4, 101,
193–98, 263–65
supports Nehru's prime ministership,
11
Gandhi, Kasturba, 21, 40, 98, 101–03,
147, 153–58, 196, 198–200, 234,
262
Gandhi, Maganlal, 35, 80, 90–91, 112–13
Gandhi, Mohandas Karamchand. *See also*
Harijans; Round Table Conference
(RTC); untouchability
arrest and imprisonment, 7, 16, 21,
51, 55, 62–63, 148, 150–51,
155, 169, 172, 174, 182, 184–85,
198–99, 233, 270
assassination, 2, 281–82
Congress president, 63–64
and CR
on allegations and slurs against,
100–01, 123, 235–36
differences with, 223–24
relationship with, 1–5, 72–73,
106–09
fasts, 68–69, 151, 152, 184–90, 202,
233, 281–82
meeting with Lord Irwin (1931),
132
withdrawal from active politics and
Congress, 201–05
Gandhi, Rajmohan, 75, 101–02, 185,
209, 219, 278–82, 289–90
Mohandas, 36
The Rajaji Story, 50, 219

The Rajaji Story, 1937–1972, 101–02,
219, 278–82
Gandhi–Ambedkar agreement, 151
Gandhi–Irwin Pact, 132, 143, 147, 191
Gandhi–Jinnah talks, 275
Gokhale, Gopalkrishna, 7, 22, 99
Government of India Act, 1935, 207–08,
216, 266, 274

Habibullah, Muhammad, 116–17
Harijans, 80, 113, 166, 179, 181, 187,
220. *See also* untouchability
fund, 199–200
population, 183–84
temple-entry, 151, 159, 161
tour, 199–200
Harijan, 177–79, 183–84, 190, 209, 212,
216, 218, 223, 225, 227–28, 236
Hindi, 94, 236–37, 260
teaching in schools, 48, 94, 212–15,
248, 253
Hind Swaraj, 7, 24, 26, 29
Hindu, The, 23, 46, 126, 209, 224, 272
Hindu Mahasabha, 273
Hindu–Muslim
divisions, 215, 217–18
Simon Commission (dominion
status), 116–17
riots, 97, 291
unity efforts, 44–45, 59, 67, 114–16,
227–28, 233
Hoare, Samuel, 142, 192
Home Rule Movement, 23, 49

Independent, 49
interim (provisional) Government of
India, 8, 222–23, 240, 278
Irwin, Lord C.R., 130, 132, 147,
191–92. *See also* Gandhi–Irwin
Pact